ENGLISH WORKSHOP

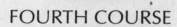

FOURTH COURSE

D1318610

HOLT, RINEHART AND WINSTON

Harcourt Brace & Company

Austin • New York • Orlando • Chicago • Atlanta
San Francisco • Boston • Dallas • Toronto • London

TABLE OF CONTENTS

GRAMMAR, USAGE, AND MECHANICS

PREWRITING: FINDING IDEAS FOR WRITING

Writing begins before you pick up your pencil. It begins when you get an idea. The following two prewriting techniques can sharpen your writing skills as well as help you to unlock writing ideas.

WRITER'S JOURNAL

A **writer's journal** is a record of what you see, hear, do, and feel. Keeping a journal will sharpen your observation powers and create a good source of ideas you can refer to at any time. Write in your journal daily, even if it's just a short paragraph, and date your entries.

- Take your journal with you to interesting places. Write about what you hear, feel, and see. You can also include your own sketches.
- Let your imagination roam freely as you write. Include dreams, daydreams, and fantasies.
- Collect stories and bits of poems and song lyrics you hear. Make a note of what you like about them or how they make you feel.
- Don't worry about spelling, grammar, or neatness. The main purpose of your writer's journal is to preserve your thoughts and feelings as vividly as you can.

FREEWRITING

To **freewrite**, you choose a subject and write whatever comes into your head.

- Set a time limit of three to five minutes, and don't stop until time is up. If you get stuck, write about feeling stuck.
- Begin with anything, perhaps a memory of a person, a place, or an experience. Or begin with a sentence you remember from a book or a conversation.
- Don't worry about writing clearly, making corrections, or using logical order. Just write!

EXERCISE 1   Using Prewriting Techniques

1. On your own paper, write a one-page entry for your journal. Begin by describing an experience you had in a place that you liked.

2. On a separate sheet of paper, freewrite for three minutes. Begin with the name of a person you know. Write whatever comes to mind about the person.

PREWRITING: BRAINSTORMING AND CLUSTERING

BRAINSTORMING

Brainstorming is a technique that frees your mind to come up with many ideas as quickly as possible. You can brainstorm alone, but the technique often works best with a group. Then you can bounce ideas off each other.

- Choose a word or subject, and write it on a piece of paper.
- Now quickly jot down every idea on the subject you can think of.
- Do not stop to judge the ideas. You can do that later.
- Keep going until you run out of ideas.

CLUSTERING

Clustering, sometimes called *webbing*, is a process of breaking down a subject into smaller parts. Follow these guidelines for clustering.

- Write your subject in the center of your paper, and circle it.
- Write related ideas around the subject. Circle each idea, and connect them with lines to the original subject. You may also want to connect some of the ideas to each other.
- Let your mind wander. Keep adding, circling, and connecting ideas until your paper is filled.

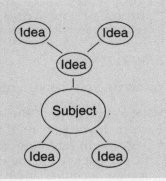

EXERCISE 2 Using Brainstorming and Clustering

Choose a subject from the list below, and brainstorm a list of related ideas on your own paper. Then choose another subject, and use it as the center of a cluster on a separate sheet of paper.

how to make new friends

a political campaign

pollution

money

a new trend in fashion

what to do when you're bored

PREWRITING: ASKING QUESTIONS

ASKING THE 5W-HOW? QUESTIONS

The **5W-How? questions** that a news reporter must answer in an article are *Who? What? Where? When? Why?* and *How?* These questions are a useful guide for anyone gathering information on a subject. Sometimes you won't need all of the questions, or you may need to ask some of the questions more than once. Here is an example of how to use the *5W-How?* questions to gather information about a sports hero.

• *Who?*	Who is Ben Roethlisberger?
	Whom does he play with?
• *What?*	What are his strengths and weaknesses?
	What awards has he won?
• *Where?*	Where did he go to college?
	Where did he grow up?
• *When?*	When did he start playing football?
• *Why?*	Why does he play football?
• *How?*	How does his record compare with those of other great quarterbacks?

OBSERVING

Suppose you want to describe a basketball game. You need to rely on your observations. What you observe with your senses—sight, hearing, touch, taste, and smell—is an indispensable source of information for writing.

touch:	hard bleachers; pushing and bumping of the crowd
hearing:	chants of cheerleaders and fans; blare of the buzzer
smell:	hot dogs and mustard; popcorn
taste:	stale, too-salty popcorn; tangy mustard
sight:	players in maroon-and-gold uniforms; colorful signs

EXERCISE 3 Collaborating to Gather Information

1. With a partner, choose a person you would like to gather information about. Work together to create *5W-How?* questions. Write the person's name and two of each type of question on the following lines.

Person: _____

Who? _____

_____

What? _____

_____

Where? _____

_____

When? _____

_____

Why? _____

_____

How? _____

_____

2. Choose a place or thing, and write down everything about it you can observe with your five senses—sight, smell, hearing, taste, and touch.

Place or thing: _____

_____

Sight: _____

_____

Smell: _____

_____

Hearing: _____

_____

Taste: _____

_____

Touch: _____

_____

IMAGINING

Imagination is one of the most powerful tools a writer has. For creative writing, letting your mind wander freely can help you generate a variety of ideas for stories and characters. For expository writing, using your imagination can help you approach your topic in varied and interesting ways. One way to get your imagination working is to ask yourself "What if?" questions.

- *What if the roles people play were reversed?* (What if I became the mayor of my town or city?)
- *What if something I take for granted vanished?* (What if I came home from school and found that my street had disappeared?)
- *What if I could change one thing in the world?* (What if I discovered a new way of communicating?)

EXERCISE 4   Using "What if?" Questions

Choose one of the questions below. Then, on your own paper, write ten more "What if?" questions about it to generate ideas or information.

1. What if a stranger left a message for someone else in your locker?

2. What if a man in an airport asked you to watch his bags and did not return?

3. What if you became separated from your group while hiking in the desert?

4. What if you got a chance to interview anybody from history?

5. What if you could change identities with someone for one day?

PREWRITING: ARRANGING IDEAS

After you have gathered ideas for a piece of writing, you need to organize them. You can choose from several approaches to arranging ideas. This chart shows four common ways of organizing ideas.

ARRANGING IDEAS		
Type of Order	**Definition**	**Examples**
Chronological	Narration: order that presents events as they happen in time	story, explanation of a process, drama, history biography,
Spatial	Description: order that presents objects according to location (near to far, outside to inside, left to right, top to bottom)	description of settings for stories, dramas, etc.; tour and travel guides
Importance	Evaluation: order that presents information from most to least important (or the reverse)	persuasion, evaluation, justification
Logical	Classification: order that presents objects or events according to groups and subgroups	definitions, classifications

EXERCISE 5   Choosing Appropriate Organization

Four writing assignments are listed below. On the line before each, identify the method you would use to arrange the ideas and details for your writing.

_____ 1. Write a newspaper article describing the new video arcade in your town.

_____ 2. Write a magazine article describing the events that led up to a district soccer championship.

_____ 3. Write a letter to your school board to persuade them to change the dress code.

_____ 4. Write a report for class about the different ethnic groups that live in the South Pacific.

WRITING A FIRST DRAFT

After you have gathered and organized your ideas, it is time to write a first draft. There is no single right way to write a draft. Some writers make detailed outlines before they begin, while others use a sequence chain or a few rough notes. Some scribble as fast as the ideas come, while others work slowly, carefully crafting each sentence. As you begin to shape your first draft, keep these suggestions in mind.

- Use your prewriting as a guide.
- Write freely, but concentrate on expressing yourself clearly.
- Feel free to adjust and expand on your original ideas as you work. Writing is a process of discovery.
- Don't worry about errors in grammar, usage, and mechanics. They can be fixed later.

Below is the first draft of a report on the American conservationist John Muir. Notice the notes the writer has made. The writer will go back to the prewriting stage to gather additional information to answer the new questions. Also notice that the draft is not a polished effort. The polishing will come later.

John Muir, a pioneer in the movement to conserve the American wilderness, was born in Scotland in 1838. [When did he come to the U.S.?] He spent [part of?] his youth in Wisconsin. He traveled about the country until, in 1868, he came to Calif. As JM tells the story, he arrived by Panama steamer in San Francisco and asked for the nearest way out of town. when he was asked where he wanted to go, he replied, "To anywhere that is wild." He went to the Yosemite Valley in the Sierra Nevadas. [how did he get there? Did he walk?] He fell in love with the valley and wrote books and articles describing it. With others [who?] he led an effort to make the govt. protect the places of great natural beauty in this country [need more details] Yosemite became a national park in 1890.

EXERCISE 6   Writing a First Draft

Here are some notes for a biography of Indian writer Rabindranath Tagore.
Use them to write a first draft of a one-paragraph biography.

Rabindranath Tagore, Indian writer

won Nobel Prize for literature in 1913

Founded an international school, Santiniketan. Purpose: for students from
around the world to learn about India, and for Indian students to learn
about the West.

was painter and composer also (Wrote national anthems of India and
Bangladesh.)

Indian children learn to read with his books.

_____

_____

_____

_____

_____

_____

_____

_____

_____

_____

_____

_____

_____

_____

_____

_____

_____

EVALUATING AND REVISING

EVALUATING

After you have finished your first draft, the next step is to *evaluate* it. When you evaluate something, you judge it by measuring it against a set of standards or criteria. Which criteria you use depends on the purpose of your writing, but the five criteria below apply to most writing.

- Is the writing interesting enough to catch and hold a reader's attention?
- Does the writing have a clear theme or main idea?
- Is the main idea supported by enough details?
- Is the material organized sensibly? Are the ideas connected smoothly?
- Does the writing omit clichés, repetitions, and unnecessary details?

Being objective about your own work is difficult. Writers learn a great deal from the opinions of others. Friends, family, teachers, editors, and classmates can give you valuable feedback about your work. Keep these strategies in mind when you are evaluating your own writing or a classmate's.

Self-Evaluation	Peer Evaluation
1. To give yourself a fresh perspective, put your draft aside for a few hours or overnight before evaluating it.	1. Begin by commenting on what works well. Writers need to know their strengths so they can build on them.
2. Read your draft several times, each time focusing on only one criterion: content, organization, or style.	2. Focus on content, organization, and style. Proofreading for mechanics and grammar comes later.
3. Read your draft aloud to discover awkward or unclear passages.	3. Make specific suggestions for revising ideas that are unclear or for adding information that is needed.
4. Keep a positive attitude. You must find the trouble spots before you can eliminate them.	

EXERCISE 7   Practicing Peer Evaluation

A classmate has written the paragraph below and has asked you to evaluate it. Use the five criteria for evaluating writing, and follow the guidelines for peer evaluation. Continue on your own paper if you need more space than the lines below for your comments.

The Hopi Niman Dance is a dance the Hopis perform for supernatural beings called *kachinas*. The Hopis believe that the kachinas live in the mountains for six months, and for the other six months they visit the Hopi. They believe the kachinas bring rain for the crops and good health for the people. The Niman Dance is the dance they perform at the end of the six months. It is called the "Going Home" ceremony. Dancers dance and sing for most of the day in this ceremony, which wishes the kachinas a good journey home and tells them to hurry back. Also, presents are given to children.

_____

_____

_____

_____

_____

_____

_____

_____

_____

_____

_____

_____

_____

_____

REVISING

Based on your evaluation, the next step is to to *revise* your work. The four basic revision techniques are adding, cutting, replacing, and reordering. Use these techniques to make the changes needed in your first draft.

REVISION TECHNIQUES	
Technique	**Example**
1. **Add.** Add information and details: words, phrases, sentences, even paragraphs.	The umbrella was invented in Mesopotamia. *ancient*
2. **Cut.** Eliminate repetitions, unnecessary words, and details that are unrelated to your main idea.	Red Giants are stars that ~~are called Red Giants because they~~ are very large and red in color.
3. **Replace.** Replace weak, unclear, or awkward words, phrases, and sentences with more precise and effective language.	He had just completed a ~~sentence~~ in New York. *prison term*
4. **Reorder.** Rearrange words, phrases, sentences, or paragraphs for variety and clarity.	Tonga is the last kingdom in Polynesia called the Friendly Islands.

EXERCISE 8   Evaluating and Revising Your Writing

Reread the paragraph you wrote for Exercise 6. Evaluate your draft, using the five criteria on page 9. Then revise your writing, using the four techniques for revision described above. Mark your changes by hand on your first draft. Finally, rewrite the revised paragraph on your own paper.

PROOFREADING AND PUBLISHING

PROOFREADING

Proofreading is the final step in preparing a piece of writing. When you proofread, you search carefully for mistakes in grammar, spelling, punctuation, and capitalization. Finding these mistakes is easier if you have put your paper aside for a while. Exchanging papers with a partner can also be useful. Use these guidelines when you proofread.

Guidelines for Proofreading
• Is every sentence a complete sentence instead of a fragment or a run-on?
• Is every sentence punctuated correctly?
• Is the capitalization correct for the beginnings of sentences, proper nouns, and proper adjectives?
• Do verbs show the correct number and tense?
• Do pronouns show the correct case, number, and gender?
• Are frequently confused words (such as *accept* and *except*) used correctly?
• Is each word spelled correctly?

Symbols for Proofreading		
≡	korea	Capitalize a letter.
/	the speed of Light	Lowercase a capital letter.
~	way which to go	Change the order of words or letters.
ℒ	the citty of Dallas	Take out a letter, word, phrase or punctuation mark.
∧	open the door	Insert a letter, word, phrase, or punctuation mark.
∨	dogs	Insert apostrophe or quotation mark.
#	birdcage	Add a space.
⌣	a water fall	Close up space.

EXERCISE 9   Proofreading a Paragraph

Proofread the following paragraph to find mistakes in grammar, spelling, capitalization, and mechanics. Use proofreading symbols to mark the errors.

Do you no what makes a rainbow. Rainbows occurr when the Sun shins through a rain showr. Rainbows usually happen erly in the morning. Or late in the after noon, when the sun is low in in the sky. each randrop acts like a little prism that seperate the white sun light into the different colors that makeup the sunlight. When all the the rain drops act together they form a big prism that shine colored light into the sky. This colored light is a raindow.

PUBLISHING

After you have revised and proofread your work, you are ready to *publish* it, to share your work with an audience.

Guidelines for Manuscript Form

1. Use only one side of the paper.
2. Type, use a word processor, or write in blue or black ink. If you type, double-space the lines. If you write, don't skip lines.
3. Leave margins of one inch at the top, bottom, and sides of each page.
4. Indent the first line of each paragraph.
5. Follow your teacher's instructions as to where to place your name, the date, and the title of your work.
6. Number all pages, except the first page, in the upper right-hand corner.
7. Make sure all the pages are neat and clean. You can often erase smudges with a regular pencil eraser. If you must use correction fluid, be sure that it is barely noticeable.

Suggestions for Publishing

- Submit your work to your school newspaper, yearbook, or literary magazine.
- Enter a writing contest. Your teacher or guidance counselor probably knows about contests for students.
- Submit letters to the editor of your local newspaper.
- Post items on a bulletin board in your school or local library.

EXERCISE 10   Preparing a Final Copy

Proofread and correct the paragraph you revised for Exercise 8. Then prepare a clean, final copy of your paper, using the manuscript guidelines on the preceding page. Meet with a small group of your classmates, and take turns reading your papers. Discuss ways that each of you might publish your writing.

EXERCISE 11   Collaborating to Identify Publishing Opportunities

Suppose you have just completed the writing projects described below. Work in a group to brainstorm two ideas for publishing each piece.

1. Transcriptions of your grandmother's stories about her life as a child growing up in Poland

2. An eyewitness account of the dramatic rescue of people trapped inside a burning apartment building

3. A humorous poem about your first music lesson

4. An article about the correct way to brush your teeth

5. A review of your favorite movie

Animal Crackers reprinted by permission: Tribune Media Services.

MAIN IDEAS AND TOPIC SENTENCES

Most paragraphs are organized around one *main idea*. All the sentences work together to make that main idea clear. In the following paragraph, the sentences are all related to one main idea: the writer learned about his grandfather's childhood when they visited Mexico together.

> I learned a lot about my grandfather when I visited Mexico with him last summer. We saw the house where he was born and stayed in the village where he grew up. I met people who had known him when he was a boy. They had great stories to tell me.

THE TOPIC SENTENCE

A *topic sentence* states the main idea of a paragraph. A topic sentence may come anywhere in the paragraph, but it often appears at the beginning. Some paragraphs have no topic sentence. For example, a narrative paragraph that relates a sequence of events usually does not have a topic sentence.

In the following paragraph the topic sentence is at the end. It summarizes the writer's main idea: a first backpacking experience was full of adventure.

> We hiked until late in the afternoon. We noticed that storm clouds were rolling in. Soon the wind became wild. The sky was dark by the time we pitched our tent. Squashed inside our tiny space, we ate a cold dinner. The tent collapsed during the night, and a nosy bear took my trail mix. My first backpacking experience was quite an adventure!

EXERCISE 1   Identifying Main Ideas and Topic Sentences

On the lines after each of the following paragraphs, state the main idea of the paragraph. If the paragraph has a topic sentence, underline it.

1.   The Tuareg people live in the Sahara, the largest desert on earth. Using camels as their method of transportation, the Tuareg move frequently to find water. They travel great distances to trade salt and dates for items that they don't have in the desert. They carry with them their homes, which are made of dried grasses and camel leather. The Tuareg people certainly lead a nomadic life!

_____

_____

_____

2.   Stepping cautiously into the cave, Hector found it darker than he'd
expected. He could see the faint outline of bats hanging from the
ceiling, but nothing else. The air felt cold and damp. Something
swooped through the air uncomfortably close to his head. He jumped
back. Shaken, he called to the others. "Let's get out of here!"

_____

_____

_____

3.   The height of a mountain could depend on how you measure it.
Mount Everest, the Himalayan giant, rises to a height of 29,028 feet
above sea level—the highest in the world. If, however, you measure a
mountain from its base to its summit, there is one mountain that
surpasses Everest. Mauna Kea is a volcano that is part of the Hawaiian
Islands. It rises only 13, 796 feet above sea level, but its base is 19,087
feet below the sea. So if you added the underwater part of Mauna Kea
to the part above sea level, its actual height would be 32,883 feet. That's
3,855 feet taller than Mount Everest. So, which is the higher mountain?

_____

_____

_____

4.   Russian explorers and traders introduced their homeland to
American Indian art. From 1741 to 1867, Russia ruled Alaska and the
Northwest Coast. As Russian explorers and traders traveled through
the territory, they collected samples of the local arts and crafts. The
headdresses, painted bowls, carved pipes and rattles, and blankets and
clothing woven from natural fibers fascinated these visitors. They took
these things home with them to Russia. So today, more than a hundred
years after Russia sold Alaska to the United States, you can still see
fine examples of American Indian art in the Saint Petersburg Museum
of Anthropology and Ethnography.

_____

_____

_____

UNITY AND COHERENCE

UNITY

When a paragraph has *unity*, all the sentences relate to the main idea. Nothing extra is added that might distract a reader. Unity is important no matter how the main idea is stated.

All Sentences Relate to a Stated Idea. In the following paragraph, the first sentence states the main idea. All the other sentences provide details related to that idea.

> When we had a visitor from Japan, we found ourselves tasting foods we had never tried before. Takayuki showed us how to prepare squid, octopus, and sea urchins. He fixed sashimi, a dish made of raw fish seasoned with soy sauce, and wasabi, which is made from spicy, green radish. My favorite was sushi, because we could use so many different ingredients.

All Sentences Relate to an Implied Main Idea. Although not stated outright, the main idea of the following paragraph is that Concord was home to some important American writers. All of the sentences provide details about those writers.

> The Old Manse, in Concord, Massachusetts, was home, at different times, to poet and essayist Ralph Waldo Emerson, writer Henry David Thoreau, and novelist Nathaniel Hawthorne. Not far from the Old Manse is Orchard House, where Louisa May Alcott wrote her famous novels, including *Little Women*. Perhaps the most famous literary landmark in this area is Walden Pond, where Thoreau lived alone in a cabin. There he wrote the journals that later became the basis for his book *Walden*.

All Sentences Relate to a Sequence of Events. The following paragraph does not have a main idea as such. But it relates a sequence of actions.

> The starting gun sounded, and Lola dove into the water. Jostled at first by the other triathletes, she slowly distanced herself from the pack. Twenty minutes later, she emerged from the water and struggled into her cycling gear. She had trained well, and the eighteen miles of flat terrain gave her little trouble. Pulling into the transition area, she mentally prepared herself for her most difficult leg of the race: the 10k run. Her legs, though tight and tired, responded to her command to keep going. With a final burst of speed, she crossed the finish line with her arms raised in exhausted victory!

EXERCISE 2   Identifying Sentences That Destroy Unity

In each of the following paragraphs, find the sentence that doesn't support the main idea. Draw a line through that sentence.

1. A surprising number of birds cannot fly, but they have other abilities that make up for their inability to fly. The ostrich has powerful legs that allow it to run swiftly. The penguin uses its flippers to swim underwater. Birds such as eagles fly to great heights. Another flightless bird, the kiwi, uses its extremely sharp sense of smell to find its prey at night.

2. For the Lovedu people of South Africa, rainmaking is an important festival, and their queen is the rainmaker. They call her the Transformer of the Clouds. They believe that she has great powers to influence the weather. When rain is needed, the people bring her gifts. In other places the rainmaker is often a man. The Lovedu queen uses secret medicines and summons the help of ancestors in trying to call forth the rain.

3. The 1971 eruption of the Italian volcano Mount Etna was its 136th recorded explosion. Etna is the oldest continuously active volcano in Europe. Hurricanes and tornadoes are other natural disasters. The Greeks recorded an eruption from Etna in 475 B.C. Today, an observatory located near the rim of the volcano can warn people in time for them to evacuate.

COHERENCE

A paragraph has *coherence* if a reader can easily follow the material and see how it is related to the main idea. You can create coherence in a paragraph by clearly organizing ideas and making connections between them.

Order of Ideas

How you *order,* or arrange, ideas in a paragraph can help a reader follow them. The subject will often suggest the best method to use. Here are four basic ways of arranging ideas.

Chronological Order. *Chronological order* relates an event or series of actions in the order in which they happen. Chronological ordering works well when you are explaining a process or telling a story.

Spatial Order. *Spatial order* describes an object's location in relation to other objects. You might describe objects from left to right, for example, or from far to near. Spatial order can help give a reader a visual impression of a room, a building, or an object, such as a car.

Order of Importance. You can arrange the details in a paragraph in *order of importance,* from the least to the most important, or from the most to the least important. You can draw your reader's attention to what you think is most important by putting it at the beginning or end of your paragraph.

Logical Order. With *logical order,* related ideas are grouped together. For example, in a paper about soccer, you might have one group of details about equipment and another group of details about rules.

EXERCISE 3   Choosing the Order of Ideas

For each topic below, identify which order of ideas would make the most sense. For some topics, more than one order might work. Write your answers on your own paper.

1. a visit to the Empire State Building
2. a discussion of blue whales and sperm whales
3. reasons to celebrate the birthday of Dr. Martin Luther King, Jr.
4. the early history of a major-league baseball team
5. how to connect the parts of a stereo system

Between Ideas

To connect ideas in a paragraph, you can make a *direct reference* to other material in the paragraph. You can also make a *transition,* or bridge, from one idea to another.

Direct References. You can make a direct reference in these three ways: (1) by using a pronoun or noun that refers to a noun or pronoun used earlier, (2) by repeating a word used earlier, or (3) by using a word or phrase that means the same thing as one used earlier. In the following paragraph, the direct references are in italics. The superscript numbers indicate the type of direct reference.

   Although spiders frighten many people, *their*[1] fearsome reputation is largely undeserved. Although thousands of species of *spiders*[2] have been identified, only a *few*[1] are any more harmful to *people*[2] than ants or beetles are. Notable among the dangerous *spiders*[2] is the black widow. Also known as the *hourglass spider*[3], the female of *this species*[1] has powerful venom.

Transitional Words and Phrases. Transitional words and phrases show a connection between facts or ideas. The following chart lists some frequently used transitional expressions.

Comparing Ideas	also, and, another, besides, in addition, other, similarly, too
Contrasting Ideas	although, but, however, in spite of, instead, nevertheless, on the other hand, still, yet
Showing Cause and Effect	as a result, because, consequently, for, since, so, therefore, thus
Showing Time	after, at last, at once, at one time, before, eventually, finally, first, for a time, meanwhile, then, when
Showing Place	above, across, around, before, beyond, from, here, in, nearby, next, on, over, there, to, under, up
Showing Importance	first, last, mainly, more importantly, then, to begin with

EXERCISE 4 **Identifying Direct References and Transitions**

On your own paper, make a list of the direct references and a list of the transitional phrases that you find in the paragraph below.

[1] The word *Inuit* means "the people," and the Inuit prefer this name for themselves. [2] At one time, other American Indians called them *Eskimos*, which means "eaters of raw meat." [3] The home of the Inuit is the North American tundra, a treeless area in the North that extends from the edges of the forests to the Arctic Ocean. [4] In this frozen, barren land the Inuit have struggled to find food and shelter. [5] Because their appearance is similar to that of Central Asian peoples, the Inuit are thought to have migrated from Asia centuries ago.

USING DESCRIPTION

One strategy, or method, of developing a paragraph is *description.* You use description when you want to show what an object, person, or place is like, or what it looks like. For example, you would use description to let your parents know what your teacher looks like or to tell your best friend what your new shoes are like. In description, you use *sensory details* as support. Sensory details are details of what you see, hear, smell, touch, or taste. These details are often arranged in spatial order.

In the following paragraph, the writer uses details of sight, sound, and smell to describe an engine room.

> The engine room of the spaceship *Orion* was cramped, cluttered, and dimly lit. Empty boxes were stacked haphazardly all around me. Their packing materials were scattered on the floor, along with a clutter of greasy pipes. On one side there was a table strewn with tools and strange, twisted bits of metal and wire. A few notes, scrawled on scraps of paper, were weighted down by bolts and screws. I glanced over the notes but still could not figure out what project was underway there. Against the back wall the computers, humming amid a tangle of colored wires, blinked red and green lights in the dark. In the air was the faint smell of burning rubber.

EXERCISE 5 Using Description as a Strategy

Choose four of the topics below. Use brainstorming or clustering to think of at least five details to describe each topic. On your own paper, arrange each group of details in spatial order.

1. a scene in a forest
2. a busy street corner
3. your school auditorium
4. a coral reef
5. your dream car

6. your classroom
7. a bicycle shop
8. a member of your family
9. your favorite food
10. a telephone booth

USING EVALUATION

You use the strategy of *evaluation* whenever you make a judgment about whether something is good or bad, interesting or dull, worthwhile or not. In a paragraph, you use evaluation to share your judgment or opinion of a subject with your audience. To let your audience know how you made the judgment, you provide reasons that support your opinion. An effective way to arrange these reasons is by *order of importance*.

In the following paragraph, the writer evaluates a book. Notice how the opening opinion is supported by details. The writer emphasizes the details by arranging the most important details first.

> Maurice Herzog's book *Annapurna* is a gripping mountain adventure story. In 1950, Herzog was one of the leaders of the first ascent of Annapurna, a gigantic Himalayan peak. Because this story is true, it is that much more exciting. He describes vividly what it is like to wander through jungles. He journeys to a mountain and battles both frostbite and mosquitoes. He brings you along on the journey. Then when the mountaineers finally reach the summit, you feel as if you were there.

EXERCISE 6   Using Evaluation as a Strategy

Evaluate two of the topics below by making a positive or negative judgment about each one. On your own paper, write your judgments or opinions, and then give two or three reasons that support each opinion.

EX.   Broad Topic: School Uniforms
      Evaluation: Schools should require uniforms.
          Reason 1: Uniforms are less expensive than a school wardrobe.
          Reason 2: You wouldn't have to decide what to wear each day.
          Reason 3: Clothing at school would no longer be an important issue
                     to regulate or worry about.

1. a requirement that all high school students take a home economics class

2. a video game you have played

3. a book you have read recently

4. a change in the minimum age (from sixteen to eighteen) for a driver's license

USING NARRATION

The stategy of *narration* enables you to look at changes over a period of time. You use narration to tell a story (what happened at the party), explain a process (how to study for a test), or describe a cause and effect (the effects of sunburn). When you use narration, you usually arrange details in *chronological order*, the order in which they occur in time.

TELLING A STORY

When you tell a story, you are telling what happened. The story can be about a real or an imaginary event. In the following paragraph, the writer tells what happened on New Year's morning.

> Mei Hua was up early. She woke up everyone else in the house and hurried them through their breakfast. She waited impatiently while the rest of her family took a dreadfully long time to dress. Didn't they understand that this was the most exciting day of the year? Finally, everyone was ready. She hurried ahead of them as they walked to the front of the parade. Quickly, she found her place beneath the huge silk dragon and waited for the New Year's parade to begin.

EXPLAINING A PROCESS

When you tell someone how something works or how to do something, you are explaining a process. Any process involves changes over time. The following paragraph tells how to make latkes. As you read, think about the changes that occur.

> To make latkes, you need potatoes, onions, eggs, and flour or matzo meal. Grate the onions with the potatoes so the potatoes won't darken. Squeeze the liquid from the grated potatoes and onions. Add the eggs, flour, salt, and pepper. Heat some oil in a frying pan until it is hot but not smoking. Slip your batter into the hot oil, and fry the pancake until it is golden brown on both sides. Use a slotted spoon to transfer the latke to a paper towel.

EXPLAINING CAUSE AND EFFECT

When you want to explain the cause or effect of something, you need to relate a sequence of actions over a period of time. The following paragraph uses the strategy of narration.

> The predictions had been for rain, high tides, and "some high winds." This report, we thought, was no cause for worry, and so we stayed in the cottage by the ocean. By midafternoon, however, it was clear that the storm was going to be much wilder than anyone had expected. The fierce winds were shaking the fragile cottage, and the waves, whipped into a frenzy by these winds, were breaking at the edge of our deck. The power went out, and we huddled around a transistor radio. In the dark, we heard that the roads were flooding, and power lines were down all over. We were now trapped in our cottage.

EXERCISE 7   **Using Narration as a Strategy**

Use narration as a strategy to develop the lists below. Write your lists on your own paper.

1. Have you ever met a famous person? Has something exciting happened at your school recently? What happened in the last movie you saw? Choose one of these subjects, and list at least three actions that took place.

2. Can you prepare tacos? Do you know how to do the backstroke? Can you parallel park a car? Choose one of these subjects, and list at least three steps in the process.

3. Has something changed recently in your neighborhood? Has someone moved away? Has a business closed or opened? Choose one of these events, and identify at least three causes or effects of the event.

USING CLASSIFICATION

When you use *classification*, you look at a subject as it relates to other subjects in a group. There are three ways to classify. You can divide a subject into parts, define it, or compare and contrast it with something else.

DIVIDING

With some subjects, the best way to explain the whole is to divide it into parts. For example, to explain the U. S. Congress, you may have to divide it into two parts: the Senate and the House of Representatives. The following paragraph uses the strategy of dividing to explain the parts of a wheat kernel.

> In the making of whole wheat flour, the entire kernel of wheat is used. Each of the three parts of the kernel offers valuable nutrients. The *bran*, a protective outer covering, provides fiber and many B vitamins. Underneath the bran is the starchy *endosperm*, the largest part of the kernel. The endosperm contains iron, protein, and B vitamins. The *germ*, found at one end of the grain, occupies only a small portion of the kernel. Besides having a high fat content, the germ is rich in vitamin E and thiamine.

DEFINING

When you *define* a subject, you identify it as a part of a larger group or class. Then you identify the features that make it unique. In the following paragraph, the first sentence identifies the group to which Paraguay belongs, South American countries. The remaining sentences include details about Paraguay that tell how it is different from other South American countries.

> Paraguay is a country that is located almost in the center of South America. Surrounded by Brazil, Bolivia, and Argentina, its only access to the sea is river systems. The people of Paraguay speak Spanish and Guarni, the language of the Guarni Indians, who were the original inhabitants of this land.

COMPARING AND CONTRASTING

Another way to classify subjects is to explain how they are alike (*comparing*) or how they are different (*contrasting*). Depending on your purpose, you can compare, contrast, or both compare and contrast. The following paragraph compares and contrasts two sisters.

> Although Jenna and Maryssa are sisters, you might never guess it. Jenna is tall; Maryssa is short. Jenna has curly black hair. Maryssa's hair is red and straight. Jenna loves any kind of sport, particularly baseball and in-line skating. Maryssa is studious, and her idea of a game is one she can play on a computer. Both sisters, however, love travel and adventure. This love is a good thing, since both their father and mother are in the military, and the family moves frequently.

EXERCISE 8   Using Classification as a Strategy

Follow the directions telling which classification strategy to use for developing each main idea below. Work in a small group with two other classmates. Choose one member of your group as the recorder, and then work together to list ideas. After you've finished your lists, discuss the strategies. Which one was the most difficult to use? Which was the easiest? How did the strategies help you stay focused on your subject?

Main Idea	Classification Strategy
1. Magazines currently available cover just about every interest a person might have.	Examine the subject of magazines by dividing them into types. List five details for each type to support the main idea.
2. Sports spectators add color and excitement to sporting events.	Define who is included among "sports spectators." List five of their characteristics, and describe how they differ from other audiences.
3. Working in the supermarket and volunteering at the hospital are both rewarding ways to spend after-school hours.	Compare and contrast the two kinds of jobs by listing five of their likenesses and differences.

PLANNING A COMPOSITION

Writing a composition, like writing a single paragraph, requires planning. Before you begin to write, you need to complete several steps.

   You must first choose a topic and decide on your main idea. Next, you gather information related to your topic and main idea. Then you need to organize the information in a way that will make sense to your reader. An **early plan**, or **rough outline**, can make organizing your ideas easier.

EARLY PLANS

To create an *early plan*, or *rough outline*, sort your ideas or facts into groups. Then arrange the groups in some order that makes sense of your ideas.

GROUPING.   After you have gathered details on your topic, group the details that have something in common. Write a heading for each group to show how the details in that group are related. (Details that don't fit into any group may be useful later. For now, put them in a separate list.)

ORDERING.   Next, put the details within each group in order, and then order the groups themselves. There are several ways to order, or arrange, ideas.

Chronological (time) *order* presents events in the order that they happen.
Spatial order presents details according to where they are located.
Order of importance presents details from most important to least important, or vice versa.
Logical order presents your topic by dividing it into parts, by defining it, or by comparing and contrasting it with something else.

EXERCISE 1   Creating an Early Plan

Here are some notes for a composition about how women gained their right to vote. Work with a partner to organize the notes into two separate groups. On your own paper, write a heading for each group to show what the notes in that group have in common. Finally, arrange the notes within each group in a sensible order.

two hundred years ago, women had few rights and couldn't vote

1848—the first women's rights conference in the United States calls for women to be given the right to vote

1800s—women in Britain begin to protest for suffrage, the right to vote in elections

Emmeline Pankhurst (British) calls for action to gain the vote
British women chain themselves to public buildings to gain publicity for their cause; many are jailed
early 1900s—women can vote in many states in the Midwest and the West, places where women pioneers had worked alongside men
1800s—American women like Sojourner Truth and Susan Anthony lead the movement for voting rights for women
British newspapers call the women "suffragettes" to make fun of them; the women adopt the name
1914–18—women work in factories in Britain while men fight in World War I
1918—women over thirty granted voting rights in Britain
after World War I—U.S. women campaign with meetings, parades, and speeches
1920—U.S. women who are thirty and older can vote in all states

FORMAL OUTLINES

A *formal outline* is a highly structured, clearly labeled writing plan. It divides a subject into main headings and subheadings that are labeled with letters and numbers. There are two kinds of formal outlines. A *topic outline* states ideas in words or brief phrases. A *sentence outline* states ideas in complete sentences. The following topic outline is for a composition about changes in our lives.

Title: How Inventions and Information Have Changed Our Lives
Main Idea: Although new inventions have changed the way we live in the United States in the last fifty years, we have also been affected by new Information.

I. Inventions
  A. Computers
  B. CDs and DVDs
  C. Microwave ovens

II. New Information
  A. Health
    1. Changing eating habits
    2. Changing exercise habits
  B. Environment
    1. Recycling
    2. Conserving natural resources

EXERCISE 2   Creating a Formal Outline

Using the early plan you made for Exercise 1, create a formal outline on your own paper. You can use a topic outline or a sentence outline. Add a title and a statement of your main idea.

WRITING INTRODUCTIONS

A composition begins with an *introduction*, which must do three important things.

1. **CATCH THE READERS' INTEREST.** The introduction should make your readers want to keep reading. It should arouse your readers' interest and curiosity.

2. **SET THE TONE.** The introduction should also set the composition's *tone*, or general feeling. For example, the tone might be serious and formal or humorous and lighthearted.

3. **PRESENT THE THESIS.** Most important, your introduction should tell readers what your composition is about. In other words, it should present a *thesis statement*, a sentence or two that announce your main idea. Often, but not always, the thesis statement comes at the end of the introduction.

WAYS TO WRITE INTRODUCTIONS

Writers use a variety of techniques to grab their readers' attention in the introduction. Here are five.

- **Begin with an example or an anecdote.** An example or an anecdote (a short, interesting, or humorous story) will draw readers in with concrete, vivid details. These details not only spark the reader's interest, but also can include important aspects of the topic.

> I was the only one who had studied Chinese, and so I thought I'd show off a little when the waiter brought the menu. I pointed to an item and said, "That would be very good." With a twinkle in his eye, the waiter agreed. "It is very good. It says we accept credit cards." How foolish I felt, but the desire to impress makes people do unusual things!

- **Begin with a startling fact or opinion on a topic.** Curious readers will keep reading to discover more about your topic.

> In Ghana, the humble yam determines the beginning of the new year. At harvest time the Ewe people hold a yam festival for a week, filling their towns with drumming and dancing. At the end of the week, the farmers bring in the new crop of yams in a parade—The new year has begun!

- **Use an appropriate quotation.** You might use someone else's words in an introduction if their words are interesting and make an important point. Quotes from experts, authors, or someone mentioned in the composition build your readers' interest in the topic.

> "Star light, star bright, first star I see tonight . . ." Have you ever said these words to make a wish? In fact, the first "star" of the evening is likely to be the planet Venus.

- **Give some background information.** Providing background details can help your readers understand the thesis, help them recall what they already know about the topic, or simply help them build their interest.

> Peru is one of the largest South American countries, both in size and population. The Andes Mountains cross Peru, with many of its twenty million people living on mountain farms.

- **Begin with a simple statement of your thesis.** You may wish to state your thesis plainly, without fuss or fanfare. This technique immediately focuses your readers' attention on your composition's main idea.

> When the Soviet Union broke up in 1992, many people learned for the first time that it had been made up of many distinct nations. Azerbaijan, Kazakhstan, and Turkmenistan were unfamiliar places where languages, customs, and lifestyles differed greatly from those of the well-known Soviet state, Russia.

NOTE The body of a composition contains paragraphs that support the main idea stated in your thesis. In supporting the main idea, these paragraphs should all work together to achieve **unity** and **coherence.** For information on these two elements, see pages 17–20.

EXERCISE 3   Identifying Types of Introductions

On the line after each following introduction, write the technique the writer uses to get the readers' attention.

1. When the rice harvest in Malaysia is over, it is time for the top-spinning season. In Malaysia, top-spinning is a traditional art. The tops measure six inches across and weigh more than five pounds each. A skillful player can make a top spin for as long as two hours. The art of making and spinning tops is passed from generation to generation.

2. "If it ain't one thing, it's two," my great-uncle Chris used to say. This original version of the old saying never seemed truer than on the first day of this year's lizard-spotting contest.

3. One morning my brother decided he was a frog. He wouldn't walk. He hopped everywhere. It took half an hour for him to hop to the playground. He wouldn't say anything either—just "Ribbet," even when I offered him a cookie. After a morning of this, I began to realize how powerful a small child's imagination can be.

4. Rhinoceroses have existed for thirty million years, but today they are among the most endangered animals on the planet. They are killed for their horns, which many people believe have medicinal properties. Because of this, all the species of the rhino are on the endangered-species list.

5. Alfred Nobel was the founder of the Nobel Prize. He was a Swedish chemist who invented dynamite. He disliked the fact that his invention was used for warfare, so he left money in his will to establish prizes for people who work to make the world a better place. The first Nobel Prizes were given in 1901. Since then they have been given each year to people around the world who have made outstanding contributions in physics, medicine, chemistry, economics, literature, and peace.

EXERCISE 4 Working Cooperatively to Write an Introduction

Work with a partner to draft two introductions to a composition based on the formal outlines you created in Exercise 2. Each introduction should use one of the techniques for writing introductions discussed in this lesson. Write your introductions on your own paper.

WRITING CONCLUSIONS

The *conclusion* is the last part of your composition. Your conclusion should leave your readers feeling satisfied that the composition is complete. To create this sense of completion, your conclusion must reinforce the main idea while bringing the composition to a definite close.

WAYS TO WRITE CONCLUSIONS

Writers use many methods to end their compositions. Here are six.

- **Restate your main idea.** The most direct way to end your composition is to restate the thesis in different words. Try to find a newer, stronger wording. The following conclusion restates in different words the idea that backpacking, although difficult, has its rewards.

> Backpacking is not a luxurious vacation. It can be difficult, unpredictable, and downright uncomfortable. Still, it is one of the best ways to get in touch with nature and discover the wilderness.

- **Summarize your main points.** Emphasize the major points of your composition by summarizing them.

> The area called the Middle East actually consists of fifteen countries. Even though they all differ, sometimes greatly, the discovery of oil in this region affected every one of them.

- **Close with a final idea or example.** You can reinforce or pull together your main points by using a final example.

> When you go hiking, be prepared for anything. The weather may change; a hike may take longer than expected; or you may need emergency first aid. You may not need rain gear, extra food, a flashlight, or a first-aid kit; but why take a chance? After all, the unexpected is part of what makes hiking an adventure!

- **Make a final comment on the topic.** Give a sense of completeness to your composition by ending with one final comment on your topic. You can provide a thoughtful observation, give a personal reaction, or project a vision of the future.

> King was assassinated before he could complete his work. Each year on Martin Luther King Day, however, people pause to remember the words of his now-famous speech, "I have a dream . . ." By doing this, they make sure that his dream stays alive.

- **Refer to your introduction.** Your conclusion may make a direct reference to something in the introduction. For example, the following conclusion refers to the introduction on page 29.

> People may choose to mark the new year by celebrating the yam. However they choose to celebrate, it is a time of reflection and thanksgiving.

- **Call on your readers to take action.** If you are writing a persuasive essay, use your conclusion to urge the reader to do something or to accept a belief. This approach, called the direct appeal, also works for other kinds of compositions.

> Although the destruction of the rain forests continues, it has been slowed because of the tremendous public outcry against it. As people continue to take interest in the fate of a place that may be far from their own homes, the future of the rain forest looks somewhat brighter.

EXERCISE 5   Writing a Conclusion

Read the introduction and body of the composition on the following page. On your own paper, write a conclusion, using one of the techniques on this page or the previous page. Then get together with a small group of classmates and answer the following questions about your conclusions. Why did you choose one particular technique over another? Which conclusion works best with the composition? What are the strengths and weaknesses of each conclusion?

Spiders are creatures that people see as spooky, frightening, and deadly. These busy, resourceful creatures often don't deserve this reputation.

Of about 35,000 known species of spiders in the world, few are harmful to people. Spiders are carnivores, or meat eaters, but their food is mostly insects. Although some large spiders native to South America have been known to catch and eat birds, most of the time their diet is made up of worms, mice, and large insects. Without spiders, it's possible that the world would be overrun with insects, including pesky flies.

Spiders can be clever engineers and architects. Many spiders catch their food in webs that they spin. Not all webs resemble the commonly seen orbed web of the garden spider. The trapdoor spider, for example, makes a tunnel in the ground and spins a silk lining for it. The spider waits in the tunnel beneath a trapdoor. When it hears an animal nearby, the spider springs out to prey on it.

An old name for spiders is <u>attercop</u>, which means "poison head." Spiders do have venom, or poison, which they inject through their jaws when they bite their prey. Most spiders, however, do not have jaws strong enough to break human skin. They cannot give a large enough dose to harm a person.

The fearful reputation of spiders is based on the few spiders that can harm a person. These include the brown recluse spider, the Australian funnel web spider, and the black widow. These spiders have a venom that, even in a small dose, makes a person very ill. In some cases this venom can be fatal. On the other hand, a spider's size does not determine how harmful a spider is. Tarantulas are large, hairy spiders that live in North and South America. Although their bite may be painful to humans, it is less poisonous than that of the much smaller black widow.

Even though people sometimes call them insects, spiders are actually members of the animal group called arachnids. Spiders have eight legs, whereas insects have six. Also, in contrast to the body of an insect, the body of a spider is divided into only two parts, and spiders have no antennae. The word <u>arachnid</u> comes from Greek. In Greek mythology, Arachne was changed into a spider because she challenged the goddess Athena to a weaving contest.

A FAMILY HISTORY

"Who am I?" This question has no simple answer, but your family history is one place to start looking. After author Alex Haley asked himself this question, he traced his ancestors back to Africans who had been captured and brought to the United States as slaves. Haley turned his family history into the blockbuster book and television miniseries *Roots*. Below is another example of a family history, written by a high school student.

My Family

by Miguel Wharton

I am an adopted child. I was born Miguel Antonio Ramírez-Cuadros, in Lima, Peru. In 1979, when I was eight months old, I was adopted by a couple from the United States—Philip and Sara Wharton. So I guess you might say that I have two families, one in North America and one in South America.

My biological mother's name is Guadalupe Vanessa Ramírez. She is an American Indian woman from a large family. When I was born, she lived with her brothers, sisters, parents, and grandparents in the village of Cajamarca, north of Lima. Her family was very poor, and she gave me up for adoption so that I could have a better life. I have a picture of her, which my adoptive parents took when they were in Peru. She is very beautiful, with black hair and copper-colored skin like mine. I would like very much to meet her someday. My biological father's name is Carlos Cuadros. That's all I know about him. I often wonder what he was like.

My adoptive parents decided to keep my Spanish first and middle names: Miguel Antonio. They believe that it's important for me to remember and honor my heritage. Of course, I have their last name, Wharton. They have been the best parents anyone could ever want. My dad, Philip Wharton, is an art teacher in a middle school. He likes to take me to the park so I can practice my sketching. He helps me a lot with school projects. My mom, Sara Wharton, is a lawyer. She is really busy, but we still talk almost every day about school or my friends.

When people hear that I'm adopted, they often ask me if I know anything about my real parents. I feel that Philip and Sara Wharton are my real parents. After all, they've been there for me all these years. They're the ones who have loved me and cared for me. They're the ones who taught me to walk, and who sat up with me at night when I was sick. They've given me a lot: a nice house and nice clothes. But more than that, they've given me love.

Still, I often wonder about the life that I might have lived in Peru. I've read a lot about the Incas. Every time I hear a news report about something that's happening in Peru, I wonder again. I'm proud of being an American and an Indian from Peru. Someday, when I'm older, I want to go back to Peru to learn more about where I came from.

Thinking About the Model

The model shows you how one writer explored his unique family history. Your family history is unique, too, and—like Miguel—you'll be exploring and writing about some part of that history. Before you begin your exploration, take a closer look at Miguel's essay by writing answers to the following questions.

1. Why does Miguel say that, in a way, he has "two families"? Who are the people he names and discusses in the history, and what are their relationships to him?

   _____

   _____

   _____

   _____

2. What kinds of information does Miguel give you about these family members? List two specific details about each person. (This won't be possible for one family member.)

   _____

   _____

_____

_____

3. Miguel's essay is an example of **expressive writing**. People write expressively to explore what they think and feel. For example, what thoughts and feelings does Miguel say he has about his parents who live in Peru?

_____

_____

_____

4. In the last two paragraphs of the essay, Miguel draws personal conclusions about what his family history means to him. For each paragraph, state his conclusion in your own words, and give one detail he uses to support the conclusion.

   Paragraph 4. Conclusion about his adoptive parents: _____

   _____

   _____

   Supporting detail: _____

   _____

   Paragraph 5. Conclusion about his birth in Peru: _____

   _____

   Supporting detail: _____

   _____

   _____

ASSIGNMENT: WRITING A FAMILY HISTORY

Trace part of your "family tree" by writing a brief history of some of your family members. (*Family* means the people you share your life with: parents, guardians, or other special people in your household.) Gather information to tell readers who the family members are and what they're like. Be sure to make the record personal by expressing what the family history means to you.

Prewriting

Who will you write about—which "branch" of your tree? Putting family members into a tree diagram will be one of your prewriting steps, so look at the sample tree below. This is meant to show how one family tree might look. Your tree may be smaller or larger; all families are different.

A Sample Family Tree

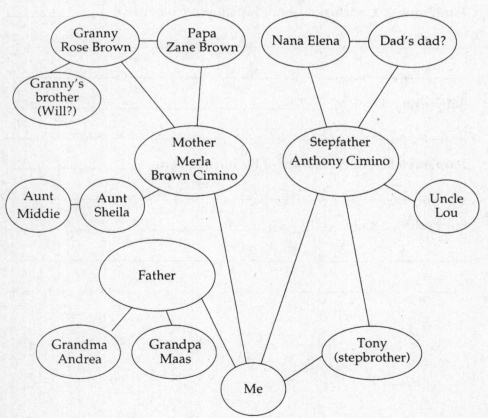

Step 1: Now, on your own paper, start making your own family tree. This is just brainstorming, so don't worry about knowing all the names, including every relative, or getting branch lines perfect. Begin with your closest family member or members. Then branch out to others you know, have heard about, or wonder about.

Step 2: Now narrow your focus: Choose the specific family members you'll write about. Here are some guidelines to help you:

- **Choose one family member as a starting point, and write about** *connecting* **relations**. For example, in the sample tree, the writer wouldn't start with Aunt Middie and then go to Nana Elena—her mother's sister and her stepfather's mother. They're too far apart in the tree. But the writer could start with her mother and then move to her mother's sisters—Aunt Middie and Aunt Sheila.

- **Write about at least two people, but do not include too many**. Four family members may be your maximum number, so that you can include good details. (Note that writing about two parents and *their* parents equals six people. You can do it, but you'll need to write more.)

- **Write about one generation or about two**. Looking at a family tree, this means you can go sideways or up and down. For example, you could write about your mother and father (the same generation), your mother and her sisters (the same generation), or your stepfather and his mother (two generations).

- **Choose family members that attract your interest**. Perhaps you're close to them or curious about them.

- **Choose family members that you know well or can easily find out about**. If your personal knowledge isn't enough to give you facts you can write about, be sure you will be able to talk to the people or to someone who knows them.

Once you have decided which family members you will write about, draw circles around their names on your family tree. Then write their names below.

_____

_____

Step 3: Next, gather information about the people you've chosen. Take a separate piece of paper for each person, and write the name at

the top. Start your research by freewriting whatever you know—
or don't know—about each person. Next, interview the family
members themselves (or people who know about them) and take
notes. Look for the following information.

- places they were born, grew up, or lived as adults
- their immediate family: sisters, brothers, husband, wife,
  children, etc. (you may not wish to use all this information)
- appearance
- work
- interesting details: talents, interests, unusual adventures, most
  vivid personality traits

Writing

Review your freewriting and research notes. (You may want to circle or
star important facts and details about each family member.) Then write a
rough draft of your family history. The guidelines below will help you.

Beginning	• Introduces yourself and the family member who is the starting point for your history. • Catches the reader's interest. You could use an unusual description, a personal thought, or a hint of interesting facts to come.
Body	• Presents information about one or two people in each paragraph. Names them, explains their places in the family tree, and gives facts about their lives. • Offers some details that make family members and your feelings about them come alive for readers: a vivid description of appearance, an important action or event, your favorite memory of them. • Discusses the family members in an order easy for readers to follow. For example, you'll use chronological order (present to past, or vice versa) for discussing a parent and a grandparent. You could use "age order" (youngest to oldest, or vice versa) for discussing your foster mother and her two brothers.
Ending	• Tells your thoughts and feelings—what you've learned from writing the history, why the people are important to you, or other personal observations.

Evaluating and Revising

To evaluate your family history, reread it to decide where the writing works well and where it could be improved. A classmate will also review your essay. Use the questions below for both of your evaluations.

Questions for Evaluation

1. Does the beginning introduce the writer and one or more family members? Does it catch the reader's attention? If not, what facts, details, or thoughts could be added or changed?

2. Does each paragraph in the body give information about one or two family members? Does the information mix facts, vivid details, and the writer's thoughts and feelings? If not, what could be cut? What kinds of details could be added?

3. Is the information presented in a clear order? If not, how could the family members, or what is told about each one, be reordered?

4. Does the writer end with a personal statement? If not, what could be said about what the writer learned, found surprising, believes is important, or is still curious about?

Peer Evaluation

Exchange rough drafts with a classmate, and follow these steps.

Step 1:   Read the family history carefully.

Step 2:   Answer the **Questions for Evaluation** on a separate sheet of paper.

Self-Evaluation

Use these steps to evaluate your own paper.

Step 1:   Read or listen to your classmate's evaluation. To remember good ideas for revising, you may want to star or circle items on the written evaluation, ask questions, or make additional notes.

Step 2:   Write your own answers to the **Questions for Evaluation**.

Now revise your rough draft, using these hints:

- Before you begin, think carefully about both your own evaluation and your classmate's evaluation of your essay.
- Revise directly on your draft, or recopy it with changes.

- Go back to any prewriting step—such as talking again with your family—if you need to. Even start over.
- Revise more than once. Don't think you have to go from rough draft to "hand-in" paper in one step.

Proofreading and Publishing

Step 1: Read your revised family history *more than once* for errors in spelling, grammar, usage, and mechanics. Refer to the **Proofreading Guidelines** on page 12, and also be alert for errors you make often.

Step 2: Correct the errors. Check a dictionary or grammar reference source whenever you're uncertain about a correction. If possible, ask a classmate to proofread your changes.

Step 3: Make a clean, final copy of your corrected paper.

Step 4: Publish your family history. Some suggestions follow, and you can invent others. Ask classmates how they plan to share their family stories.

a. Show what you've written to your family: the people you've written about or interviewed, as well as any others.

b. Find family photographs of the people and places in your history. (You might also find magazine pictures of places.) For an Autobiography Day in class, create an illustrated copy of your essay, or make a poster display.

c. Save what you've written. It is family history that you, others, and even your children can enjoy years from now.

> **FOR YOUR PORTFOLIO**
>
> Respond to the following items on your own paper. Then place the answers with your family history in your writing portfolio.
>
> 1. Which of the people in your family history would make interesting characters in a story or novel? Why?
> 2. Write briefly about the experience of interviewing. Was it hard, fun, or both—and why? What would you do differently next time?
> 3. If you were continuing your family history, who would you write about next? Why are these people important to you?

A LETTER POEM

People can be creative in many ways. They can use watercolors to create a beautiful picture, write the words and music to a song, write a short story, or write a poem. Here's an example of creative writing in a form that might surprise you. It's a poem in the form of a letter. As you read it, think about what makes it creative. What makes it a poem rather than simply a letter?

19 Laurel Road
Marblehead, MA 01945
September 10, 2008

Dear Washing Machine,

OK. That's it. I've had enough.
We've lived inthesamehouse for three years now,
And I've never once complained about all the noise you make,
All that gurgling and chugging and thumping
Like a badly played tuba.
And I didn't even mind that you ate a few socks.
I figured, OK, the life of a washing machine is pretty boring,
The same old round, day in, day out,
And you probably get a kick out of these occasional pranks,
And maybe it's just a cycle you're going through.
But splashing black ink all over white sheets and underwear?
Well, that completely burst my bubble,
Sent me into a spin.
I mean,
Really,
I look like a Dalmatian.
I've got this sinking feeling.
Our relationship's going down the drain.
This has to stop, Washpot. If it doesn't, I'll pull the plug.
I'll wear dirty clothes and tell the other appliances,
"It's not my fault. I have this irresponsible washing machine."
So what do you think of that?

Fretfully yours,
Kim

Thinking About the Model

Now that you have read the model letter poem, you can use these questions to clarify your thinking.

1. How is the model poem like a letter?

   _____

   _____

2. One way poets use language creatively is by repeating sounds—beginning sounds (place/pens/pockets), ending sounds (fluffy/sleepy), or rhymes (fluffy/huffy). What sounds are repeated in the model letter poem?

   _____

   _____

3. Another way to use language creatively is to compare two very different things. In the model poem, what does the writer compare the washing machine to? How is this surprising?

   _____

   _____

4. In poetry, a writer might break a line in the middle of a sentence. Or the writer might even put a word all by itself on a line. Writers also play with spacing—bunchingwordstogetherlikethis or drawing them out like this. What examples of creative arrangement or spacing can you find in the model poem?

   _____

   _____

   _____

5. What is the writer's message—what does he want to tell the washing machine? What is his attitude toward the washing machine?

   _____

   _____

ASSIGNMENT: WRITING A LETTER POEM

This is your chance to be creative, to free yourself to think in new ways. Write a poem in the form of a letter. Your goal is to be creative with language and to say something interesting.

Prewriting

Step 1: A letter is from someone (or something) to someone (or something). For example, the model letter poem is from a person to a thing—a washing machine.

If you were to write a letter to an object or a thing, what would you write to? A storm, a pencil, a football, honesty? Perhaps you remember some object from your childhood and have strong feelings about it. Brainstorm a list of ten or twelve objects or things.

_____   _____

_____   _____

_____   _____

_____   _____

_____   _____

_____   _____

Step 2: Now look back at the list you made in Step 1. Which object or thing is most interesting to you? If you wanted to be serious, which one would you choose? If you wanted to be funny or silly, which one would you choose?

In the space below, write the name of the object or thing you would most like to write your letter poem to.

_____

Step 3:   What do you want to say to this thing or object? Are you like Kim, who has "had enough" of the washing machine's behavior? Or do you have something totally different to say? Perhaps you want to show your respect (for the United States flag, for example) or your sense of wonder (for a tornado or a raging river, for example). Use the following questions to explore what you want to say.

- How do you feel about this object or thing? Do you cherish it, respect it, fear it, resent it? Jot your feelings on the lines below.

  _____

  _____

  _____

- How do you want to express your feelings? Do you want to joke about them, be serious about them, show your anger about them? For example, Kim seems to be joking about his relationship with the washing machine. Sure, he's frustrated, but he's exaggerating to be funny. In the space below, describe how you want to handle your feelings about the object or thing.

  _____

  _____

  _____

  _____

- What is your message to the object or thing? What are some things you could tell it? For example, Kim says he hasn't complained about the noise, he understands the machine's life is boring, and he's upset by the splashing black ink. Jot down a list of four or five things you might say. You might include some examples of what you like or dislike.

  _____

  _____

  _____

  _____

  _____

- Remember the comparison of the washing machine to the tuba in the model poem? In his comparison Kim says the washing machine is *like* a badly played tuba. Here are two other ways he could have stated his comparison:

  The washing machine is as irritating *as* a badly played tuba.
  The washing machine *is* a badly played tuba, noisily gurgling and chugging and thumping.

  What unusual comparison could you use in your poem? Brainstorm a list, or freewrite to think of something that, while very different from the thing or object you are writing to, has one interesting feature in common with it. Use the space below for your list or your freewriting.

  _____

  _____

  _____

  _____

  _____

  _____

 ## Writing

Before you begin the first draft of your letter poem, think of some things you could do to make it less like a letter and more like a poem. Here are some ideas to consider.

1. Repeated sounds—beginning sounds, ending sounds, or rhymes—add interest. They also help to emphasize words or ideas.

2. The lines of a poem don't have to go all the way to the right margin. You can end some lines with sounds you want to repeat or words you want to stress.

3. The way you use space is important. By setting a word apart, running words together, or spreading words out, you can add interest or emphasize words or ideas.

Now, use the following basic framework to draft a letter poem on your own paper.

A Letter Poem

- begins with "Dear _____ ,"
- is imaginative
- communicates your feelings and your attitude as well as a message to the thing or object
- is no longer than one page
- ends with a closing and signature

 ## Evaluating and Revising

Your first draft is not the best you can do. Professional writers always evaluate and revise. When you are ready to evaluate your poem, you can use the following **Questions for Evaluation.**

Questions for Evaluation

1. Has the writer identified the thing or object the poem is addressing? If not, what should be added?

2. Does the poem reveal the writer's feelings and attitude toward the thing or object? If not, what could the writer add or change?

3. Does the writer share a message or say anything of interest to the thing or object? If not, what could the writer say?

4. Does the poem include any unusual comparisons? If not, what could the writer compare the object or thing to?

5. Does the writer use sounds in a creative way? If not, what sounds could be repeated, changed, or added?

6. Does the writer use space to emphasize words or ideas? If not, what words could be set apart, run together, spread out, and so forth?

Peer Evaluation

Exchange rough drafts with a classmate. Then follow these steps.

Step 1:   Read your partner's letter poem carefully. Concentrate on content, on how the letter works as a poem.

Step 2:   Answer the **Questions for Evaluation** on page 48, adding as many specific suggestions as you can think of. Then give the poem back to the writer.

Self-Evaluation

Follow these steps to evaluate your own poem.

Step 1:   Read or listen to your classmate's comments. Note any of the suggestions you want to use when you revise your poem.

Step 2:   Reread your poem. Then use the **Questions for Evaluation** on page 48 to evaluate it yourself.

Now use your evaluation to revise your poem. Make the changes you have decided are necessary to improve it. When you have completed that revision, reread it one additional time.

- Look for ways to tighten your language. Find places where you could take out two or three words and replace them with one word. (For example, you could change *ink from a black pen* to *black ink*.)

- Replace dull, vague words with vivid, concrete ones. (Instead of *good*, use *spicy* or *angelic*; *instead* of *rough*, use *craggy* or *dimpled*.)

Proofreading and Publishing

After making a few final touches, you will be ready to share your poem.

Step 1:   Use the **Proofreading Guidelines** on page 12. Look for and correct any errors in spelling, capitalization, punctuation, and usage.

Step 2:   Make sure you have capitalized the first word in each line. Most poems follow this pattern of capitalization. For help with capitalization, see pages 261–272.

Step 3:   Take advantage of this opportunity to practice the manuscript form for a friendly letter. Make a final copy of your letter poem,

Heading. Imagine a vertical line dividing the letter in half. Begin the heading to the right of that imagined line. The heading of a friendly letter includes three lines:

- your street address
- your city (followed by a comma), state, and ZIP Code
- the date (with a comma between the day of the month and the year)

Salutation. *Salutation* is another word for *greeting*. Leave about a one-inch margin at the left of your letter poem (or any other friendly letter). Begin your greeting at that margin. Place a comma after the greeting, and capitalize the first word and all nouns.

Closing and Signature. Write the closing so that it is aligned with the heading. The closing can be very informal—*Your friend, Always, Love.* (Since the model letter poem was somewhat humorous, the writer decided to close with *Fretfully yours.*) Always sign your name, even if you type or word process the body of the letter. Only the first word of a closing should be capitalized.

Step 4:   Share your poem with classmates by holding an in-class poetry reading. Or look for a poetry-writing contest you could enter. Your teacher or librarian might be able to help you identify some contests.

FOR YOUR PORTFOLIO

If you are keeping a portfolio, you might want to try one or both of these suggestions.

1. Write a second letter poem. This time, write to a famous person, alive or dead. For example, you might write to Cleopatra or to Shaquille O'Neal.

2. Think about these questions, and write the answers on your own paper: How does writing poetry differ from writing prose (a regular letter, a composition, a story, a newspaper article)? Which kind of writing do you like best? Why?

I-SEARCH PAPER

In a report, you gather information about a topic and present that information to your readers. An *I-Search* paper is a special type of report that you do to find out something for yourself. First, you think of a topic that you want to know about for personal reasons. Next, you research the topic to gather information about it. Finally, you write a report that focuses the story of your search for information. As you read the following I-Search paper, ask yourself why Kerrie researched the making of pottery.

How Memories Are Made
by Kerrie Kasamoto

On the dresser in my room at home is a very special object, a cup made by my grandmother on my father's side. Grandma Kasamoto was a potter. Years ago, when I was five, I saw this pretty cup sitting on a shelf in Grandma's pottery shop. It was white, with delicate green stems and leaves painted on it. The stems curled up the sides of the cup and ended in tiny purple flowers. I tried to grab it, and my mother told me not to touch it because it might break. However, my grandmother stopped her, sat me down, and handed me the cup to look at. From then on, whenever I visited my grandmother, she would give me that cup to drink from. Last year, my grandmother died of a stroke at age sixty-four. She left the cup to me to remember her by. I've thought ever since that I would like to learn how the cup was made. I've felt that doing so would make me feel closer to my grandmother, whom I loved very much.

The pottery shop that my grandmother owned now belongs to someone else, a professional potter named Claude Mackey. I decided to start my research by going to visit Mr. Mackey's shop. I told him who my grandmother was and asked him if he would tell me how pots and cups and other ceramics are made.

I showed Mr. Mackey my grandmother's cup. He explained ceramics like that are made from molds. He showed me the large sink where he mixes the clay. This clay is then poured into plaster molds. After a while, the clay around the edge of the mold hardens a bit and the extra clay is poured out of the mold. The ceramic is then taken out of the mold. It is a light gray color and is very soft.

The next step is to carve a design onto the clay using little knives that look like a dentist's tools. The design is then painted with special paint that has clay in it. The ceramic is allowed to dry. Then it is placed in a very hot oven, called a *kiln*. It hardens the ceramic. Finally, the ceramic is coated with a glasslike liquid called a *glaze*, and is baked in the kiln a second time. The whole process takes about five days.

After talking to Mr. Mackey, I was still curious about the design on my cup. I asked my mother where Grandma had gotten her ideas for decorating her pottery. Mom explained that, in addition to being a potter, Grandma had studied the Japanese art of flower arranging. She modeled the flower designs on her ceramics after her favorite flower arrangements. I decided to go to the library to find out more about Japanese-style flower arranging.

The librarian helped me find two books on the subject. One of these books, called *Japanese Decorative Arts*, was a large picture book. The section on flower arrangements was quite beautiful, but it didn't provide a lot of information. The second book, however, was very useful. It was called An *Introduction to Ikebana*. From that book I learned that flower arranging is an ancient Japanese art, and that in Japanese it is called *ikebana*. People must study ikebana for many years before they master it. The purpose of *ikebana* is to create an arrangement of flowers or other plants that looks ordered and balanced but not artificial. The arrangement is supposed to look natural, as though it might have happened by accident.

I learned that my grandmother had combined pottery with the ancient craft of ikebana to make my cup. My grandmother was proud of her Japanese heritage, and so am I. My research has increased my interest in pottery making and in flower arranging. I hope to study both in the future, in honor of my grandmother and of my heritage.

Thinking About the Model

On your own paper, answer the following questions.

1. What personal reason does the writer give for her research?

2. In an I-Search paper, information is presented in *chronological,* or time, order. The writer tells what he or she did to find out about the topic, from beginning to end. What steps did the writer of the model take to find out about her topic?

3. The conclusion of an I-Search paper sums up what the writer learned. What did Kerrie learn from her research? What does she plan to do in the future as a result of this experience?

4. A Works Cited is a list of the sources the writer used to write the paper. What kinds of sources did Kerrie use? The list below shows the sources Kerrie used to write her paper.

Hanabata, T. C. An introduction to Ikebana. Rockport, MA: Wordworks Publishing . 2003.

Kasamoto, Sara. Personal Interview. 30 Sept. 2008.

Mackey, Claude. Personal Interview. 23 Sept. 2008.

Philanger, Marc, and Toshiro Hirakawa. *Japanese Decorative Arts.* New York: Rittinger House, 2007.

ASSIGNMENT: WRITING AN I-SEARCH PAPER

Find a topic that is important to you personally, and research it using several different sources. Write a paper telling about your research and what you learned from it.

Prewriting

Step 1:   Think of a topic that you would like to know more about for personal reasons. What do you want to know about? This is your chance to research something that is really important to you. You could use one of the following topics, or think of one of your own.

- You own a particular kind of dog or cat and want to know more about that breed.
- You want to purchase a portable CD player and want to know which is the best brand.
- You want to lose or gain weight and would like to know the best program to follow.
- Your family is considering a move, and you want to know about the area you might live in.
- You have a friend who is ill, and you want to know more about the illness.

On the lines below, brainstorm for a list of possible topics for your paper.

_____

_____

_____

_____

_____

Step 2:   From your list above, choose a topic you feel you need to find information about. Write the topic on the line below. Then freewrite on your own paper about why that topic interests you personally.

_____

Step 3:   On the lines below, list the people whom you could interview to find out more about your topic. These people might be teachers, local business or professional persons, people at a local college or university, or anyone else who would know a lot about your topic.

_____

_____

_____

Step 4:   Go to the library, and find at least two other sources of information on your topic. These sources could be books, magazines, newspapers, brochures, movies, videotapes, CD's, or audiocassette tapes. List these sources below. For a book, include the name(s) of the author(s), the title, the place of publication, the publisher, and the date of publication.

_____

_____

_____

Step 5:   Take notes from your sources. Write these notes in a notebook or on index cards. Include one main idea or piece of information on each card.

Step 6:   On the lines below, use the *5W-How?* questions to write at least five questions to ask the person or persons whom you plan to interview. Make an appointment for the interview. Show up on time. Ask your questions politely, and take notes on a pad of paper.

_____

_____

_____

_____

Step 7:   Review your interview notes and circle the important points. Reflect on the information you've gathered so far. Is there any new information you need or any more details about information you've already gotten?

Step 8:   Once you've finished your research, freewrite on your own paper about what you have learned. What discoveries did you make? Do not stop at this point to worry about grammar, spelling, or mechanics. Simply get the main things that you've learned down on paper. Be sure to include enough details so that your readers can experience your search with you.

 ## Writing

Now it's time to dive in and write a first draft of your I-Search paper. The following guidelines will help you structure your report.

Beginning	• Begins with a paragraph that tells what you researched and why that topic was personally interesting to you.
Middle	• Should be written as a ***personal narrative***, or story about what you did. Presents your research in chronological order. • Tells what you did to find out about the topic, in the order that it occurred. • Shares with your reader the discoveries that you made along the way. • Includes information from at least one interview and from one additional source. • Uses transitional words such as *first, second, third, next, finally,* and *then* to tell what happened and in what order.
Ending	• Summarizes the paper and explains what you learned from your research.
Works Cited	• Includes, in alphabetical order, a complete list of the sources that you used in your paper.

Evaluating and Revising

To evaluate your writing, look critically at what you have written. When you evaluate your I-Search paper, you will use the following guidelines.

Questions for Evaluation

1. Does the report identify your topic in the first paragraph? If not, add a sentence that includes the topic.

2. Does the report explain, in the first paragraph, why that topic was chosen? If not, add sentences that explain.

3. Does the body of the report describe the process of researching the topic? If not, add details of the process.

4. Does the report use transitional words such as *first*, *second*, and *third* to show the chronological order of the search? If not, add transitional words where appropriate.

5. Does the body of the paper present the major discoveries that the writer made during his or her research? If not, add details about the discoveries.

6. Does the report include information from one personal interview and at least one other source? If not, add the necessary information.

7. Does the ending summarize the paper and explain what the writer learned from the research? If not, add sentences that summarize and show the significance of the research.

8. Does the writer include a list of works cited at the end of the paper? Is this list complete and in alphabetical order? If not, add the necessary sources, or arrange them in alphabetical order.

Peer Evaluation

Step 1:   Read the I-Search paper, and, on your own paper, answer the **Questions for Evaluation** given above.

Step 2:   If any part of the paper is unclear to you, underline that part and write a question mark next to it. If you need additional information, write "More info needed."

Self-Evaluation

Step 1:   Read or listen to your peer evaluator's comments.

Step 2:   Answer the **Questions for Evaluation** for your own paper.

Step 3: Look for places where more information needs to be added to make the paper clear to the reader. Also, look for places where the order of events needs to be made clearer. You might want to move some sentences around. You might also need to add transitional words or phrases to tell the order in which the events you are describing happened.

All the problems you discovered in evaluating can be corrected. Based on the peer and self-evaluations, now revise your I-Search paper. If necessary, you might even return to the prewriting stage and do additional research to add missing information.

Proofreading and Publishing

Step 1: Read the paper carefully for errors in spelling, grammar, usage, and mechanics. Refer to the Guidelines for Proofreading on page 12.

Step 2: Make a clean, error-free final copy. Include your Works Cited list.

The following guidelines tell you how to record the necessary information for different types of sources.

- Center the words *Works Cited* one inch from the top of your paper (if Works Cited is on separate sheet).
- List your sources by the author's last name. If no author is given, alphabetize by the first important word of the title or by the last name of the person interviewed.
- Begin each listing at the left margin. If the listing continues onto the next line, indent all following lines five spaces.
- Use the following format for each entry.

    1. Book with one author
       Author's last name, Author's first name. Title of Book. Place of Publication: Publisher, Year of Publication. (See page 52 for example.)

    2. Interview
       Interviewee's Last name, Interviewee's first name. Type of Interview. Day, Mo., Year of Interview. (See page 52 for example.)

Step 3: Share your I-Search paper with classmates, friends, or relatives who might be interested in the subject that you have researched.

FOR YOUR PORTFOLIO

Answer the following questions on your own paper. Place the answers, along with your finished paper, in your writing portfolio.

1. How does an I-Search paper differ from other types of writing you've done? Which type of writing do you think is the most interesting? Why?

2. Which sources of information were most useful to you? Which ones were least useful? Which sources might you consult to find out more about your topic?

3. What was the hardest part of this writing assignment? What was the easiest part?

DENNIS THE MENACE

"IF KIDS HAVE KIDNEYS, DO BUGS HAVE BUGNEYS?"

AN ADVICE LETTER

Have you ever offered your opinion on an important issue, such as having an open campus during your school's lunch hour? Have you ever helped a friend solve a difficult problem? In either situation, you probably explained your ideas for solving the problem and then used persuasion to prove the advantages of your solution. You can find this kind of persuasion in an *advice letter.* Here is an example of a request for advice, followed by a columnist's advice to the letter writer. What does Ms. Marie try to persuade Desperate to do?

1501 Mountainview Dr.
Greenfield, WI 53221
September 23, 2008

Dear Ms. Marie:

I am having a major disagreement with my parents. They don't think I should get a part-time job, but I think I have time right now. To get money during summer vacation and on holidays, I have done odd jobs for my neighbors. But the idea of having my own spending money year-round makes getting a job very tempting!

My biggest problem is that my math class this year is harder than the one I had last year, and I am having to study more to keep my grades up. My parents think that I won't have time to study and to work at a job. So far, I haven't been able to convince them to let me get the job.

I just don't know what to say to my parents anymore. Please help me figure this problem out. I am

Desperate

Dear Desperate:

It is natural for your parents to worry about your getting a job, especially if your grades were to fall. However, I think there is hope for you.

To persuade your parents, you will first have to get and keep good grades in your classes. If you are worried about your math grade, you could set up a buddy system with someone in your class so that you can help each other. Also, check with your school counselor to see if you could work with a tutor from time to time.

You could also explain to your parents that earning extra spending money would take some of the financial responsibility off them. They might not have thought about this aspect of your earning money. To convince them, keep track of the amount of spending money they give you so that you will have specific figures to show them.

When you look for a job, look for ones that fit your schedule. You could ask about job openings at your school, at local stores, and at your area community center.

Proving your responsibility and determination to your parents should be a strong influence in persuading them to allow you to work. Begin now to plan what you will do. And write to me again soon. Let me know how you are getting along. I expect to hear great news!

Good luck,

Ms. Marie

Thinking About the Model

The advice columnist has several solutions for Desperate's problem. Think about how Ms. Marie analyzes the problem, explains her solutions, and convinces Desperate the solutions are good. Answer the following questions on the lines provided.

1. The first thing an advice letter does is to identify the problem. What is Desperate's problem?

_____

_____

_____

2. Based on the letter she received, Ms. Marie makes several suggestions to Desperate. She describes and explains the proposed solutions. On the lines below, list the things she tries to persuade Desperate to do.

_____

_____

_____

_____

_____

3. To be persuasive, you often have to give the reader reasons for doing what you propose. What reasons does Ms. Marie give for setting up a buddy system in math? for keeping track of spending money?

_____

_____

_____

_____

_____

4. The conclusion of the letter should summarize the writer's points and possibly give a *call to action*—what you might want the reader to do as a result of your suggestions. How does Ms. Marie end her letter?

_____

_____

_____

_____

_____

ASSIGNMENT: WRITING AN ADVICE LETTER

Write an advice letter in response to one of the following topics taken from several letters. As you write, think about identifying the problem and proposing solutions to the problem.

a. Bob has been asked by Maria to share his history homework with her because she has been making bad grades in that class. He wants to help her, but he doesn't think sharing his homework is okay. What should he do?

b. Susan and Katy are friends. Susan wants to be friends with Ruthanne, too. However, Katy doesn't like Ruthanne and has told Susan that their friendship will be over if Susan befriends Ruthanne. What should Susan do?

c. Lydia and several of her friends from Lincoln High School think their principal should allow students from other schools to attend Lincoln school dances. School policy prohibits this practice now. What should Lydia and her friends do?

d. Identify a problem you would like to write about.

Prewriting

Step 1:   From the list above, choose the problem you want to write your advice letter about. Write the letter of the problem you choose on the lines below. If you choose Topic d., explain what the problem is.

_____

_____

Step 2:   Now that you have chosen the problem, you're ready to analyze it for possible solutions. First, be sure that the advice you offer is appropriate to the person you're answering. For example, Ms. Marie offers solutions that are appropriate for someone in high school. To help you think of solutions, freewrite about the following questions.

What are the causes of the problem?

_____

_____

_____

What are the effects of the problem?

_____

_____

_____

What can be done to eliminate the causes of the problem?

_____

_____

_____

Besides the solutions you listed in the previous question, what is the most unusual way you can think of to solve the problem? the easiest way?

_____

_____

_____

_____

Step 3: To choose the best solutions from the preceding answers, answer the following questions.

What are the strengths and weaknesses of each solution?

_____

_____

_____

Good solutions are supported by reasons. What reasons can you give for each of your solutions?

_____

_____

_____

Step 4: Now you must explain how each solution will be helpful. Think about what you need to say to persuade someone to accept your solutions. To help you think through each solution, fill out the following chart.

Problem:		
Possible Solutions	Strengths/Reasons	Steps to Implement

 ## Writing

You are ready to use your prewriting notes to write a first draft of your advice letter. Use the format of a business letter. Follow the guidelines below as you write this draft on your own paper.

Beginning	• Clearly states problem

Middle	• Gives proposed solutions, supported by persuasive examples and reasons • Gives necessary steps for implementing solutions

Ending	• Restates proposed solutions • Offers possible call to action

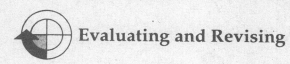

Evaluating and Revising

Now that you have written the first draft of your advice letter, you need to evaluate it. Use the following **Questions for Evaluation** to help you find the strengths and weaknesses in your writing and in the writing of a classmate. Write your answers on your own paper.

Questions for Evaluation

1. Does the beginning clearly state the problem? If not, add a sentence that states the problem.

2. Are possible solutions given and explained? If not, add solutions, with explanations.

3. Does the letter support the solutions with persuasive examples and reasons? If not, add examples and reasons.

4. Does the letter give the necessary steps for implementing the solutions? If not, add the steps.

5. Does the ending offer a possible call to action? If not, what can be added?

Peer Evaluation

Exchange rough drafts with a classmate. Ask the classmate to follow these steps.

Step 1:   Read the rough draft carefully.

Step 2:   Answer the **Questions for Evaluation** on a separate piece of paper.

Self-Evaluation

Now complete your evaluation of your own rough draft. Follow these steps.

Step 1:   Reread your own rough draft carefully.

Step 2:   Think about the suggestions you made for your classmate's rough draft. Do any apply to your own draft?

Step 3:   Answer the **Questions for Evaluation** for your rough draft.

Step 4:   Study your classmate's suggestions. Note the suggestions you would like to use in your revision.

Use your answers to the **Questions for Evaluation,** together with your classmate's suggestions, to revise your draft until you are satisfied with it.

Proofreading and Publishing

Your letter will be taken more seriously if it is polished and free of errors. Use these steps to prepare your final version.

Step 1: Check the spelling of each word. Use a dictionary if you are unsure about a word. To help you check your spelling, see pages 309–316.

Step 2: Check for correct punctuation, grammar, usage, and capitalization.

Step 3: Make a clean and error-free copy. Refer to the guidelines for correct manuscripts on page 13.

Step 4: You can publish your advice letter by submitting it to a local or school newspaper; sending it out as a memo; posting it on a wall, bulletin board, or refrigerator; or reading it out loud.

FOR YOUR PORTFOLIO

1. Ask people to respond orally or in writing to express how they feel about your letter. Did you convince anyone? If not, why? Have you seen any results because of your letter? Keep a record of the responses and of your observations with the letter. Put these in your writing portfolio.

2. Find examples of advice letters in the newspaper, and put your favorites in your portfolio.

SENTENCE FRAGMENTS

> **8a** A *sentence fragment* is a group of words that is only a part of a sentence.
>
> FRAGMENT   Ends the professional baseball season. [The subject is missing. *What* ends the professional baseball season?]
>
> SENTENCE   The World Series ends the professional baseball season.
>
> FRAGMENT   The Boston Red Sox and the Pittsburgh Pirates. [The verb is missing. *What* did the Boston Red Sox and the Pittsburgh Pirates do?]
>
> SENTENCE   The Boston Red Sox and the Pittsburgh Pirates played in the first World Series, in 1903.
>
> FRAGMENT   When one team wins four games. [This group of words has a subject and a verb but does not express a complete thought.]
>
> SENTENCE   The World Series is over when one team wins four games.
>
> **NOTE**   By itself, a sentence fragment doesn't express a complete thought. But a fragment can make sense in writing if it is clearly related to a sentence that comes before or after it.
>
> EXAMPLE   All day we waited, listening to weather reports. Finally, it hit. The storm. Fiercer and wilder than we had imagined. A hurricane.
>
> As you can see, the sentence gives the fragments meaning. It fills in the missing parts.

EXERCISE 1   Identifying Sentence Fragments

On the line before each of the following sentences, write *s.* if the subject is missing, *v.* if the verb is missing, or *C* if the sentence is complete.

EX. ___*v.*___ 1. The Amazon rain forest, one of the earth's last frontiers.

_____ 1. Covers an area almost as large as the continental United States.

_____ 2. The Amazon River flows through the center of this rain forest.

_____ 3. Is over 3,500 miles long.

_____ 4. At the foot of the Andes, the Amazon.

_____ 5. Includes one third of the earth's tropical rain forests.

_____ 6. In this region, thousands of people.

_____ 7. Have seen large fish, pirarucú, swimming in the Amazon.

_____ 8. The Amazon basin is home to thousands of species of animals, plants, and insects.

_____ 9. One main tributary of the Amazon.

_____ 10. Are burning the jungles of the Amazon basin.

EXERCISE 2   Revising Fragments in a Paragraph

Correct the fragments in the paragraph below. On the lines provided, form sentences by changing the punctuation and capitalization or by adding needed words. Some sentences need no revision.

EX.   [1] The seafaring Maoris. [2] How arrived at New Zealand?
       How did the seafaring Maoris arrive at New Zealand?
_____

[1] The Maoris were the first inhabitants of New Zealand. [2] A culture rich in legends. [3] One legend. [4] How the Maori people discovered New Zealand. [5] According to the legend, a group of Maoris who lived on another island in the South Pacific. [6] Set out in seven canoes. [7] Were separated by a storm. [8] Landed in different places. [9] What we now call the Northern Island of New Zealand. [10] Called the island Aotearoa.

_____

_____

_____

_____

_____

_____

_____

_____

_____

_____

_____

_____

PHRASAL FRAGMENTS

8b A *phrase* is a group of words that does not contain a subject and a verb. Three kinds of phrases are often mistaken for sentences: verbal phrases, appositive phrases, and prepositional phrases.

A *verbal phrase* contains a word that is made from a verb but is used as another part of speech. This could be a word that ends in *–ing, –d,* or *–ed* and does not have a helping verb (like *is, were,* or *have*). It could also be an infinitive, a verb with the word *to* in front of it (*to run, to help*).

FRAGMENT   To go to a movie.
SENTENCE   Felicia and Tony decided to go to a movie.

FRAGMENT   Agreeing on a film.
SENTENCE   They had trouble agreeing on a film.

An *appositive phrase* is, a group of words that identifies or explains a nearby noun or pronoun in the sentence.

FRAGMENT   Tony's favorite neighbor.
SENTENCE   Felicia, Tony's favorite neighbor, wanted to see a comedy.

A *prepositional phrase* is a group of words consisting of a preposition, a noun or pronoun that serves as the object of the preposition, and any modifiers of that object.

FRAGMENT   After a long debate.
SENTENCE   After a long debate, Tony agreed to Felicia's choice.

EXERCISE 3   Revising Phrasal Fragments

Create a sentence from each of the following fragments. You may add the fragment to a complete sentence or develop the fragment into a complete sentence by adding a subject, a verb, or both.

EX.   1. walking by the ocean
             Walking by the ocean, I watched the sailboats.
or   I enjoy walking by the ocean.

1. a fine day for a walk _____

_____

2. in the sand _____

_____

3. surprised to see _____

_____

4. under a rock _____

_____

5. to touch the animal carefully _____

_____

6. washed ashore _____

_____

7. talking with a fisherman _____

_____

8. on the horizon _____

_____

9. blown by the wind _____

_____

10. a perfect seashell _____

_____

11. to go for a swim _____

_____

12. after a picnic lunch _____

_____

13. living in tide pools _____

_____

14. of noisy sea gulls _____

_____

15. before leaving for the day _____

_____

SUBORDINATE CLAUSE FRAGMENTS

8c   A *subordinate clause* does not express a complete thought and cannot stand alone as a sentence.

A *clause* is a group of words that contains a subject and a verb. One kind of clause, an *independent clause*, expresses a complete thought and can stand alone as a sentence, but a subordinate clause is a fragment.

FRAGMENT   Which you should enjoy. [*What* should you enjoy?]
SENTENCE   Let's watch the movie, which you should enjoy.

FRAGMENT   Who can teach science. [This fragment would be a complete sentence if the punctuation were changed to a question mark. As a statement, it doesn't express a complete thought. It doesn't tell *who* can teach science.]
SENTENCE   Several countries have requested volunteers who can teach science.

NOTE   A subordinate clause telling *why, where, when*, or *how* (an adverb clause) may be placed before or after the independent clause. When you combine sentences by inserting an adverb clause, try the clause in both positions to see which use gives the meaning that you want.

EXAMPLES   Because Jani has always wanted to visit Africa, she will probably accept the invitation to work in Kenya.

or

Jani will probably accept the invitation to work in Kenya because she has always wanted to visit Africa.

EXERCISE 4   Revising Subordinate Clause Fragments

On your own paper, rewrite the following paragraph, combining the subordinate clauses with independent clauses. Change the punctuation and capitalization as necessary. (You may combine two subordinate clauses with one independent clause.)

EX.   [1] Although changing careers in midlife is not uncommon.
        [2] Annie Smith Peck's career change is a dramatic example.

    Although changing careers in midlife is not uncommon, Annie Smith Peck's career change is a dramatic example.

[1] When Annie Smith Peck was forty-five years old. [2] She changed

careers. [3] Because she found it was hard to teach Latin and climb mountains. [4] She decided just to climb mountains. [5] When she was born, in 1850. [6] Women mountaineers were unusual. [7] While traveling in Switzerland in 1885. [8] She first saw the Matterhorn. [9] Which is a famous peak in the Alps. [10] She climbed several smaller mountains. [11] Before she returned to the United States. [12] Although she began teaching Latin at Smith College. [13] She also gave lectures so that she could afford to travel. [14] After she stopped teaching entirely. [15] She became the first woman to climb the Matterhorn. [16] She went on to climb many other mountains. [17] When she climbed Mount Coropuna, in Peru, at the age of sixty-one. [18] She planted a "Votes for Women" flag on the summit. [19] When she was eighty-two years old. [20] She made her last climb.

EXERCISE 5   Using Subordinate Clauses in Sentences

Write a complete sentence with each of the subordinate clauses below. Change the punctuation and capitalization as necessary.

EX.   1. because Akio grew up in Hawaii
          Because Akio grew up in Hawaii, he is familiar with the sea.

1. when Akio visits the volcano _____

    _____

2. if a hurricane comes _____

    _____

3. who once taught native dances _____

    _____

4. since he lives on an island _____

    _____

5. where his ancestors lived _____

    _____

RUN-ON SENTENCES

8d A *run-on* sentence is two or more complete sentences that are written as one sentence.

The two kinds of run-on sentences are the fused sentence and the comma splice. In a *fused sentence*, the writer has joined two or more complete sentences, with no punctuation mark between them.

RUN-ON   The heart of Amish country is Pennsylvania there you can see samples of beautiful Amish quilts.

CORRECT   The heart of Amish country is Pennsylvania. There, you can see samples of beautiful Amish quilts.

In a *comma splice*, the writer has joined two or more sentences, using only a comma to separate them.

RUN-ON   Amish quilts use unexpected combinations of bold colors, the results are striking.

CORRECT   Amish quilts use unexpected combinations of bold colors. The results are striking.

There are several ways to revise a run-on sentence. You can always make two separate sentences. But you can also make a compound sentence if the independent clauses in the run-on are closely related.

(1) You can make a compound sentence by adding a comma and a coordinating conjunction (*and, but, nor, or,* or *yet*).

RUN-ON   Food is scarce for birds in the winter you can help by feeding them.

REVISED   Food is scarce for birds in the winter, but you can help by feeding them.

(2) You can make a compound sentence by adding a semicolon.

RUN-ON   There are many types of bird feeders many of these you can make yourself.

REVISED   There are many types of bird feeders; many of these you can make yourself.

(3) You can make a compound sentence by adding a semicolon and a *conjunctive adverb*—**a word such as** *also, however, instead, meanwhile, nevertheless, still,* **or** *therefore.* **A conjunctive adverb needs to be followed by a comma.**

RUN-ON   Hang your bird feeder where you can watch the birds, keep it out of the reach of cats.

REVISED   Hang your bird feeder where you can watch the birds; however, keep it out of the reach of cats.

EXERCISE 6   Revising Run-on Sentences

On your own paper, revise each run-on sentence. If the sentence is correct, write C.

EX.   1.   Tecumseh was a leader of the Shawnee group of American Indians his name means "shooting star."

    1.   Tecumseh was a leader of the Shawnee group of American Indians. His name means "shooting star."

1. Tecumseh was born around 1768 in what is now Ohio the Shawnee lived throughout the midwestern states.

2. His father was a leader he was killed when Tecumseh was a child.

3. Tecumseh's brother Cheeseekan taught him the ways of Shawnee warfare he also taught Tecumseh leadership and speaking skills.

4. Tecumseh wanted to unite all of the peoples from the Great Lakes region.

5. He was recognized as a leader when he was young, he was only sixteen when he took part in his first battle.

6. Cheeseekan was killed in a battle, Tecumseh became chief.

7. Tecumseh hated the practice of torture he would not permit it when he was leader.

8. Tecumseh and another brother, Tenskwatawa, built a village for their people on the Tippecanoe River, people from many places came to live in the village.

9. Tecumseh traveled, organizing a league of American Indians, while he was away, his village was destroyed in the Battle of Tippecanoe.

10. Because an American general burned the village, Tecumseh supported the British in the War of 1812 he was killed in that war.

REVIEW EXERCISE

A. Identifying Fragments and Run-on Sentences

Identify the fragments and run-on sentences below. On the line before each word group, write *frag.* for *fragment* and *r.o.s.* for *run-on sentence*. If the sentence is correct, write C.

EX. <u>frag.</u> 1. Wherever you can find an empty seat.
<u>r.o.s.</u> 2. That burn was serious it hurt so much that Taka thought she would faint.

_____ 1. Odessa likes to read she reads all the time.

_____ 2. At a busy corner during rush hour in Atlanta.

_____ 3. The sound of thunder that rattled the windows.

_____ 4. He is learning how to fly he has always wanted to do this.

_____ 5. When the test is over.

_____ 6. The game is scheduled.

_____ 7. If you want to go there.

_____ 8. The capital of France is Paris, it is in Europe.

_____ 9. They are preparing a feast, it is for everyone.

_____ 10. When you come to the intersection, look for a green house.

B. Revising Fragments and Run-on Sentences in a Paragraph

On your own paper, rewrite the following paragraph to correct fragments and run-on sentences. Change the punctuation and capitalization wherever necessary.

EX. [1] We always have piñatas at Christmas, I thought they were invented in Mexico.
    We always have piñatas at Christmas. I thought they were invented in Mexico.

[1] The piñata originally came from Italy it was called a *pignatta*. [2] It was used for a game. [3] In which an earthen pot was filled with sweets and messages. [4] A blindfolded person tried to break the pot open. [5] While it was suspended overhead. [6] The idea was adopted in Spain the name was changed to *piñata* Spanish explorers brought the game to

Mexico. [7] Hundreds of years ago. [8] Today, piñatas are often made from papier-mâché. [9] Shaped like stars, flowers, rainbows, or animals. [10] The game, however, has not changed, the piñata is still filled with treats and surprises everyone wants to be the lucky one to break it open.

C. Recreating a Message

You just received a postcard from a friend who is on a holiday in Greece. Before you could read it, however, your puppy got hold of it and tore it to bits. From the groups of words below, try to re-create your friend's message on your own paper.

EX.   Yesterday
      to the beach
      Yesterday, we went to the beach.

having fun	I like the outdoor cafes
three days in Athens	wonderful food
the capital of Greece	Next, we will go
lots of ancient ruins	Delphi, where we will
everywhere we go.	famous temple of the Greek god Apollo.

Shoe, by Jeff MacNelly, reprinted by permission: Tribune Media Services.

COMBINING BY INSERTING WORDS

8e **You can combine short sentences by taking a key word from one sentence and inserting it into another sentence.**

ORIGINAL   Lupe showed us her weaving. She had just finished it.
COMBINED   **Finished**, Lupe showed us her weaving.

To fit one word into another sentence, you may need to change the form of the word.

ORIGINAL   Lupe chose colors that reminded her of the desert. She chose them with **care.**
COMBINED   Lupe **carefully** chose colors that reminded her of the desert.

NOTE   When you change the form of a word before inserting it into a sentence, you often add an ending that makes the word an adjective or an adverb. The endings you'll use most frequently are *–ed, –ful, –ing,* and *–ly.*

EXERCISE 7 Combining Sentences by Inserting Words

Combine each of the following sets of sentences by inserting the italicized word(s) into the first sentence. The directions in parentheses tell you how to change the form of the word if you need to. Rewrite the sentences on your own paper.

EX.   1. The discovery of the fish called coelacanth is a fascinating story. It is like a *detective* story.

    1. The discovery of the fish called coelacanth is a fascinating detective story.

1. In 1938, the manager of a museum in Africa found the body of a fish mixed in with a shipment of sharks. It was a *strange* fish.

2. She could not identify the fish. It was *huge* and *blue*.

3. She sent drawings to a famous fish expert. It was a *puzzle* to her. (Add *–ed*.)

4. The expert recognized a coelacanth, a fish that had previously been seen only in fossilized impressions. These impressions were *ancient*.

5. Scientists thought the coelacanth had died out with the dinosaurs, but it had not. It was *amazing* that it had not. (Add *–ly*.)

6. News of the discovery spread. It was an *international sensation*.

7.   Dr. Smith wanted to find another coelacanth. He decided to *search for* it.

8.   He offered a reward for another specimen of the fish. The reward was *$400*.

9.   Finally, another man found one in the Comoro Islands. This man was a *Sea Captain*.

10. More coelacanths have been found since then, but scientists still have questions about how this species managed to survive. These questions are *unanswered*.

EXERCISE 8   Combining Sentences by Inserting Words

In Exercise 7, the key words were italicized for you. Now you must decide which words to insert. Rewrite the sentences on your own paper, changing the form if you need to.

EX.   1.   Iditarod is a dog sled race. It is the longest dog sled race in the world.

    1.   Iditarod is the longest dog sled race in the world.

1.   It is held each year. It takes place in Alaska.

2.   The race goes from Anchorage to Nome, 1,609 kilometers. It is a challenge to compete in it.

3.   The top twenty racers share the prize. It is more than $100,000.

4.   The mushers need eight to eighteen dogs to pull the sleds carrying supplies. They need well-trained dogs.

5.   The mushers often have to battle snowdrifts and winds of up to sixty miles per hour. Winds at this speed have a lot of power.

6.   Each dog sled carries food for the team and for the musher. The sled must carry enough food.

7.   In addition, supplies include snowshoes and some booties for the dogs' feet. They also include a sleeping bag.

8.   The huskies' feet need protection. It must be constant.

9.   The race may take anywhere from eleven to thirty-two days. It is a long race.

10. A new record time was set in 2002. The time was eight days, twenty-five hours and forty-six minutes.

COMBINING BY INSERTING PHRASES

You can combine two closely related sentences by reducing one sentence to a phrase and inserting it into the other sentence.

8f You can combine sentences by inserting a prepositional phrase.

A *prepositional phrase* is a group of words consisting of a preposition, a noun or pronoun that serves as the object of the preposition, and any modifiers of that object. Usually, you can insert a prepositional phrase into a sentence without changing it in any way.

ORIGINAL   I have just finished reading *The Call of the Wild*. It was written by Jack London.

REVISED   I have just finished reading *The Call of the Wild* **by Jack London.**

8g You can combine sentences by inserting a participial phrase.

A *participle* is a word that is formed from a verb but is used as an adjective. Participles usually end in *–ed* or *–ing*. A *participial phrase* contains a participle and words related to it. The whole phrase acts as an adjective in the sentence.

ORIGINAL   London wrote popular adventure stories. He drew from his own experiences.

REVISED   **Drawing from his own experiences,** London wrote popular adventure stories.

8h You can combine sentences by changing one sentence into an appositive phrase and inserting it into the other.

An *appositive phrase* is made up of an appositive and its modifiers. An appositive phrase should be placed directly before or after the word it modifies. It is set off by commas.

ORIGINAL   Jack London wrote stories with settings all around the world. He was a native of California.

REVISED   Jack London, **a native Californian,** wrote stories with settings all around the world.

EXERCISE 9   Combining Sentences by Inserting Prepositional Phrases

Combine each pair of sentences into one sentence by building upon the first sentence and by eliminating needless words. Use prepositional phrases to make the combinations, and punctuate the combined sentences properly. Write your answers on your own paper.

EX.   1. Salvadore and his brother live in a small town. The town is near Dallas, Texas.
    1. Salvadore and his brother live in a small town near Dallas, Texas.

1. We stored our new video games. We stored them in the bookcase.
2. Chunks fell from the trunk. The chunks were ice.
3. The car costs more. The car has racing stripes.
4. We saw my teacher and his wife. We saw them at the mall.
5. The waiter brought the food. He brought it to the table.

EXERCISE 10   Combining Sentences by Inserting Participial Phrases and Appositive Phrases

Combine each pair of sentences by making one sentence of each pair a participial phrase or an appositive phrase. Punctuate the combined sentences correctly. Write your answers on your own paper.

EX.   1. Inez rode her bicycle to school. She wanted to arrive early.
    1. Wanting to arrive early, Inez rode her bicycle to school.

1. Marcus waited for somebody to help him. He tapped his fingers on the counter.
2. Ms. Early wants to will her estate to the school. Ms. Early was the wife of the first mayor of our town.
3. Leslie and Nathan washed his car. They wanted to surprise their brother.
4. The students are Holly and Zia. They are organizing the talent show.
5. Walt Disney produced the first full-length cartoon feature. He was born in 1901.
6. Alfred Nobel invented dynamite in 1866. He founded the Nobel Prize.
7. Alice Walker wrote the novel *The Color Purple*. She was born in Georgia.
8. A woman offered a suggestion. She was wearing a green overcoat.
9. We finished the job easily. We used the proper tools.
10. Samantha rushed down the hall. She was frightened by the sudden, loud noise.

COMPOUND ELEMENTS

8i **You can combine sentences by creating compound subjects and compound verbs.**

Use a coordinating conjunction (*and, but, for, nor, or,* or *yet*) to make a compound subject, a compound verb, or both.

ORIGINAL   Aretha is in high school. Tamara is in high school.
REVISED   **Aretha and Tamara** are in high school. [compound subject]

ORIGINAL   They both play tennis. They both like tennis.
REVISED   They both **play and like** tennis. [compound verb]

ORIGINAL   Aretha walks and rides her bicycle to school. Tamara walks and rides her bicycle to school. They rarely drive.
REVISED   **Aretha and Tamara walk and ride** their bicycles to school, **but rarely drive**. [compound subject and compound verb]

EXERCISE 11   **Combining Sentences by Creating Compound Subjects and Compound Verbs**

Combine each set of sentences below by creating a compound subject, a compound verb, or both. Write the new sentences on your own paper.

EX.   1.   We often watch birds at the shore. We also photograph the birds.
    1.   We often watch and photograph birds at the shore.

1.   Auks are diving birds. Puffins are diving birds.
2.   The cormorant is a bird that dives. The cormorant swims to great depths.
3.   Gulls fly to catch their food. Gulls swim to catch their food. Pelicans fly to catch their food. Pelicans swim to catch their food.
4.   Penguins can swim well. Penguins cannot fly.
5.   The cormorant swims gracefully. The cormorant dives gracefully. The cormorant walks awkwardly.
6.   We also like to explore at the ocean. We look for other forms of life.
7.   Small fish often live in tide pools. Hermit crabs do too.
8.   My sister collects seashells. I collect seashells.
9.   Last week many perfect sand dollars were scattered on the beach. Clam shells were scattered there, too.
10.   I collected some but left most of them in the sand. My sister did the same thing.

8j   You can create compound sentences by linking two sentences with a coordinating conjunction, a semicolon, or a semicolon and a conjunctive adverb.

If the thoughts in two sentences are related to one another and are equal in importance, you can combine the sentences to form a compound sentence.

ORIGINAL   Cesar was not sure his idea would work. It won first place in the science fair.

REVISED   Cesar was not sure his idea would work, **but** it won first place in the science fair.

or

Cesar was not sure his idea would work; **it** won first place in the science fair.

or

Cesar was not sure his idea would work; **however,** it won first place in the science fair.

NOTE   *So* is often overused as a coordinating conjunction. Think twice before using it.

☞   **REFERENCE NOTE:** For a list of conjunctive adverbs, see page 291.

EXERCISE 12   **Combining Sentences into Compound Sentences**

Turn each set of sentences below into a compound sentence. Use each of the three methods described above at least once. Write the new sentence on your own paper, adding punctuation where necessary.

EX.   1.   Nancy Ward was a remarkable Cherokee woman. She became famous when she was sixteen years old.

1.   Nancy Ward was a remarkable Cherokee woman; she became famous when she was sixteen years old.

1.   In 1755, the Cherokees were fighting off an attack by neighboring warriors. The Cherokees were losing.

2.   Nancy's husband was killed in this battle. She fought on.

3.   Her courage rallied the Cherokee warriors. They drove off the invaders.

4.   During the Revolutionary War, Nancy Ward warned white settlers of coming attacks. She helped them when they were taken captive.

5.   Nancy Ward also helped negotiate a peace treaty. She was a spokesperson for the Cherokees.

COMBINING SENTENCES THROUGH SUBORDINATION

If two sentences are unequal in importance, you can combine them by forming a *complex sentence*. Just turn the less important idea into a subordinate clause, and attach it to the other sentence.

8k You can make a sentence into an adjective clause by replacing its subject with *that*, *which*, or *who*.

ORIGINAL   The financial aid advisor spoke to our class yesterday. She said that all qualified students should apply to college.

REVISED   The financial aid advisor, **who spoke to our class yesterday**, said that all qualified students should apply to college.

8l You can make a sentence into an adverb clause by adding a subordinating conjunction (such as *after*, *although*, *because*, *if*, *when*, or *while*).

ORIGINAL   We asked the advisor many questions. We asked them after she spoke.

REVISED   We asked the advisor many questions **after she spoke**.

8m You can make a sentence into a noun clause by adding a word like *how*, *that*, *what*, *whatever*, *who*, or *whoever*.

ORIGINAL   She will come back for another visit. She told Atul this news.

REVISED   She told Atul **that she would come back for another visit**.

EXERCISE 13   Combining Sentences into a Complex Sentence

Revise each pair of sentences by turning one sentence into a subordinate clause and inserting it into the other sentence. Write the revised sentence on the lines after each sentence.

EX.   1. Wilton doesn't know. Monday is a holiday.

   Wilton doesn't know that Monday is a holiday.

1. Eli will take us to the museum. He will take us if he has time. _____

   _____

2. The storm was unexpected. It caught many sailors off guard. _____

   _____

3. Who wrote this book? I want to know. _____

   _____

4. Sook can prepare Vietnamese specialties. Her grandmother taught her how to do this. _____

     _____

5. Ms. Bevan lives in the green apartment building. It is across from the bakery. _____

     _____

6. Ramon is going to the festival. He said he is. _____

     _____

7. We went to the Aztec ruins. Then I decided I liked them best of all the things we'd seen in Mexico. _____

     _____

8. Marcus doesn't like mathematics. He works hard at it. _____

     _____

9. Laura is taking good care of her kitten. It was the runt of the litter. _____

     _____

10. We went camping in August. We saw a moose. _____

     _____

11. Sam took the photographs. They were highly praised. _____

     _____

12. Vanya wants to go to law school. He told me he wants to go. _____

     _____

13. Cara planned the party. It was a great success. _____

     _____

14. The runners were very tired. They decided to take a less strenuous route back. _____

     _____

15. Ikaika lives in Hilo. Hilo is a town in Hawaii. _____

     _____

USING PARALLEL STRUCTURE

USING PARALLEL STRUCTURE

8n When you join several equal or related ideas in a sentence, use the same grammatical form to express them.

For example, you pair a noun with a noun, a phrase with a phrase, and a clause with a clause. This kind of pairing is called **parallel structure.**

NOT PARALLEL	A good friend is loyal, sensitive, and showing consideration. [two adjectives and a phrase]
PARALLEL	A good friend is loyal, sensitive, and considerate. [three adjectives]
NOT PARALLEL	I like to fish for trout, to hunt for deer, and hiking. [two phrases and a noun]
PARALLEL	I like fishing for trout, hunting for deer, and hiking in the forest. [three phrases]
NOT PARALLEL	Mona told me that I had won an award for my poem and to pick it up on Saturday. [a clause and a phrase]
PARALLEL	Mona told me that I had won an award for my poem and that I should pick it up on Saturday. [two clauses]

EXERCISE 14 Revising Sentences to Create Parallel Structure

Rewrite each of the following sentences, giving it parallel structure. Write the revised sentence on the lines after each sentence.

EX.　1.　Peaceful farms, mountain villages, and living in modern cities are all things that you can see in Switzerland.

　　1.　Peaceful farms, mountain villages, and modern cities are all things that you can see in Switzerland.

1. Visitors go to Switzerland to hike, to ski, and visiting fine museums. ___

_____

2. In Switzerland people speak German, French, and Italian is spoken. ___

_____

3. Mountains and farming the land occupy much of the country. _____

_____

4. Switzerland is famous for its clocks, watches, and making cheese. _____

_____

5. The mountain villages stay open throughout the year and offering beautiful views. _____

    _____

6. Thelma answered the challenging question confidently, completely, and with carefulness. _____

    _____

7. Being naturally outgoing and because he knows everything about animals, Lani will be a good veterinarian. _____

    _____

8. The sponsor suggested a spaghetti dinner being held and that we take a group photograph. _____

    _____

9. Melba loves to play tuba, to march, and going to the games. _____

    _____

10. Losing the contract was discouraging for our competitors, but it also caused great excitement for our company. _____

    _____

11. Tawna spoke unsurely but with sound arguments to the PTA. _____

    _____

12. Cheye liked browsing in the library and to sit by the lake. _____

    _____

13. Convincing Luke to take me to the fair is easy but to convince my father is impossible. _____

    _____

14. The selection in our local market is better than many larger stores. _____

    _____

15. Evaluate the books you read by considering their prose style, and having lasting meaning. _____

    _____

IMPROVING SENTENCE STYLE

REVISING STRINGY AND WORDY SENTENCES

8o A *stringy sentence* **has too many independent clauses strung together with coordinating conjunctions like** *and* **or** *but.*

Because the ideas are all treated equally, it's difficult to see how they are related to one another. To fix a stringy sentence you can (1) break the sentence into two or more shorter sentences or (2) turn some of the independent clauses into subordinate clauses or phrases.

ORIGINAL	I rang the doorbell, but no one came to the door, and I was sure that this was the right address, so I waited, and then I saw a curtain move.
REVISED	I rang the doorbell, but no one came to the door. I was sure that this was the right address. While I waited, I saw a curtain move.

8p A *wordy sentence* **uses more words than it needs to clearly convey its meaning.**

Here are three tips for creating sentences that aren't too wordy: Don't use more words than you need to. Don't use fancy, difficult words where simple, plain ones will do. Don't repeat words or ideas unless it's absolutely necessary to do so.

WORDY	This kit has a lot of complicated and complex directions.
IMPROVED	This kit has complicated directions.

EXERCISE 15 Revising Stringy Sentences

Revise each of the following stringy sentences on your own paper.

EX. 1. Gwendolyn Brooks is shy, and she does not stand out in a crowd, yet she is a well-known American poet.

1. *Gwendolyn Brooks, a shy woman who does not stand out in a crowd, is a well-known American poet.*

1. Gwendolyn Brooks wrote poetry, and she was an African American, and she was the first African American to win the Pulitzer Prize for poetry.

2. She was born in Kansas, but she moved to Chicago, and she studied at Wilson Junior College in Chicago.

3. She won praise for her first book of poetry, *A Street in Bronzeville*, and, for this same book, she won a merit award from *Mademoiselle* magazine, and the magazine named her outstanding woman of the year.

4. She wrote other books of poetry, and she wrote a novel, and she has won many prizes and awards for her work.

5. Her poetry is about sights and sounds of Chicago's South Side, and her poetry gives a picture of life in this urban area.

EXERCISE 16   Revising Wordy Sentences

Revise each wordy sentence below on your own paper. If a sentence is not wordy, write C.

EX. 1. Astronomy is the study of the sky that is all around us and the study of the mysterious objects in the vast reaches of space.

   1. Astronomy is the study of the sky and the mysterious objects in it.

1. The reason I would like to study astronomy is because I like stars and would like to learn all about them.

2. A star is an extremely large, gigantic ball of hot, burning gaseous materials.

3. The closest star to earth is the sun.

4. Because it is the star closest to earth, we know more about the sun than we know about other stars that are farther away.

EXERCISE 17   Revising Stringy and Wordy Sentences

Revise each sentence below by breaking it into two or three sentences, or by changing an independent clause into a subordinate clause or a phrase.

EX. 1. My dad likes his new job, and he goes to interesting places all the time, but my mom is upset because he's never at home, and she asked him to quit and they have been discussing the problem.

   1. My dad likes his new job, which takes him to interesting places all the time, but my mom is upset because he's never home. She asked him to quit, and they have been discussing the problem.

1. Charlie wandered back and forth across the room, and he was waiting for an important phone call, which was to come from the captain of the debate team.

2. Marthe had traveled to every ski area in California and in Colorado and in Utah and in Idaho, for she competed on her college ski team, and she did not like surprises on the slopes.

3. Mom told me to go to Uncle Fred's store on the corner and to buy some milk and to buy biscuit mix for dinner, and I told her I didn't have any money, and she told me to get some from the top of her dresser.

4. When I was a child, I liked books by Dr. Seuss, but now that I am older, I prefer a different sort of book; I guess I like adventure stories best, but I also like to discover new authors.

VARYING SENTENCE BEGINNINGS

8q To add interest to your writing, use a variety of sentence beginnings.

Instead of beginning every sentence with the subject, you can try these variations.

VARYING SENTENCE BEGINNINGS
Single-Word Modifiers
Frightened, John slammed the door. **Excitedly**, Lisa accepted the award.
Phrases
Unable to wait any longer, Aki opened the box. [participial phrase] **With trembling hands**, Jane reached for the light switch. [prepositional phrase]
Subordinate Clauses
Because Tao had waited so long, her success was even sweeter. **Although it was late at night**, Chim answered the telephone.

EXERCISE 18 Varying Sentence Beginnings

On your own paper, rewrite each sentence below, using a variety of sentence beginnings. The hint in parentheses suggests how to begin the sentence.

EX. 1. Leotie was delighted when she heard that she had won first place. (single-word modifier)

    1. Delighted, Leotie heard that she had won first place.

1. The house was designed to look like a castle, and it was built on a hilltop. (phrase)
2. Ruby joined the school band today. (single-word modifier)
3. The sailboat race was postponed because of the high winds. (phrase)

4. Kwam has just started writing poetry, yet some of it is quite good. (clause)

5. The teacher solved the argument by allowing the whole class to discuss the problem. (phrase)

6. The lights came on when the storm was over. (clause)

7. The dog ate its food noisily. (single-word modifier)

8. Halaku has ridden in a dozen rodeos, including the one today. (phrase)

9. The children listened to Kim's stories, and they were enchanted. (single-word modifier)

10. We went to the showers after the game was over. (clause)

EXERCISE 19   Revising a Paragraph to Create Sentence Variety

Using what you've learned about combining sentences and varying structure, revise the paragraph below to make it smoother and more varied. Rewrite the paragraph on your own paper.

EX.   [1] Chico Mendes was a rubber tapper. [2] He worked in the rain forest of Brazil.

  Chico Mendes was a rubber tapper who worked in the rain forest of Brazil.

[1] Mendes was born in Brazil. [2] He began working as a rubber tapper when he was nine years old. [3] His father tapped rubber, too. [4] Rubber tappers had worked for many years in these forests. [5] Rubber tappers collect a substance from the rubber trees that grow in the rain forest. [6] This substance is called *latex*. [7] Latex is used to make tires and other rubber products. [8] It doesn't harm the trees or the forest. [9] Mendes wanted to improve the lives of the tappers. [10] They worked for long hours with low pay. [11] Mendes was also one of the tappers who saw that the rain forest was being destroyed by others. [12] It was being cut down to make cattle ranches. [13] This is called deforestation. [14] Mendes knew that deforestation would not just take away the rubber tappers' work. [15] Deforestation could affect the entire planet. [16] Mendes led protests against deforestation. [17] He helped bring the problem to the attention of the rest of the world. [18] Mendes died in 1988. [19] He had already done a great deal of work. [20] He had already done much to save the rain forest.

CHAPTER REVIEW

A. Proofreading a Paragraph for Fragments and Run-on Sentences

Proofread the paragraph below for fragments and run-on sentences. On your own paper, rewrite the paragraph to correct the errors.

EX. [1] Some plants are insect eaters and they eat insects because they cannot get enough nitrogen from the ground.

Some plants are insect eaters. They eat insects because they cannot get enough nitrogen from the ground.

[1] One insect-eating plant. [2] Called the pitcher plant. [3] It grows in tropical forests. [4] Shaped like a pitcher. [5] The plant has a slippery rim. [6] A leaf grows as a lid over the top of the pitcher and the lid opens and insects come close to it. [7] Attracted by its color. [8] If an insect lands on the rim. [9] It can fall into the pitcher. [10] It cannot get out and it is trapped and there it is dissolved and it is digested by the plant.

B. Revising a Paragraph by Combining Sentences

Revise the following paragraph by combining sentences. Write the revised paragraph on your own paper.

EX. [1] Cecilia Beaux was a portrait painter. [2] She was an American.

Cecilia Beaux was an American portrait painter.

[1] Cecilia Beaux grew up in West Philadelphia. [2] She lived with her grandmother. [3] She was taught at home until she was fourteen. [4] Her aunts taught her. [5] About then she started studying drawing. [6] At twenty-eight, she had her own studio. [7] She painted her first full-length portrait. [8] It won a prize at the Pennsylvania Academy of Fine Arts. [9] Beaux painted portraits of women and children. [10] She became well known for these paintings. [11] She often painted mother-and-child portraits. [12] A portrait of her niece was bought by a museum. [13] The Metropolitan Museum of Art in New York City bought it. [14] Her painting technique was polished. [15] Her technique makes painting look easy. [16] She repainted a canvas many times. [17] Her work was praised

by the critics. [18] Beaux was one of America's most distinguished
painters. [19] Her autobiography was published in 1930. [20] It is called
Background with Figures.

C. Revising a Paragraph

Revise the paragraph below on your own paper. Make sure that each
sentence has parallel structure, no wordy or stringy sentences, and a variety
of sentence beginnings.

EX.   [1] I like to learn about my ancestors, hear about their lives, and
       reading about the places where they lived.

       I like to learn about my ancestors, hear about their lives, and read
       about the places where they lived.

[1] My great-grandmother was a member of the Cheyenne people, and
so I've always wanted to learn more about the Cheyennes. [2] We have
unfortunately always situated and lived at a great distance from any place
where any Cheyenne people live, and I thought I could not form an
acquaintance with anyone who could inform me of more about the
Cheyenne people. [3] I decided that the way to find out more about the
Cheyennes was to use books. [4] I went to the library, to the bookstore in
town, and writing for catalogs of books about American Indians. [5] I
asked for help at the library. [6] The librarian asked me why I was
interested in the Cheyennes and I told her about my great-grandmother,
and she told me that she had always been interested in them, because her
grandfather was a Cheyenne, too. [7] It was an amazing and surprising
thing. [8] We have become friends now. [9] I go to the library. [10] When I
go there, we talk about books we have read and loaning each other books
we have discovered.

FORMAL AND INFORMAL ENGLISH

English is a very adaptable language, and it is suitable for a variety of situations. The kinds of language that you use in different situations are called *levels of usage*. These vary from the very formal to the very informal.

FORMAL ENGLISH   The game is starting, so **be alert**.
INFORMAL ENGLISH   The game is starting, so **look lively**.

Each level of language has an appropriate use. The following chart lists some of the uses of formal and informal English.

Uses of Formal and Informal English		
Speaking	Formal	formal, dignified occasions, such as banquets and dedication ceremonies
	Informal	everyday conversation at home, school, work, and recreation
Writing	Formal	serious papers and reports
	Informal	personal letters, journal entries, and many newspaper and magazine articles

The main differences between formal and informal English are in sentence structure, word choice, and tone.

Features of Formal and Informal English		
Sentence Structure	Formal	long and complex
	Informal	short and simple
Word Choice	Formal	precise; often technical or scientific
	Informal	simple and ordinary; often includes contractions, colloquialisms, and slang
Tone	Formal	serious and dignified
	Informal	conversational

EXERCISE 1   Revising a Paragraph Containing Informal Language

On the lines provided, rewrite the following paragraph. Change all informal language to language that is appropriate for a written report.

EX.   [1] Sarah Breedlove was one sharp chick!

1. Sarah Breedlove was a very intelligent woman.

[1] Sarah Breedlove didn't come from money. [2] When she was born, her folks were poor African American farmers. [3] This lady was no stranger to tough duty. [4] When she was still a bitty thing, she was washing clothes for people. [5] One day she had some kind of brainstorm. [6] She came up with making shampoos and conditioners specially for black women. [7] She started in her kitchen but soon outgrew the place. [8] Within a few years she had three thousand sharp-looking dudes and dudettes wearing her uniform. [9] By 1914 she was a millionaire, rolling in money. [10] She wasn't tightfisted, though; she gave bundles to charity and homes for old folks.

_____

_____

_____

_____

_____

_____

_____

_____

_____

_____

_____

_____

_____

_____

COLLOQUIALISMS AND SLANG

Colloquialisms are the colorful expressions of conversational language. They add a friendly, informal tone to speaking and writing.

EXAMPLES   I thought my parents would **have a fit**, but they didn't.
We waited until the rain **let up**, and then we left.

Many colloquialisms are also idioms. An *idiom* is a word or phrase that means something different from the literal meanings of the word or phrase. For example, *to drop by* has the colloquial meaning "to pay an unannounced visit." The literal meaning is "to fall near or next to."

Slang is highly informal English. It consists of made-up words or of old words used in new ways. Slang is usually clever and colorful. Slang words are often a special vocabulary for close-knit groups, such as students, musicians, or army personnel.

EXAMPLES   The **bottom line** is that we lost.
Don't get **hyper** if you see a snake.

EXERCISE 2   Translating Slang and Colloquialisms into More Formal English

On the lines after each sentence, rewrite the informal language to say the same thing in more formal English. Use a dictionary to find the meaning of any slang or colloquialism that you don't understand.

EX.   1.   I got paid today, so I have money to burn!
I got paid today, so I have extra money!

1.   Knock it off, or I'm leaving. _____

_____

2.   Farid will show you around, because he knows the ropes. _____

_____

3.   My mother works the graveyard shift at the factory. _____

_____

4.   It's too hot to cruise all over town. _____

_____

5.   Mr. Lam gives everyone a fair shake. _____

_____

6. I'm psyched; Mom agreed to take us to the amusement park! _____

_____

7. Let's go to the mall and check out the new threads. _____

_____

8. Do we have enough dough to rent a movie and buy some snacks? _____

_____

9. James says that Maria is in the know. _____

_____

10. I like hanging out with Marcus because he's cool. _____

_____

EXERCISE 3   Replacing Slang and Colloquialisms with More Formal English

In each sentence below, underline the word or phrase in parentheses that has the same meaning as the word or phrase in italics. Use a dictionary to find the meaning of any slang or colloquialism that you don't understand.

EX.   1. Ask Blythe to help you, because she's a real *hotshot* on the computer. (*typist, expert*)

1. Don't buy that ring; it looks *phony*. (*expensive, fake*)

2. My uncle Raúl was very sick, but it looks as if he'll *pull through*. (*recover, work hard*)

3. I painted doors all day, and I'm *dead*. (*tired, experienced*)

4. Come into the kitchen; we can *chat* while I make dinner. (*snack, talk*)

5. This meeting is serious, so don't try any *monkey business*. (*strange noises, foolish behavior*)

6. My brother just came home after a *hitch* in the army. (*job finished, time served*)

7. Those two have become rather *buddy-buddy* lately. (*friendly, tight*)

8. Don't sit in front of the *tube* all evening. (*stereo, television*)

9. If you are caught plagiarizing, Ms. Weeks will *throw the book at you*. (*physically harm, severely punish*)

10. Your friend certainly *got a charge* out of that movie. (*was shocked by, enjoyed*)

LOADED WORDS AND EUPHEMISMS

A word that has a very strong connotation, either positive or negative, is said to be **loaded**. Loaded words appeal to our emotions, so they are often used to influence our thinking. Advertisers, politicians, and writers of editorials tend to use loaded language.

EXAMPLES   This point of view is **totally irresponsible**. [loaded words]
             This point of view **does not address important issues**.

             The **mob shouted down** the speaker. [loaded words]
             The **crowd was so loud** that the speaker could not be heard.

In contrast to loaded words, *euphemisms* are agreeable words that are used in place of ones that might be considered offensive. For example, car salespeople know that the phrase *used car* has negative connotations. Therefore, some have started using the euphemisms *previously owned* and *experienced vehicle* instead.

NOTE   Keep in mind the emotional effect your words are likely to have. Euphemisms and loaded words can be effective in writing, but you need to choose them carefully. Avoid words that may mislead your readers.

EXERCISE 4   Analyzing Loaded Words

Underline the loaded words and phrases in the following restaurant review. On your own paper, rewrite the paragraph. Make this review more upbeat by replacing words that have a negative connotation with words that have a more positive connotation.

EX.   [1] We stepped into a murky room.

1. We stepped into a dimly-lit room.

[1] There was a cavelike feeling in the thirty-seat restaurant. [2] The food server arrived abruptly and took our order. [3] As we waited, we chewed on some dry crackers and a gooey cheese spread. [4] Then a stale, cold loaf of bread arrived at our table. [5] The band was making a racket, so it was difficult to talk. [6] My friend ordered the boneless Creole chicken, which set his mouth on fire. [7] Another member of our party ordered the tasteless, chewy shrimp stir-fry. [8] I had the stew, which was

full of overcooked vegetables. [9] The portions were skimpy, and the food's appearance on the plate was boring. [10] The desserts were limited to dishes made only with fresh fruit. [11] Two people in our group ordered the uninteresting, sour-tasting strawberry cake. [12] My wife was served an overripe, tiny slice of cantaloupe. [13] We asked for our bill, and it arrived twenty minutes later. [14] The food server waited impatiently for us to examine the items on the bill. [15] If you like overpriced food and poor service, we recommend that you try this restaurant.

EXERCISE 5   Translating Euphemisms into Straightforward English

On the line after each euphemism below, write its meaning in straightforward English. Use a dictionary if necessary.

EX. 1. offender   _criminal_____

1. meet your Maker   _____

2. tummy   _____

3. beauty mark   _____

4. powder room   _____

5. have words with   _____

6. dentures   _____

7. indisposed   _____

8. previously owned car _____

9. late bloomer   _____

10. misrepresentation   _____

11. fixer-upper   _____

12. smeller   _____

13. beat around the bush _____

14. additional revenues _____

15. under the weather   _____

CHAPTER REVIEW

A. Identifying Formal English

For each sentence below, underline the word in parentheses that is formal English.

EX. 1. Come in and meet my (*mother*, *ma*).

1. We're only a few minutes late, so (*relax*, *chill*).

2. Anyone who uses the pool after hours is a (*dead duck*, *person in trouble*).

3. That man (*is a dead ringer for*, *resembles*) Ray Charles.

4. One of the rings is (*a phony*, *an imitation*) emerald.

5. Stop (*bothering*, *hassling*) me about the tickets.

6. I'm sorry I saw that movie, because it (*upset me*, *gave me the creeps*).

7. What this job needs is a (*very ambitious person*, *go-getter*).

8. The play is a (*smash hit*, *complete success*), so the tickets sold out early.

9. If you help me now, I'll (*get off your back*, *stop asking you*).

10. Don't get (*upset*, *bent out of shape*) just because the bus is late.

11. I'm hungry; let's get some (*food*, *chow*).

12. My brother had to (*shell out*, *pay*) fifty dollars for his new shirt!

13. Lana really (*lucked out*, *was fortunate*) when she won the raffle.

14. Coach Ramírez likes to give (*a pep*, *an inspirational*) talk before an important game.

15. It's important to remember your (*roots*, *heritage*).

B. Revising Informal English

On the lines after each of the following sentences, rewrite the sentence using formal English.

EX. 1. Be careful, because I smell a rat.
   Be careful, because I think something is suspicious.

1. I sure get a kick out of skateboarding! _____

   _____

2. It's the last day of vacation, so live it up. _____

   _____

3. Takao is really into computer games. _____

_____

4. Before the play, Paula had butterflies in her stomach. _____

_____

5. Most people were excited, but one dude was as cool as a cucumber.

_____

_____

C. Revising an Advertisement

The automobile dealer who wrote the advertisement below tried to be extemely honest in describing the cars. However, the description would probably not be effective as a selling tool. On your own paper, revise the advertisement to make it more appealing to buyers. Include loaded words and euphemisms whenever you think they would influence buyers.

EX. [1] Center City Automotive is offering good cars at low prices.

[1] Center City Automotive is offering you the chance of a lifetime!

[1] In addition to its new cars, Center City Automotive is now offering seventeen used cars. [2] These automobiles will all sell at dealer cost. [3] They are not beautiful, but they are reliable. [4] They are guaranteed for six months from the date of purchase. [5] They will appeal to buyers who have little cash but need transportation. [6] Each car is approximately eight to ten years old and was used as a trade-in. [7] Many of these cars are discontinued models. [8] Some show signs of wear on the surface, but all have been checked for mechanical and electrical problems. [9] If you have the time and skill to polish one of these older models, it will be hard to distinguish from a newer car. [10] This offer will be in effect only for the months of February, March, and April.

NOUNS

The Eight Parts of Speech			
noun	adjective	pronoun	conjunction
verb	adverb	preposition	interjection

10a A *noun* is a word used to name a person, place, thing, or idea.

Persons	carpenter, Ray Charles, sister, child
Places	canyon, Kenosha, neighborhood, basement
Things	desk, train, footprint, Pulitzer Prize, dog
Ideas	courage, happiness, truth, fairness, generosity

10b A *common noun* names a class of things. A *proper noun* names a particular person, place, or thing.

Common Nouns	Proper Nouns
planet, state, river	Venus, Idaho, Rio Grande
artist, president	Henri Matisse, Thomas Jefferson
monument, building	Vietnam Veterans Memorial, Empire State Building
ship, airplane	*Merrimack*, *Kitty Hawk*

10c *Concrete nouns* name an object that can be perceived by the senses. *Abstract nouns* name a quality or an idea.

Concrete Nouns	cat, moon, lightning, cotton, banana, George Washington, money, China, flower, book
Abstract Nouns	freedom, strength, gentleness, failure, love, anxiety, pride, hope, intelligence, honesty, admiration

EXERCISE 1   Identifying and Classifying Common and Proper Nouns

In each of the sentences below, underline the common nouns, and circle the proper nouns.

EX.   1. A sari is a garment worn by women in India.

1. One book talked about the crash of the *Titanic* into an iceberg in the Atlantic.

2. Karen and Leon are coming to my house to watch the Super Bowl.

3. The surprise was four tickets to Hawaii.

4. Judge Miller decided that both men should pay for damages.

5. *Jahdu* is the name of the hero in a story by Virginia Hamilton.

6. Her attitude was pleasant, but her remarks were not.

7. Members of the Neighborhood Merchants Association met to nominate officers for the coming year.

8. *Calvin & Hobbes* is a cartoon strip distributed across the country.

9. *The Joy Luck Club*, a novel by Amy Tan, was made into a movie.

10. After leaving office, President James Madison spent his later years at Montpelier, his estate in Virginia.

EXERCISE 2   Identifying and Classifying Concrete and Abstract Nouns

In each of the sentences below, underline the concrete nouns, and circle the abstract nouns.

EX.   1. Our dog loves the freedom of our large yard.

1. Harriet Tubman risked her safety to help runaway slaves.

2. Vincent van Gogh is the artist who painted *The Starry Night*.

3. James appreciated the patience and kindness shown by his teacher.

4. Ramona dreamed that she won the role in the movie and shared her fame and fortune with her family.

5. Edgar Allan Poe is considered a master of mystery and suspense.

6. The actress wept with joy and gratitude when she won a Tony Award.

7. Mrs. Baron refused to allow the noise to ruin her speech.

8. What contributed to the causes of the Vietnam War?

9. Sonia has gained an appreciation of music.

10. I appreciate the faith and trust that my parents have in me.

COMPOUND NOUNS

> **10d** *Compound nouns* are made up of two or more words put together to form a single noun. Some compound nouns are written as one word, some as two or more words, and some with hyphens.
>
> | One Word | lighthouse, lifetime, clothespin |
> | --- | --- |
> | Two or More Words | Cape Cod, Mr. Li, tug of war |
> | Hyphenated Word | son-in-law, forty-eight, runner-up |
>
> When you are not sure how to write a compound noun, look in a dictionary.

EXERCISE 3   Identifying Compound Nouns in Sentences

Underline the compound nouns in the sentences below.

EX. 1. Good friends can help build a person's <u>self-esteem</u> and <u>self-confidence</u>.

1. This restaurant has the best egg rolls in New London.

2. Mr. Thomasino, who teaches Spanish at the high school, also coaches football.

3. Zhai said that the annual Moon Festival is an important holiday in China.

4. Tammy was appointed spokesperson for the group.

5. The Sproutful Seed Company, which is located downtown, employs eighty-five workers.

6. The star of the city ballet is the daughter of a famous playwright.

7. Mom got tickets to the Book and Author Luncheon this afternoon.

8. The police officer stayed with the lost child until the child's grandmother came.

9. Cleon was away over the weekend, so he recorded some of his favorite programs on a videocassette.

10. The nurse measured the man's blood pressure and took his temperature before bringing his food.

EXERCISE 4   Identifying Compound Nouns in a Paragraph

Underline the compound nouns in the paragraph below.

EX.   [1] Dad told me about a thrilling moment in baseball.

[1] That moment came in the eighth inning of the first game of the 1954 World Series. [2] Thousands of excited fans crowded the stands of the Polo Grounds in New York City to watch New York battle Cleveland. [3] The level of excitement increased when Vic Wertz, the first batter in the lineup, stepped up to home plate. [4] The first baseman swung hard, sending the ball into the outfield. [5] The hopes of the Cleveland fans soared like skyrockets. [6] Surely this blast would bring in two base runners. [7] The fans' confidence was crushed, however, when the center fielder for New York made a spectacular catch. [8] Willie Mays quieted the cheers of those fans as he caught the ball and spun around. [9] With the talent and skill that had made him famous, he hurled the ball to the infield. [10] It was the game of a lifetime.

BORN LOSER® by Art and Chip Sansom

Born Loser reprinted by permission of NEA, Inc.

PRONOUNS

10e   A *pronoun* is a word used in place of a noun or more than one noun.

Personal Pronouns	I, me, my, mine, we, us, our, ours, you, your, yours, he, him, his, she, her, hers, it, its, they, them, their, theirs
Relative Pronouns	who, whom, whose, which, that
Interrogative Pronouns	who, whose, what, whom, which
Demonstrative Pronouns	this, that, these, those
Indefinite Pronouns	all, another, any, anybody, anyone, anything, both, each, either, everybody, everyone, everything, few, many, more, most, much, neither, nobody, none, no one, one, other, several, some, somebody, someone, something, such
Reflexive Pronouns	myself, ourselves, yourself, yourselves, himself, herself, itself, themselves

NOTE Pronouns such as *my, your, his, her, ours,* and *their* are considered possessive pronouns in this book, rather than adjectives. Follow your teacher's instructions in referring to such words.

A word that a pronoun stands for is called its ***antecedent***. A pronoun may appear in the same sentence as its antecedent or in a following sentence.

EXAMPLE   Pauli enjoyed making yogurt for **his** friends. **He** was glad that **they** enjoyed **it**. [*Pauli* is the antecedent of *his* and is in the same sentence as *his*. In the following sentence, *Pauli* is the antecedent of *He*, *friends* is the antecedent of *they*, and *yogurt* is the antecedent of *it*.]

EXERCISE 5　Identifying Pronouns

Underline the pronouns in the sentences below.

EX.　1.　I asked Frank to bring in the mail when <u>he</u> came inside.

1.　He kept two letters for himself and handed me a large envelope.

2.　It was from a friend of mine in Colorado.

3.　The envelope had seven stamps on the outside, and each was different from the others.

4.　Looking at them was like looking at a mini-history lesson.

5.　Among the stamps was one with a picture of Harriet Quimby on its face.

6.　She was a female pilot who was also a pioneer in the history of aviation.

7.　Another had a picture of Margaret Mitchell, who, I recall, wrote the novel *Gone with the Wind*.

8.　Everyone knows her book was made into a movie.

9.　Who is the man pictured on the stamp next to hers?

10.　That is Luis Muñoz Marin, who served four terms as governor of Puerto Rico and greatly influenced its history.

EXERCISE 6　Identifying Pronouns and Their Antecedents

Underline the pronouns in the paragraph below. Circle the antecedent of each pronoun.

EX.　[1] The basket (maker) fanned <u>herself</u> with <u>her</u> fan.

[1] In Charleston, South Carolina, the basket makers visit among themselves as they sit, weaving their baskets. [2] The basket makers practice an art that is three hundred years old. [3] It has been passed from one generation of women to another. [4] The baskets themselves were once made to store rice harvested by slaves. [5] Later, they were used to carry vegetables and fruit. [6] People who stop to watch a basket being made understand the skill and labor that basket weaving takes. [7] Even the smallest basket requires hours of work, making it expensive. [8] Tourists seem willing to pay the price without complaining about it. [9] They appreciate the fine workmanship. [10] The three hundred families who make baskets today are proud of their tradition.

ADJECTIVES

10f   An *adjective* is a word used to modify a noun or pronoun.

Adjectives make the meaning of a noun or a pronoun more definite. Words used in this way are called *modifiers*. An adjective may modify a noun or pronoun by telling *what kind*, *which one*, or *how many*.

What kind?	**red** paint, **new** friend, **light** rain
Which one?	**this** room, **those** books, **that** car
How many?	**five** feet, **ten** musicians, **many** hours

An adjective may be separated from the word it modifies by other words.

EXAMPLE   The salad was **delicious.**

The most frequently used adjectives are *a, an,* and *the.* These words are usually called *articles*.

A and *an* are *indefinite articles*. They indicate that a noun refers to one of a general group. *A* is used before words beginning with a consonant sound; *an* is used before words beginning with a vowel sound. *An* is also used before words beginning with the consonant *h* when the *h* is not pronounced.

EXAMPLES   **A** car pulled up beside us.
Have you ever seen such **an** unusual painting?
Parsley is **an** herb.

The is the only *definite article*. It indicates that a noun refers to someone or something in particular.

EXAMPLE   **The** chorus sang **the** song cheerfully.

EXERCISE 7   Identifying Adjectives in Sentences

Underline the adjectives in each of the following sentences, and circle the word each adjective modifies. Do not include *a, an,* or *the.*

EX.   1.   A blast of <u>cold</u> (wind) came through the <u>open</u> (door).

1.   The small plane made several attempts to land safely.

2.   What lucky fishing group caught those trout?

3.   Gertrude has developed an interesting and successful plan to save money.

4. Ancient glaciers have created a large wilderness in northern Labrador.

5. The fox dashed across the grassy meadow, looking for some food.

6. The prizewinning photographer said that his best shots were unusual.

7. Seven generations of my family have lived in the isolated village along the Pecos River in New Mexico.

8. The tired tourists walked around the foggy capital, but they did not complain about the bad weather.

9. The audience was surprised when ten members of the cast flew on invisible wires around the theater.

10. That castle in the Czech Republic is famous for its mahogany walls and stained-glass windows.

EXERCISE 8   Identifying Adjectives in Sentences

Draw a line under each adjective in the sentences below. Above it, write *indef.* for *indefinite article*, *def.* for *definite article*, or *adj.* for *adjective*.

EX.   1. We are going to New England to see the spectacular fall foliage.
                                                          def.   adj.   adj.

1. If you want to see the best show of fall colors, travel to New England.

2. Only a few places in the world present this incredible spectacle.

3. Japan is one, along with New England, the mid-Atlantic states, and the Appalachian Mountains.

4. These places have the ideal combination of climate and native trees.

5. During the summer, certain trees make yellow colors in their leaves.

6. These remain hidden by the green chlorophyll in the leaves.

7. When fall comes and the chlorophyll disappears, the hidden yellows are revealed.

8. A tree may change sugar and other substances into vivid red chemicals.

9. This process seems magical.

10. A wet summer tends to result in a more beautiful fall show of leaves, which you should see.

PRONOUNS AND NOUNS USED AS ADJECTIVES

10g   Some words may be used either as adjectives or as pronouns.

To tell adjectives and pronouns apart, keep in mind what they do. Adjectives *modify* nouns; pronouns *take the place of* nouns. If a word is used as an adjective, a noun must closely follow it.

Adjective	Pronoun
These shoes are tight.	**These** are tight shoes.
Will **some** people not approve?	Will **some** not approve?
I'd like **that** book.	I'd like **that**.

10h   Some words may be used either as nouns or as adjectives.

When a noun is used as an adjective, call it an adjective. Proper nouns used as adjectives are called *proper adjectives*.

Common Nouns	Common Nouns Used as Adjectives
cheese	**cheese** omelet
city	**city** streets
silver	**silver** bracelet
Proper Nouns	**Proper Nouns Used as Adjectives**
Japanese	**Japanese** language
Malaysia	**Malaysian** economy
Beethoven	**Beethoven** symphony

EXERCISE 9   Identifying Nouns, Pronouns, and Adjectives

Classify each italicized word in the following paragraph. Above the word write *n.* for *noun*, *pron.* for *pronoun*, or *adj.* for *adjective*.

EX.   [1] A *New York City* vacation is *one* your family will always
      remember.

    [1] *New York City* has so *much* to see and do that you will be busy from

the moment you arrive. [2] When my family and *I* visited the *Big Apple* last summer, we stayed at the Mayflower Hotel. [3] Our rooms were on the *seventh* floor, overlooking *Central Park*. [4] What an *ideal* place *that* is to watch people! [5] On *Monday* morning, we got up early and took a *subway* train to *Battery Park*. [6] There we purchased tickets for a *ferry* ride to the Statue of Liberty and *Ellis Island*. [7] The *copper* statue was awesome and rather frightening because of its huge *size*. [8] The *Ellis Island* portion of the trip reminded me that *America* is a land of *immigrants*. [9] Photographs of *some* of the twelve *million* people that passed through Ellis Island are displayed in its main building, *which* was recently renovated. [10] Later *that* day, we went over to *Manhattan* for dinner.

EXERCISE 10   Revising Sentences by Using Appropriate Adjectives

Add a variety of adjectives to make two entirely different sentences from each sentence below. Rewrite the sentences on your own paper.

EX.   1. With a smile, the boy greeted the dog.
    1. With a wide smile, the friendly boy greeted the dog.
    1. With a timid smile, the boy greeted the yapping dog.

1. The clouds hung over the city for days.
2. As guests began to arrive, the host spoke to the staff.
3. Under the porch was a chest stuffed with jewelry and coins.
4. Cora traveled on the bus to her job in the city.
5. The teacher gave a presentation to the students.
6. As Coco put the dishes on the table, Tim prepared a salad.
7. That author tells stories about people.
8. The people waited on the platform for the train to arrive.
9. The man who entered the room wore a mask and a coat.
10. Using a tool, the mechanic fixed the car.
11. The river flowed under the bridge.
12. When the cat leaped, the audience gasped.
13. Take the coat to the child.
14. We sat around the fire, telling stories.
15. Those apples aren't for eating, but these melons are.

REVIEW EXERCISE

A. Identifying Nouns, Pronouns, and Adjectives

On the line before each sentence below, identify the italicized words by writing *n.* for *noun, pron.* for *pronoun*, or *adj.* for *adjective*. Circle the word each adjective modifies.

EX. __*adj.; n.*__ 1. Those are *my* (cousins) from *Florida*.

_____ 1. Floridians enjoy a *warm* climate for most of the *year*.

_____ 2. Although the *thought* of warm weather is appealing, *I* am not sure *I* would like to deal with giant insects.

_____ 3. *Florida* officials have reported seeing *huge* grasshoppers.

_____ 4. *Who* told you about *this*?

_____ 5. I read about the *five-inch* grasshoppers in *a* magazine.

_____ 6. At *the* time, only *five* had actually been seen.

_____ 7. *These* creatures are native to places like *Costa Rica* and Brazil.

_____ 8. Hungry grasshoppers can eat a tremendous *amount* of *sugar cane*.

_____ 9. Because of *this* appetite, state officials expressed *concern*.

_____ 10. The *sugar cane* crop is *important* to the area's agricultural industry.

B. Identifying Nouns, Pronouns, and Adjectives

Underline each noun, pronoun, and adjective in the following sentences. In the space above each underlined word, classify the word by writing *n.* for *noun, pron.* for *pronoun*, or *adj.* for *adjective*. Circle the word each adjective modifies. Do not include the articles *a, an,* or *the.*

      n.   pron.   n.   adj.   n.

EX. 1. The <u>voyage</u> took <u>them</u> from <u>Japan</u> to the <u>California</u> (<u>coast</u>).

1. The newborn chicken ate its first meal eight hours after it hatched.

2. The dealer purchased the Monet painting for an anonymous collector.

3. Aviva felt great satisfaction as she accepted the first-place award.

4. The bald eagle is a symbol of freedom for many United States citizens.

5. A visual illusion can make you believe you are seeing an object even though it is not there.

6. The ancient Mayan cities of El Mirador and Tikal are protected areas.

7. The pretty tune that she is humming is a Brahms lullaby.

8. Whenever I have to speak in front of a crowd, anxiety sets in.

9. Thea enjoys stand-up comics, and Bill Cosby is one of her favorites.

10. Because of their generosity and kindness to the community, the new library was named for the Lopezes.

C.   Working Cooperatively to Write a Travel Advertisement

Work with a partner to create a travel brochure for a Caribbean vacation.

1. Choose an island in the Caribbean. Gather specific information about the island. You will probably want to learn about the climate, the beaches, the local culture, and the most popular tourist attractions and activities. On your own paper, make notes on your research.

EX.   JAMAICA

an island in the Greater Antilles in the West Indies

named Xaymaca by Arawak Indians; name means "island of springs"

tropical climate with refreshing ocean winds

temperatures along the coast between 80° and 86°

beautiful sandy beaches

places to see: Montego Bay, Ocho Rios

things to do: snorkeling, scuba diving, exploring, sailing

2. Organize your notes. Work together to decide on the most appealing way to present the information. Then create a travel brochure of at least ten sentences, using a variety of nouns, pronouns, and adjectives. When you have finished, underline each noun, pronoun, and adjective. Above the words, write *n.* for *noun*, *pron.* for *pronoun*, and *adj.* for *adjective*. Do not label the articles *a*, *an*, and *the*.

n.

JAMAICA

pron.   n.   adj.   adj.   n.   pron.

EX.   Forget your troubles. Let tropical Jamaican breezes whisk them away.

VERBS

10i   A *verb* is a word that expresses action or a state of being.

Words such as *take, speak, run,* and *drive* are ***action verbs***. Some action verbs express actions that cannot be seen—for example, *think, trust, recognize,* and *remember*.

EXAMPLES   She **lifted** the box.
Should we value your judgment?

10j   A *transitive verb* expresses an action directed toward a person or a thing named in the sentence.

EXAMPLES   Mark **hugged** his parents. [The action of the verb *hugged* is directed toward *parents*.]
Does Sheilah **write** poetry? [The action of the verb *writes* is directed toward *poetry*.]

10k   An *intransitive verb* expresses action or a state of being without referring to an object.

EXAMPLES   The crowd **cheered**.
The plane **landed** on the runway.

The same verb may be transitive in one sentence and intransitive in another. An intransitive verb is often used when the emphasis is on the action rather than on the person or thing affected by it.

EXAMPLES   Carrie **waved** her arm. [transitive]
Carrie **waved** quickly. [intransitive]

EXERCISE 11   Identifying Action Verbs

Underline the verb in each sentence below.

EX.   1. Rudy <u>raked</u> the leaves in the back yard.

1. A cold wind whipped through the trees.

2. Mary expects an important letter in the mail.

3. Because of the drought, the farmer worried about his vegetable crop.

4. Mrs. Tsao poured hot Chinese tea from the porcelain teapot.

5. Coreen recited the poem aloud for the class.

EXERCISE 12 Identifying Transitive and Intransitive Verbs

In the sentences below, identify each italicized verb as transitive or intransitive. Write *trans.* for *transitive* or *intr.* for *intransitive* on the line before each sentence.

EX. 1. _intr._ Robert *arrived* late.

_____ 1. That rude remark *irritated* her.

_____ 2. The squirrel *jumped* from the tree branch onto the bird feeder.

_____ 3. When the commotion started, *did* Bill *walk* out?

_____ 4. She *analyzed* the relationship of the two main characters.

_____ 5. The cats *sat* silently and watched the hawk soaring above them.

_____ 6. We listened while Mr. Siadat *read* the opening verses of the poem.

_____ 7. The English language *borrows* words from many cultures.

_____ 8. Buffalo no longer *roam* freely over the Great Plains.

_____ 9. Jo and Ina piled the necessary provisions into the canoe and *pushed* off.

_____ 10. The writer N. Scott Momaday *spent* a part of his youth on Apache, Pueblo, and Navajo reservations.

_____ 11. The lost explorers *wandered* aimlessly through the jungle.

_____ 12. Miguel *gave* a rousing campaign speech to the student body.

_____ 13. In chemistry class we *did* an experiment with sulfuric acid.

_____ 14. The teacher *turned* to me and said, "Did you do your homework?"

_____ 15. *Have* you *picked* a bushel of apples?

EXERCISE 13 Writing Sentences with Transitive and Intransitive Verbs

For each verb below, write two sentences on your own paper. In one sentence, use the verb as a transitive verb, and underline the person or thing the action is directed toward. In the other sentence, use the verb as an intransitive verb.

EX. 1. sang
    1. Denise sang the school song.   1. Denise sang sweetly.

1. kept	6. moved
2. taught	7. left
3. whispered	8. rested
4. painted	9. learned
5. climbed	10. drove

LINKING VERBS

101 A *linking verb* links, or connects, the subject with a noun, a pronoun, or an adjective in the predicate. The verb *be* may express a state of being without having a complement.

A *complement* is a word or group of words that completes the meaning of a predicate.

The most commonly used linking verbs are forms of the verb *be*.

Forms of *Be*			
be	being	will be	shall be
am	can be	would be	should be
are	could be	have been	shall have been
is	may be	has been	should have been
was	might be	had been	will have been
were	must be	could have been	would have been

Other Commonly Used Linking Verbs			
appear	grow	seem	stay
become	look	smell	taste
feel	remain	sound	turn

EXAMPLES   Lynda Sagor **is** my doctor. [Lynda Sagor = doctor]
Why **does** that **sound** familiar? [familiar that]
The flowers **smell** exotic. [exotic flowers]
Our dog **can** sometimes **be** a nuisance. [dog = nuisance]

Many linking verbs can be used as action (nonlinking) verbs as well.

EXAMPLES   The tree **grew** tall. [linking verb: tall tree]
The tree **grew** several new branches. [action verb]

Even *be* is not always a linking verb. It may be followed by only an adverb. In the sentence *They are here,* the word *here* is an adverb. It does not refer to the subject, *They.* To be a linking verb, the verb must be followed by a noun, a pronoun, or an adjective that refers to the subject.

EXERCISE 14   Identifying Linking Verbs

Underline the linking verb in each sentence below. Then circle the two words that each verb links.

EX.   1. The (guitarist) was (pleased) with the applause.

1. Marguerita feels peaceful after a long run.

2. The tacos on that platter smell delicious.

3. Virgil seemed anxious before class today.

4. Wanda's older brother is my math tutor.

5. That story became a myth among the Seneca people.

6. Good friends have always been important to me.

7. That was a childish prank.

8. The stone statues almost looked alive in the moonlight.

9. Gladys might someday become a dancer with a jazz troupe.

10. Does that story sound fishy to you?

11. That could have been Ronald up there.

12. You may be right, but I doubt it.

13. We were being too noisy.

14. I am sure you had it a moment ago.

15. My sister's green eyes gradually turned brown.

EXERCISE 15   Writing Sentences Using Verbs as Both Linking and Action Verbs

On your own paper, write two sentences for each of the verbs below. In the first sentence, use the verb as a linking verb. Underline the two words that the verb connects. In the second sentence, use the verb as an action verb.

EX.   1. become

    1. According to the rules, the person with the most points becomes the winner.

    1. This straw hat becomes you.

1. feel
2. sound
3. taste
4. grow
5. remain
6. appear
7. smell
8. stay
9. turn
10. look

VERB PHRASES

10m A *verb phrase* consists of the main verb and its *helping verbs* (also called *auxiliary verbs*).

Commonly Used Helping Verbs				
can	do	has	might	should
could	does	have	must	will
did	had	may	shall	would

The forms of the verb *be* are also helping verbs.

EXAMPLES   **Would** Alfred **like** some help?
You **should have offered** sooner.
I **did** not **get** home until a few minutes ago.
We **shall** probably **be finished** in an hour.

NOTE   The word *not* in a phrase such as *could not go* is not a helping verb. Both *not* and the contraction *–n't* are adverbs.

EXERCISE 16   Identifying Verb Phrases

Underline the verb phrase in each of the following sentences. Circle the helping verbs in each verb phrase. One sentence contains two verb phrases.

EX.   1. *Miss Saigon* (was) performed at the Wang Center in Boston.

1. You may have heard of the youth workshops at the Wang Center.

2. During the run of *Miss Saigon*, hearing-impaired students from the Horace Mann School could participate in the Young at Arts program.

3. This program was established in 1988.

4. More than 65,000 young people have been introduced to the arts through these workshops.

5. How did the *Miss Saigon* workshops help the students?

6. The acting games may have increased their awareness of the Vietnam War.

7. Wasn't the story of *Miss Saigon* based on events in the Vietnam War?

8. Discussions with the cast and crew members before and after the play must have been enjoyable.

9. The Young at Arts program has also prepared study guides.

10. These guides should have stimulated students' interest in the play.

11. Have you seen the play yet?

12. The Wang Center has served the entire community.

13. Will the theater be making changes to the entrances?

14. The center does offer performances that are interpreted in American Sign Language.

15. I have liked learning that language.

EXERCISE 17   Using Verb Phrases

Complete the sentences below by rewriting them on your own paper. Add helping verbs to the verbs in parentheses to create verb phrases.

EX.   1. I _____ (*read*) a book about opera.

   1. I have been reading a book about opera.

1. My aunt _____ (*want*) to take me to the opera for a long time.

2. She _____ (*tell*) me that I limit my musical experiences.

3. She _____ (*know*) that I wasn't wild about attending the opera.

4. That _____ (*be*) why she ordered the two tickets for *Carmen* without telling me.

5. I _____ (*act*) nicer when she told me, but I never hide my feelings.

6. However, she _____ (*pay*) for the tickets, and my conscience warned me to be more agreeable.

7. So I said I _____ (*go*), but I dreaded it.

8. Well, I _____ (*be*) the first person to admit it when I am wrong.

9. I _____ (*expect*) to be miserable.

10. From the moment the curtain _____ (*raise*), I was thrilled with the colorful costumes, the lively music, the characters, and the story.

ADVERBS

10n An *adverb* is a word used to modify a verb, an adjective, or another adverb.

Adverbs modify by telling *how, when, where,* or *to what extent.*

How?	Sadie opened the package **very carefully**.
When?	The catalogs arrived **yesterday**.
Where?	Tonya and Webster came **inside**.
To what extent?	I **almost** forgot your birthday. She is **extremely** beautiful.

Just as adjectives modify nouns and pronouns, adverbs modify verbs. An adverb makes the meaning of the verb clearer and more definite.

EXAMPLES   The dog was barking **outside**. [*where*]
The dog barked **today**. [*when*]
The dog barked **loudly**. [*how*]
The dog **always** barked. [*to what extent*]

EXERCISE 18   Identifying Adverbs and the Verbs They Modify

Underline the adverbs in each of the following sentences. Then circle the verb each adverb modifies. A sentence may have more than one adverb.

EX.   1. The police (searched) everywhere for Heta's bracelet.

1. The first-graders willingly participated in the geography contest.

2. That map of the world was brilliantly painted.

3. Claudia spoke endlessly about her summer vacation.

4. You left your jacket here.

5. Tecumseh was a Shawnee leader who fought tirelessly to preserve his people's heritage and land.

6. Today the mail arrived early, something that is unusual.

7. You can completely depend on Liz because she always works hard.

8. Dr. Martin Luther King, Jr., firmly opposed the use of violence in the civil rights movement and often spoke against it.

9. Kathy and Lynette constantly try to outdo each other.

10. Granddad exercises frequently and eats well.

11. Don't wander aimlessly around the room.

12. Now we must reach a decision about a movie.

13. The librarian does not allow pens here.

14. Diego nearly lost his hat.

15. Fortunately, school ends early on Wednesday.

EXERCISE 19   Using Adverbs

Complete each sentence below by writing an appropriate adverb on the line provided. The word or phrase in parentheses tells you what information the adverb should give about the verb.

EX.   1. She patted the frightened dog ___gently___ (how).

1. Kwam dived into the lake's cold water _____ (how) and swam _____ (where).

2. Halona _____ (to what extent) relives her experiences during the hurricane.

3. Cobb will change the flat tire _____ (when), but he will complain _____ (to what extent) about it.

4. Mai looked _____ (where) and waved _____ (how) when she spotted us.

5. The mechanics couldn't locate the necessary part _____ (where), so they can't fix the car _____ (when).

6. Michael speaks Spanish _____ (how).

7. The bird sang _____ (to what extent) _____ (where).

8. Steve _____ (how) imagined what it would feel like to win the marathon _____ (when).

9. Ada May _____ (how) described to everybody what happened _____ (where).

10. Kito spoke _____ (to what extent) and _____ (how) about recycling.

ADVERBS MODIFYING ADJECTIVES AND OTHER ADVERBS

Adverbs may modify adjectives.

EXAMPLES   It was a **breathtakingly** beautiful sunset. [The adverb *breathtakingly* modifies the adjective *beautiful*.]
Did you leave because of the **extremely** long line? [The adverb *extremely* modifies the adjective *long*.]

 NOTE The most frequently used adverbs are *too, so,* and *very*. Try to avoid these overused words in your writing. Instead, think of more precise adverbs to make your meaning clearer.

Adverbs may modify other adverbs.

EXAMPLES   She explained **quite** carefully. [The adverb *quite* modifies the adverb *carefully*, telling *how* carefully.]
They will leave **early** tomorrow. [The adverb *early* modifies the adverb *tomorrow*, telling *when* tomorrow.]

 NOTE Many adverbs end in *–ly*. However, not all words ending in *–ly* are adverbs. For instance, the following words are adjectives: *homely, kindly, lovely, deadly*. To determine a word's part of speech, look at how the word is used in the sentence. Do not rely on spelling alone.

EXERCISE 20   Identifying Adverbs and the Adjectives They Modify

Underline the adverbs in each of the following sentences. Then circle the adjective each adverb modifies.

EX.   1.   Inez was <u>especially</u> (kind) to her young cousin.

1. After exercising at the gym, Patsy was thoroughly exhausted.

2. Neil expressed concern that the crowd might become quite wild.

3. His uncle was a truly generous individual.

4. Isn't this hot-and-sour soup especially spicy?

5. The highwire routine was clearly dangerous.

6. George Shortsleeve's surprisingly accurate predictions about the mayoral race won him points among the voters.

7. That is an extremely heavy box; please, be careful lifting it.

8. Our family spent the night in a barely adequate hotel.

9. Rather ominous clouds hovered on the horizon.

10. Lucia wrote a particularly thoughtful paper analyzing the poem composed by Maya Angelou.

11. Is Liang unusually polite when she is tired?

12. Bao and Cam were completely sure about the directions they gave us.

13. When I am on a boat, my face is rarely green.

14. The overly choosy batter watched the pitches fly by.

15. Turn off the burner if the milk is almost hot.

EXERCISE 21   Identifying Adverbs and the Adverbs They Modify

Underline the adverbs in each of the sentences below. Then draw an arrow from one adverb to the other adverb it modifies.

EX. 1. Sal spoke rather slowly.

1. Utina explained quite precisely what occurred at City Hall.

2. Lucas sailed his small boat into the harbor late yesterday.

3. Arlene leaned alarmingly far over the ledge.

4. The people on the bus complained extremely loudly about the delay.

5. I awoke somewhat early, which is unusual for me.

6. Those plants in the greenhouse look especially healthy.

7. I am going to the hospital almost daily.

8. Megan travels to Montana quite often, doesn't she?

9. Barry hardly ever sees puffins on the shore.

10. Increasingly often I am finding toads in the yard.

11. Did you run even faster than last time?

12. "I thank you most sincerely, Ma'am."

13. I told my story perfectly calmly.

14. He was breathing terribly hard when he reached the summit.

15. The host of the party was rather fashionably dressed.

PREPOSITIONS

10o   A *preposition* is a word that shows the relationship of a noun or a pronoun to some other word in the sentence.

In the examples below, notice how the prepositions show six different relationships between *city* and the verb *flew*.

EXAMPLES   We flew **over** the city.   We flew **across** the city.
We flew **toward** the city.   We flew **around** the city.
We flew **beyond** the city.   We flew **into** the city.

A preposition always introduces a *phrase*. The noun or pronoun that ends a prepositional phrase is the ***object of the preposition***. In the previous examples, the object of each preposition is *city*.

Commonly Used Prepositions				
aboard	before	by	like	through
about	behind	concerning	near	to
above	below	down	of	toward
across	beneath	during	off	under
after	beside	except	on	until
against	besides	for	onto	up
along	between	from	outside	upon
among	beyond	in	over	with
around	but (meaning	inside	past	within
at	*except*)	into	since	without

Prepositions may also be compound.

Compound Prepositions		
according to	in addition to	instead of
because of	in front of	on account of
by means of	in spite of	prior to

NOTE   Depending on its use in a sentence, the same word may be either an adverb or a preposition.

EXAMPLES   Vince walked **inside**. [adverb]
Vince walked **inside** the house. [preposition]

EXERCISE 22 Using Prepositions

Use the charts on page 123, and write a preposition on each line to complete the sentences below.

EX. 1. Charlotte read a fictional story __about__ the Civil War.

1. The weary soldiers marched slowly _____ the field.

2. They had fought a mighty battle _____ their country.

3. Many of their comrades had died _____ yesterday's battle.

4. These remaining soldiers were grateful _____ their survival.

5. Many of them had not eaten _____ several days.

6. Several stopped to rest _____ the large rocks or tree stumps.

7. They considered their accomplishments _____ their failures.

8. When they finally reached the farmhouse, the youngest _____ them collapsed on the ground.

9. The farmers helped carry the boy _____ the house.

10. They would feed the soldiers and give them a place to sleep _____ the next morning.

11. When the sun came up, the young soldier was still _____ any strength.

12. The rest _____ the troop decided they could not wait for him.

13. His friends waved as they walked _____ his window.

14. _____ a few days, the young man was well enough to travel.

15. He told the farmers he had survived only _____ their kindness.

EXERCISE 23 Writing Sentences with Prepositions and Adverbs

On your own paper, write two sentences for each of the words below. In the first sentence, use the word as a preposition, and underline the prepositional phrase. In the second sentence, use the word as an adverb, and circle the word the adverb modifies.

EX. 1. before
    1. Don't eat anything before dinner.
    1. I heard that story before.

1. below	5. over	8. in
2. near	6. around	9. above
3. under	7. outside	10. down
4. up		

CONJUNCTIONS AND INTERJECTIONS

10p   A *conjunction* **is a word used to join words or groups of words.**

Conjunctions that join equal parts of a sentence are called *coordinating conjunctions*.

Coordinating Conjunctions
and   but   for   nor   or   so   yet

EXAMPLES   Yesterday, we went to a movie **and** a play.
Did you see the western **or** the comedy?
I wanted to see the play, **for** Hoa directed it.

Conjunctions that are used in pairs are called *correlative conjunctions*. Like coordinating conjunctions, correlative conjunctions join equal parts of a sentence.

Correlative Conjunctions		
both . . . and	neither . . . nor	whether . . . or
either . . . or	not only . . . but also	

EXAMPLES   **Neither** my mother **nor** my father would reveal the secret.
Both my aunt **and** my grandfather showed up unexpectedly.
Their presence **not only** pleased us **but also** gave away the surprise.

10q   An *interjection* **is a word that expresses emotion and has no grammatical relation to other words in the sentence.**

An *interjection* is usually followed by an exclamation mark. An interjection that shows only mild emotion is set off from the sentence by a comma.

EXAMPLES   **Yuck!** That tastes terrible.
If they aren't here soon, **well,** I don't know what I'll do.

EXERCISE 24   Identifying Coordinating and Correlative Conjunctions

Underline the conjunctions in the paragraph below. In the space above the word, write *coor.* for *coordinating conjunction* or *corr.* for *correlative conjunction.*

> coor.
EX. [1] I enjoy art, but I am not sure I understand it.

[1] Whether you understand art or not, you will appreciate the work of Jacob Lawrence. [2] His paintings reflect not only his own life experiences but also the life experiences of many African American people. [3] The figures in paintings such as *Builders #1* often express a particular state of mind or an emotion. [4] Lawrence was born in 1917 in Atlantic City and grew up in Harlem. [5] There he developed his interest in and fascination with African American history. [6] He studied history at the YMCA in Harlem, for he wanted to learn more about his culture. [7] Today Jacob Lawrence is a celebrated American artist, but his first painting job was with the Works Progress Administration. [8] During the Great Depression, the WPA both created jobs for people and paid the workers. [9] Neither the WPA nor Lawrence himself could have predicted that his work would become so famous. [10] Among his most famous paintings are portraits of Frederick Douglass, Harriet Tubman, and John Brown.

EXERCISE 25   Using Interjections

On your own paper, write a sentence using each of the interjections below. When punctuating your sentences, use both commas and exclamation points.

> EX. 1. ouch
> 1. Ouch! That really hurt!

1. ah
2. wow
3. great
4. yikes
5. incredible
6. no
7. terrific
8. yeah
9. fantastic
10. hey

CHAPTER REVIEW

A. Determining the Parts of Speech of Words

In the paragraph below, identify the part of speech of each italicized word or expression. On the line before each sentence, write *n.* for *noun*, *adj.* for *adjective*, *pro.* for *pronoun*, *v.* for *verb*, *adv.* for *adverb*, *prep.* for *preposition*, *conj.* for *conjunction*, and *intj.* for *interjection*.

EX. [1] __adv.; n.__ We *gladly* attended the concert of the West African group Farafina at the *Sanders Theater*.

[1] _____ We were *extremely fortunate* to attend Saturday night's performance. [2] _____ *Farafina* is an African musical troupe *from* Burkina Faso. [3] _____ Since *their* formation in 1977, the group *has continued* to compose, arrange, and perform music in the traditional manner of their country. [4] _____ They plan to maintain this strong tie to tradition, *yet* they admit that they are always *open* to new influences. [5] _____ Farafina has been *popular* in Europe *for* a long time because audiences understand the music.

[6] _____ *Oh*, how exciting the *performance* was! [7] _____ *As* the audience settled *down*, the music began. [8] _____ The soft, melodic tones of the reed flute *were* soon *joined* by the more exotic sounds of the balafon, an *African* xylophone. [9] _____ Before the singing or the dancing began, several *different* kinds of African drums, the doumdou'ba, the bara, the tama, *and* the djembe, added their rhythmic sounds. [10] _____ I learned the names of these ancient African instruments *after* the performance was *over*.

B. Writing Sentences Using Words as Different Parts of Speech

On your own paper, write a sentence, using each of the following words or phrases. Above the word or phrase, identify its part of speech. Write *n.* for *noun*, *adj.* for *adjective*, *pro.* for *pronoun*, *v.* for *verb*, *adv.* for *adverb*, *prep.* for *preposition*, *conj.* for *conjunction*, and *intj.* for *interjection*.

EX. 1. gold   adj.
    1. Kay bought a gold bracelet.

1. sounded
2. neither . . . nor
3. gently
4. will be going
5. in spite of
6. challenged
7. ugh
8. today
9. this
10. table
11. White House
12. smelled
13. frequently
14. her
15. climbed
16. or
17. eek
18. across
19. must have known
20. computer

C. Determining and Writing Parts of Speech

A sailor on a pirate ship brings his captain this message about buried treasure. He found the note under the floorboards of a deserted shack on an island in the Atlantic Ocean. Unfortunately, mice have nibbled holes in the paper. For each blank, supply one word that makes sense, and write its part of speech above the word.

EX.   1   This note will lead you ___*directly*___ to the buried treasure.
                                          adv.

1   _____! If you've found this note you are a lucky person. When my

2   ship was about to sink, I _____ a chest with valuable jewels and

3   bags of golden coins. I quickly jumped into the water _____

4   somehow managed to pull the chest _____ . I have been alone on

5   this deserted island for _____ weeks and have been able to survive

6   by eating _____ . But it's time to leave. I found a small boat hidden

7   _____ the shack this morning. The chest is too heavy and big to

8   bring on the boat, so I am going to bury _____ . I'm leaving this

9   note in case I don't make it. At least someone will enjoy the treasure. I am

10 burying the chest _____ the _____ .

SENTENCES AND SENTENCE FRAGMENTS

11a   A *sentence* is a group of words that contains a subject and a verb and expresses a complete thought.

To express a complete thought, a sentence must say something that makes sense by itself. A group of words that does not express a complete thought is a *fragment*, or a piece of a sentence.

FRAGMENT   provides food and shelter for a variety of birds and other wildlife

SENTENCE   The marsh provides food and shelter for a variety of birds and other wildlife.

FRAGMENT   when we looked carefully

SENTENCE   When we looked carefully, we noticed a motionless bird standing among the reeds.

EXERCISE 1   Identifying Sentences and Fragments

On the line before each of the following groups of words, write *sent.* for *sentence* and *frag.* for *fragment.* Add correct capitalization and punctuation to the sentences.

EX.   _sent._ 1. ᔕ$he jumped over the fence and vanished

_____ 1. Shannon most enjoyed the music of the mariachi bands

_____ 2. Jorge added his name to the petition

_____ 3. Liona and another woman in my family

_____ 4. have been designed by I. M. Pei

_____ 5. I quickly put on my kneepads and helmet

_____ 6. chemistry is easier for me than biology was

_____ 7. the Chicano Training Center in Texas

_____ 8. those dogs are all trained as guide dogs

_____ 9. nodded and smiled without saying anything

_____ 10. several of the trucks at the tollbooth

_____ 11. people wanted to hear about her life as an artist

_____ 12. a deserted stretch of highway

_____ 13. crisp, green lettuce and a tomato

_____ 14. Vincent is both a drummer and a piano player

_____ 15. and after a while, each day

EXERCISE 2   Completing Sentences

Each group of words below is a fragment. To form complete sentences, add either a subject with modifiers or a verb with modifiers to each fragment.

EX.   1. Yes, ____our friend Iman____ speaks Arabic fluently.

1. In the middle of the table stood _____.

2. Only my oldest brother _____.

3. _____ is wearing a blue and gold sari.

4. My favorite breakfast food was _____.

5. The flames of the eight candles _____.

6. In July, the three-day fair _____.

7. _____ screeched to a halt in front of me.

8. _____ showed a picture of one of the ancient gods.

9. _____ asked who had painted this portrait.

10. Around his wrist was _____.

11. As the fog slowly rose, shapes of houses _____.

12. _____ cooked slowly.

13. Our two cats and the dog _____.

14. _____ closed with a crash.

15. _____ turned down the volume on the radio.

16. Included in the crafts fair were _____.

17. Sculptors, painters, and photographers _____.

18. Did _____ jump up on the stage?

19. _____ are admitted free of charge.

20. _____ enjoy eating Indian food.

SUBJECT AND PREDICATE

11b A sentence consists of two parts: the *subject* and the *predicate*.

The *subject* is the part that names the person or thing spoken about in the rest of the sentence. It may come at the beginning, the end, or even the middle of a sentence. The *predicate* is the part that says something about the subject.

	SUBJECT	PREDICATE
EXAMPLES	The pioneers	crossed the desert at night.

	PREDICATE	SUBJECT
	Long and hard was	the journey.

	PREDICATE	SUBJECT	PREDICATE
	Have	you	read the women's diaries?

In these examples, the words labeled *subject* make up the **complete subject**. The words labeled *predicate* make up the **complete predicate**. Notice in the third example that parts of the complete predicate can come before and after the subject.

EXERCISE 3   Identifying the Complete Subject of a Sentence

Underline the complete subject in each sentence below. Remember that the subject may come at the beginning, the end, or even the middle of a sentence.

EX.   1. <u>Many Japanese children</u> own Daruma dolls.

1. Did Grandma own a cornhusk doll?

2. How interesting and colorful that book on dolls is!

3. Is the wooden doll still your favorite?

4. Rare and expensive is that doll in the picture.

5. My classmate Tony owns several kachina dolls.

6. Did that old rag doll belong to a family member?

7. Would you buy an antique doll?

8. The doll on the lower shelf is more than two hundred years old.

9. Was papier mâché ever used for a doll's head?

10. These wooden dolls were used in special ceremonies.

EXERCISE 4   Identifying Complete Subjects and Predicates

In each sentence below, underline the complete subject once and the complete predicate twice.

EX.   1. The cyclists planned a two-day journey.

1. A good bike trail simplifies travel.

2. Cool and crisp was the weather.

3. The tour leader will check the equipment of each bicycle.

4. Do you wear your helmet at all times?

5. Did Mavis adjust the bicycle seat and handlebars properly?

6. A ten-speed bike is nice, but not necessary, on long trips.

7. Each person carried a small tool kit and some foul-weather gear.

8. The plastic bottle on my bike holds one liter of water.

9. You have to use hand signals and follow safety regulations.

10. For most of our trip, we traveled along country roads.

11. The reds and yellows of the fall foliage glistened in the sunlight.

12. Apples, pumpkins, and vegetables were for sale at farm stores.

13. One roadside store advertised pure cider pressed from fresh apples.

14. How could we resist a taste of that drink?

15. By Sunday evening, all the bikers were tired but happy.

16. My brother has many hobbies.

17. Last Saturday, Eric bought tomatoes at the outdoor market.

18. The woman in the front row is my aunt.

19. That lucky Bella won some beautiful prizes.

20. Mr. Daly, the art teacher, exhibited a variety of origamis that his students had made.

21. Even young children can make simple paper creations.

22. Did Felina hit a homerun?

23. Into the night roared the steam engine.

24. Our class voted on the motion for a community project.

25. Who wrote *Barrio Boy*?

THE SIMPLE SUBJECT AND THE SIMPLE PREDICATE

11c   The *simple subject* is the main word or group of words in the complete subject that tells *whom* or *what* the sentence is about.

SENTENCE	The bear on the shelf was carved out of soapstone.
COMPLETE SUBJECT	The bear on the shelf
SIMPLE SUBJECT	bear

A compound noun is considered one noun and may therefore be used as a simple subject.

SENTENCE	The white polar bear was made by an Inupiat carver.
COMPLETE SUBJECT	The white polar bear
SIMPLE SUBJECT	polar bear

NOTE   In this book, the term *subject* refers to the simple subject unless otherwise indicated.

EXERCISE 5   Identifying Simple Subjects

In each sentence below, underline the simple subject.

EX.   1.   Gwendolyn Brooks is one of my favorite authors.

1. One unit in my literature book was about African American poets of the fifties and sixties.

2. The boy in front of me read one poem with great feeling.

3. Another student in my class enjoys the poetry of Sonia Sanchez.

4. Next Friday evening a poet is speaking at our local bookstore.

5. Everyone in the class turned to the last stanza of the poem.

6. A number of the poems were about real people, including Dr. Martin Luther King, Jr., and Malcolm X.

7. The national poet laureate is Rita Dove, an English professor at the University of Virginia.

8. The title of that poem is a single word.

9. Our local bookstore has an excellent selection of poetry books.

10. The anthology on the table looks like a reprint of one that was published in 1971.

11d   The *simple predicate*, or *verb*, is the main word or group of words in the complete predicate.

SENTENCE	The bus lurched around a sharp bend in the road.
COMPLETE PREDICATE	lurched around a sharp bend in the road
SIMPLE PREDICATE	lurched

The simple predicate may be a single verb or a *verb phrase* (a verb and one or more helping verbs). When you identify the simple predicate, be sure to find all parts of the verb phrase.

SENTENCE	Have you found a pen?
COMPLETE PREDICATE	have found a pen
SIMPLE PREDICATE	have found

SENTENCE	I must have lost it here.
COMPLETE PREDICATE	must have lost it here
SIMPLE PREDICATE	must have lost

EXERCISE 6   Identifying Complete Predicates and Simple Predicates in Sentences

In each sentence in the paragraph below, underline the complete predicate once and the verb, or simple predicate, twice. Be sure to include all parts of a verb phrase.

EX.   [1] People around the world will celebrate the harvest in various ways.

[1] Here in Chicago, we sit down for a big Thanksgiving dinner.

[2] People in the Congo, though, hold a big hope of harvest festival.

[3] They believe in the festival's guarantee of a good harvest. [4] Dancers and a drummer perform an elaborate circular dance for this festival.

[5] Other people in Africa may schedule their harvest festivals during or after a harvest. [6] For example, the farmers in Ghana have a yam festival each August. [7] This festival may continue for up to two weeks. [8] I have also read about similar festivals in Burma, Syria, and many other countries.

[9] The similarities among the festivals should not surprise you. [10] After all, every nation on earth wants to have enough food for its people.

FINDING THE SUBJECT

Finding the subject of a sentence is easier if you pick out the verb first. Then ask "Who?" or "What?" followed by the verb.

EXAMPLES   A woman on my street **received** an award for heroism. [Who *received*? *A woman on my street* received. Therefore, *woman* is the subject.]

Beside the woman and her family **sits** the mayor. [Who *sits*? *The mayor* sits; *mayor* is the subject.]

11e   The subject is never in a prepositional phrase.

EXAMPLE   Two of my friends started a band. [Who started a band? *Two* started it, not *friends*, which is part of the prepositional phrase *of my friends*.]

11f   In most questions, the subject follows the verb or helping verb.

Questions usually begin with a verb, a helping verb, or a word such as *what, when, where, how,* or *why*. One way to find the subject of a question is to turn the question into a statement and find the verb. Then ask "Who?" or "What?" in front of the verb.

EXAMPLES   When will someone announce the winners?
Someone will announce the winners. [The question is turned into a statement. The subject is *Someone*.]

11g   The word *there* or *here* may begin a sentence, but it is usually not the subject. *There* or *here* may be used as expletives or as adverbs telling where.

EXPLETIVE   There is a **letter** for you. [What is for you? *Letter*. Therefore, *letter* is the subject. *There* doesn't add any meaning.]

ADVERB   Here are your **tickets**. [What are here? *Tickets*.]

11h   In requests and commands, the subject is usually not stated. In such a sentence, *you* is the understood subject. If the sentence includes a person's name, the name is not the subject. The name is called *a noun of direct address.*

REQUESTS   (You) Please open the door.   (You) Please pass the milk.
COMMANDS   (You) Help me, Tyler.   (You) Come here, Sam.

EXERCISE 7   Identifying Subjects and Verbs

In each sentence in the paragraph below, underline the subject once and the verb twice.

EX.   [1] On the postcard is a picture of Nellie Cashman.

[1] As a teenager, Nellie Cashman came to the United States. [2] From Ireland to San Francisco she traveled. [3] In 1877, this woman traveled to Alaska with a group of gold miners. [4] There, Nellie looked for gold. [5] In addition, she ran a boardinghouse for other miners. [6] During the fall, a dangerous illness hit the camps. [7] This disease, scurvy, can be deadly. [8] People with scurvy must have fresh produce or some other source of Vitamin C. [9] Despite the freezing cold, Nellie, with six others, traveled to Victoria and back. [10] With her came almost a ton of lifesaving vegetables.

EXERCISE 8   Identifying Subjects and Verbs

In each sentence below, underline the subject once and the verb twice. If the subject is understood, write (*You*) on the line before the sentence.

EX.   (You)   1. Look in the nutrition book on the top shelf.

_____ 1. Does orange juice have many vitamins?

_____ 2. Eat fresh fruits and vegetables whenever possible.

_____ 3. Look at all the jars in the canning cupboard of this old house.

_____ 4. How can someone store apples for a long time?

_____ 5. Your home freezer should keep foods at 0°F for best results.

_____ 6. There isn't enough space in the freezer for those peaches.

_____ 7. Here is a jar of homemade pickles for our picnic.

_____ 8. Why does that log cabin have a root cellar?

_____ 9. Put the milk in the coldest part of the refrigerator.

_____ 10. There is no way for us to finish this assignment by today.

COMPOUND SUBJECTS AND COMPOUND VERBS

11i A *compound subject* consists of two or more subjects that are joined by a conjunction and have the same verb. The conjunctions most often used to link the parts of a compound subject are *and* and *or*.

EXAMPLES **Mr. Pong** and the **clerk** shook hands. [Who shook hands? *Mr. Pong* and the *clerk*.]

Mr. Pong or the **clerk** will help you. [Again, the two parts of the compound subject are *Mr. Pong* and *clerk*.]

11j A *compound verb* consists of two or more verbs that are joined by a conjunction and have the same subject.

EXAMPLES On Tuesday I **brought** my history book home and **studied** chapter four.

Josh **called** but **did** not **leave** a message.

(You) **Come** inside and **have** dinner.

 NOTE If the helping verb is the same for the two verbs in a compound verb, it may or may not be repeated. Both the subject and the verb may be compound.

EXAMPLE **Rosa** and **Pang will meet** you and **show** you around.

EXERCISE 9   Identifying Compound Subjects and Compound Verbs

In each of the following sentences, underline the subject once and the verb twice. If the subject is understood, write (*You*) on the line before the sentence.

EX. <u>(You)</u> 1. Visit a market and buy some handcrafts.

_____ 1. My sister and I shopped at several different Friendship Stores.

_____ 2. Some Chinese stores display and sell everything from herbal medicines to television sets and cameras.

_____ 3. Beijing and Shanghai attract numerous visitors every year.

_____ 4. At free markets many farmers buy and sell both handcrafts and foods.

_____ 5. Shop carefully and compare prices for any expensive purchases.

_____ 6. In Tianjin you and I can buy beautiful carpets or lovely glass.

_____ 7. My friend Tamala wanted a silk blouse but could not find the right color.

_____ 8. Eric and I looked at a sandalwood fan but bought a silk one instead.

_____ 9. Some stores can wrap your purchases and mail them anywhere in the world.

_____ 10. After dinner my uncle or I will call and make plans for Friday and Saturday evening.

EXERCISE 10   Writing Compound Subjects and Verbs

Complete each sentence below by writing either compound subjects or compound verbs in the blanks. You also may add any necessary modifiers.

EX. 1. Next Friday_____ Tina _____ and _____ I _____ will make dinner.

1. Adrienne _____ the letter and _____ it.

2. _____ and _____ do not fly.

3. Before your first class, _____ and _____ will tell you about the cost of safety equipment.

4. In ten minutes, _____ the potatoes and _____ them.

5. You may _____ a tuxedo or _____ one.

6. _____ or _____ will take your temperature and your blood pressure.

7. The answering machine _____ and then _____ .

8. After a long wait, the music finally _____ but then _____ .

9. Did _____ or _____ ever visit that new Mexican restaurant?

10. An eagle _____ over the mountaintops and then _____ without warning.

COMPLEMENTS

11k A *complement* is a word or group of words that completes the meaning of a predicate.

A group of words may have a subject and a verb and still not express a complete thought.

INCOMPLETE   This picture looks   The batter hit
  COMPLETE   This picture looks original.   The batter hit the ball.

Complements are never in prepositional phrases.

EXAMPLES   Carlos wrote the **poem**. [*Poem* is the complement.]
            Carlos thought about the poem. [*Poem* is part of the
            · prepositional phrase *about the poem*.]

An adverb modifying a verb is not a complement. Only nouns, pronouns, and adjectives are complements.

EXAMPLES   The train arrived **late**. [*Late* is an adverb, not a complement.]
            Rosa is **late**. [*Late*, an adjective, is a complement.]

A complement may be compound.

EXAMPLES   The concert starred **Jaime** and **Liz**.
            The weather was **cold** and **rainy**.

EXERCISE 11   Identifying Subjects, Verbs, and Complements.

In each of the following sentences, underline the subject once and the verb twice. Circle the complement if there is one.

EX.   [1] The first <u>longhorns</u> in Hawaii <u>were</u> (gifts) from a British seaman.

[1] These cattle must have looked strange among the eucalyptus trees.

[2] A gift of horses from the United States arrived on the island about ten years after the cattle. [3] These herds of cattle and horses have been destructive to vegetation. [4] Also, some of the descendants of these cattle actually attacked people. [5] During the 1830s, King Kamehameha II sent to California for vaqueros. [6] Many of them were Mexican, American

139

Indian, and Spanish cowboys. [7] The Hawaiian cowboys' name for themselves was *paniolos*. [8] These Hawaiian cowboys wore western outfits with a Polynesian look. [9] Soon the paniolos learned the necessary skills. [10] In time, Hawaii, as many Western states, had cattle drives and rodeos.

EXERCISE 12 Writing Sentence Complements

For each group of words below, write a complement to form a complete sentence.

EX. 1. After assembly, Mr. Torres introduced _____the next speaker_____ .

1. During dinner last night, Jess seemed _____
   _____ .

2. About twenty years ago, my grandmother discovered _____
   _____ .

3. The person who called wanted _____
   _____ .

4. Over the summer, Seki painted _____
   _____ .

5. At the dance, everyone looked _____
   and _____ .

6. We postponed our trip because the weather seemed _____
   _____ .

7. Using a new computer program, Carl created _____
   _____ .

8. For our fund-raising auction, Mrs. Bluehouse donated _____
   _____ .

9. First, the ballet troupe performed _____
   _____ .

10. For months, engineers planned _____
    _____ .

SUBJECT COMPLEMENTS

11l **A *subject complement* is a noun, a pronoun, or an adjective that follows a linking verb. A subject complement identifies, describes, or explains the subject.**

EXAMPLES   Paloma is my **cousin**. [*Cousin* identifies *Paloma*.]
This cocoa smells **wonderful**! [*Wonderful* describes *cocoa*.]

(1) A *predicate nominative* is a noun or a pronoun in the predicate that identifies or renames the subject of a sentence or a clause.

EXAMPLES   This tadpole will become a big **frog**. [The noun *frog* renames the subject *tadpole*.]
The captain could be **she**. [The pronoun *she* identifies the subject *captain*.]

(2) A *predicate adjective* is an adjective in the predicate that describes the subject of a sentence or a clause.

EXAMPLES   Is she **talented** also? [The adjective *talented* describes the subject *she*.]
Let's leave because this band is too **loud**! [The adjective *loud* describes *band*, the subject of the clause.]

Subject complements may be compound.

EXAMPLE   The soldiers looked **tired** and **dirty**.

 NOTE   The subject complement may come before the subject of a sentence or a clause.

EXAMPLES   What a great **pilot** you are! [*Pilot* is a predicate nominative renaming the subject *you*.]
I noticed how **tall** Avi had grown. [*Tall* is a predicate adjective describing *Avi*.]

EXERCISE 13   Identifying Subject Complements

In each of the following sentences, underline the subject complement or complements.

EX.   1. The woman on the horse might be <u>she</u>.

1. Within a few hours, the night grew noticeably colder.

2. The poet Phillis Wheatley became a free woman only after the death of her owner.

141

3. This vegetable soup seems slightly thicker than the other soup does.

4. That unusual-looking aircraft was the winner of the last competition.

5. The main character in this story is a professional musician.

6. Despite fame, Arianna remained modest and friendly to everyone.

7. Are the sneakers in the window leather?

8. In 1993, writer Toni Morrison became the first African American winner of the Nobel Prize for literature.

9. That unplanned meeting seemed successful!

10. During the last hour of practice, your violin playing sounded really professional.

EXERCISE 14   Identifying Subjects, Verbs, and Subject Complements

For each sentence in the paragraph below, identify each subject, verb, and subject complement. In the space above the word, write *s.* for *subject*, *v.* for *verb*, *p.n.* for *predicate nominative*, or *p.a.* for *predicate adjective*.

EX.   1.   The rain forests of South America are unique.

[1] For years, the resources of the rain forests seemed unlimited.

[2] After all, the area was large and isolated. [3] It did not remain isolated for long, however. [4] South American rain forests are rich sources of beautiful hardwoods. [5] Many of these woods are quite valuable to furniture makers and artists. [6] After years of harvesting these trees, the forests had become damaged. [7] Today, however, many landowners are more aware of the value of the forest itself. [8] Some parts will probably remain unspoiled national parks. [9] Other lands are becoming tree farms, where people plant trees as well as cut them. [10] With luck, these farms can survive and still become good sources of income for their owners.

OBJECTS

Objects are complements that do not refer to the subject. They follow action verbs rather than linking verbs.

☞ **REFERENCE NOTE:** For more information about action verbs, see page 113.

11m A *direct object* is a noun or pronoun that directly receives the action of a verb or shows the result of the action. A direct object answers the question "What?" or "Whom?" after an action verb.

EXAMPLES   The marchers carried the **petition** to the courthouse. [Carried *what*? *Petition.*]

Mrs. Washington asked **us** to wait. [Asked *whom*? *Us.*]

Verbs that express mental action, such as *study* and *understand*, are just as much action verbs as are verbs that express physical action, such as *climb* and *hit*.

EXAMPLE   My brother **is studying art** in college. [Is studying *what*? *Art.*]

 Direct objects are never found in prepositional phrases.

EXAMPLES   Sarah wrote two **articles**. [*Articles* is the direct object.]
Sarah writes for our newspaper. [*Newspaper* is part of the prepositional phrase *for our newspaper.*]

11n An *indirect object* is a noun or pronoun that precedes the direct object and tells *to whom* or *for whom* (or *to what* or *for what*) the action of the verb is done.

DIRECT OBJECT   Hisoka made **lunch**. [Made *what*? *Lunch.*]
INDIRECT OBJECT   Hisoka made **us** lunch. [Made *lunch for whom*? *Us.*]

If the word *to* or *for* is used in the sentence, the noun or pronoun following it is part of a prepositional phrase, not an indirect object.

EXAMPLES   Carlota gave **me** directions. [*Me* is the indirect object.]
Carlota gave directions **to me**. [*Me* is part of the prepositional phrase *to me.*]

Both direct and indirect objects may be compound.

EXAMPLE   The clerk handed **Tonya** and **me** two **bags** and a **carton**.

EXERCISE 15   Identifying Verbs and Their Direct Objects

In the sentences below, underline the verb or verb phrase once. Underline each direct object twice.

EX.   1. As a child, Florence Sabin loved books.

1. Young Florence Sabin attended Smith College and Johns Hopkins Medical School.

2. The head of the anatomy department suggested a special project to her.

3. After graduation, Dr. Sabin studied the lymphatic system.

4. For more than twenty years, she taught students at Johns Hopkins.

5. Her work in the field of medicine saved many lives.

EXERCISE 16   Identifying Direct and Indirect Objects

In the sentences below, underline the direct objects once and any indirect objects twice. [Note: Not every sentence has an indirect object.]

EX.   1. Aziza is teaching them the song.

1. The man in the corner booth sold us wonderful homemade bread.

2. At the book sale, the ticket taker handed each shopper a paper bag.

3. Before practice, the coach read the class the safety rules.

4. The previous owner had built the treehouse for his children.

5. After a long silence, my pen pal finally wrote me a long, newsy letter about his new apartment.

6. For this job, you must give the doctor a completed health form.

7. In the last few seconds of the game, Flora tossed the ball to me.

8. My grandmother gave my father a photograph album from Cuba.

9. Before he left, Chim promised me a tennis lesson Thursday afternoon.

10. Slowly and carefully, I lifted the corner of the blanket.

11. Remember your chores, Mark.

12. My oldest sister plays tennis for her school.

13. In this movie, the pirate gives the little boy the map.

14. Is she teaching herself the new dance steps?

15. Clara wrote Ms. Ching a letter after our science fair.

CLASSIFYING SENTENCES BY PURPOSE

11o **Sentences may be classified as *declarative, imperative, interrogative,* or *exclamatory.***

(1) A *declarative* sentence makes a statement. All declarative sentences are followed by periods.

EXAMPLES   Two members of the road crew set up the amplifiers.
When Ray Charles sat down to play, the audience
clapped wildly.

(2) An *imperative* sentence gives a command or makes a request. Imperative sentences usually end with periods, but strong commands may end with exclamation points.

EXAMPLES   Please hold this.   Watch my hands.   Don't!

(3) An *interrogative* sentence asks a question. Interrogative sentences are followed by question marks.

EXAMPLES   How much does this cost?   Can you tie an obi?

(4) An *exclamatory* sentence expresses strong feeling. Exclamatory sentences are followed by exclamation points.

EXAMPLES   What a display that was!   How scared we were!

NOTE   Any sentence may be spoken in such a way that it is exclamatory. In this case, it should be followed by an exclamation point.

EXAMPLES   This is a disaster! [Declarative becomes exclamatory.]
Stop that noise! [Imperative becomes exclamatory.]
How about that! [Interrogative becomes exclamatory.]

EXERCISE 17   Identifying the Four Kinds of Sentences

On the line before each of the following sentences, identify the type of sentence. Write *dec.* for *declarative, imp.* for *imperative, inter.* for *interrogative,* or *excl.* for *exclamatory.*

EX.   _inter._ 1. Is that Golda Meir?

_____   1. Look at the article I found in this history magazine.

_____   2. She was born in Russia and later moved to the United States with her parents.

_____   3. How did she become prime minister of Israel?

_____ 4. What an interesting woman she was!

_____ 5. In 1948, she was Israel's representative to the Soviet Union.

_____ 6. What an unusual coincidence!

_____ 7. Didn't she retire from government office for a period of time?

_____ 8. Golda Meir served as prime minister of Israel for five years and then retired again.

_____ 9. Read *My Life*, her autobiography, and find out why she retired.

_____ 10. Was Meir a prime minister at the same time as Indira Gandhi?

_____ 11. Gandhi learned about politics at her father's side.

_____ 12. When did she become prime minister of India?

_____ 13. Tell me why she declared a state of emergency.

_____ 14. How much power she had!

_____ 15. She was out of the country for a few years.

EXERCISE 18   Working Cooperatively to Write T-shirt Slogans

You are a T-shirt designer who has been asked to create several designs and slogans for an ecology fair in your city. Work with a partner to write four different slogans, using each type of sentence once. Then classify your sentences by purpose. Write your slogans on the lines below.

EX.   1. Have you hugged a green plant today? (interrogative)

1. _____

_____

_____

2. _____

_____

_____

3. _____

_____

_____

4. _____

_____

_____

CHAPTER REVIEW

A. Understanding the Parts of a Sentence

On your own paper, define each of the terms below and give an example to illustrate it.

EX. 1. a fragment

A fragment is a group of words that isn't a complete sentence. born in Paris in 1893 and died twenty years later

1. a sentence
2. a complete subject
3. a complete predicate
4. a simple subject
5. a simple predicate
6. a subject complement
7. a direct object
8. an indirect object
9. an understood subject
10. a predicate adjective

B. Identifying Subjects, Verbs, and Complements

On the line before each sentence, identify each of the italicized words. Write *s.* for *subject*, *v.* for *verb*, *p.a.* for *predicate adjective*, *p.n.* for *predicate nominative*, *d.o.* for *direct object*, or *i.o.* for *indirect object*.

EX. _s.; d.o._ 1. Do *you* like *tomatoes*?

_____ 1. For supper, Dad served *us* fresh *tomatoes* and *corn.*

_____ 2. *Both* of these foods were originally *natives* of Peru.

_____ 3. The ancient Incas *grew* a *number* of different tomatoes.

_____ 4. To the explorer Pizarro, the red *fruits* were *"love apples."*

_____ 5. As a cultivated crop, corn *may be* much *older* than tomatoes.

_____ 6. The ancient Incas *buried corn* with their dead.

_____ 7. The tomato *became* quite *popular* in Italy in the 1500s.

_____ 8. For years, many *people* actually *considered* tomatoes dangerous and sometimes even poisonous.

_____ 9. The *plants* were mainly *decorative* instead of useful.

_____ 10. Today people all over the world *eat* the *tomato* in a number of different forms.

C.   Classifying Sentences by Purpose

Classify each sentence below. On the line before the sentence, write *dec.* for *declarative, inter.* for *interrogative, imp.* for *imperative, or excl.* for *exclamatory.* Then supply the proper end punctuation.

EX.   _dec._   1. Everyone in this room is related

_____   1. What a wonderful idea Kessie had

_____   2. When will you have your family reunion

_____   3. We can hold it during the last week of August

_____   4. What will the theme of the party be

_____   5. Think of something that can include all four generations attending all the festivities

_____   6. I have a great idea

_____   7. Get a large piece of wrapping paper or shelf paper

_____   8. What good will that do anyone

_____   9. The older family members can name their relatives and the younger ones can draw a family tree

_____ 10. Marta, can you reproduce the finished product and give everyone a copy

D. Writing Sentences

On your own paper, write sentences according to each of the following guidelines. Underline the subject once and the verb twice in each sentence. If the subject is understood, write *(You).*

EX.   1. a sentence with a predicate adjective
          Your kimono is beautiful.

1. a sentence with an indirect object
2. an exclamatory sentence
3. a sentence with a compound verb
4. a sentence with a predicate adjective
5. a sentence with a compound subject
6. a sentence beginning with *Here*
7. a sentence with a direct object and no indirect object
8. an interrogative sentence
9. an imperative sentence
10. a declarative sentence with a verb phrase

PREPOSITIONAL PHRASES

12a A *phrase* is a group of related words that is used as a single part of speech and does not contain both a verb and its subject.

EXAMPLES　will be leaving [verb phrase; no subject]
after the World Series [prepositional phrase; no subject or verb]

12b A *prepositional phrase* is a group of words consisting of a preposition, a noun or pronoun that serves as the object of the preposition, and any modifiers of that object.

EXAMPLES　Please be quiet during the next few **minutes.** [*Minutes* is the object of the preposition *during*. The adjectives *the, next,* and *few* modify *minutes.*]
Will you get the scissors for **me?** [*Me* is the object of the preposition *for.*]

☞　**REFERENCE NOTE:** For a list of commonly used prepositions, see page 123.

A preposition may have a compound object.

EXAMPLES　with **Sasha** and **her**
under the **tables** and **chairs**

EXERCISE 1　Identifying Prepositional Phrases

Underline all the prepositional phrases in the paragraph below.

EX.　[1] Many African American soldiers helped fight the War of 1812.

[1] The War of 1812 was fought between Britain and the United States. [2] During that war, African Americans fought in battles on land and on water. [3] They saw action in battles on the Great Lakes and were especially successful fighting the Battle of Lake Erie. [4] Two African American battalions helped Andrew Jackson to win the Battle of New Orleans against the British. [5] Jackson later praised the African American soldiers for their patriotism, bravery, and enthusiasm.

EXERCISE 2   Identifying Prepositions and Their Objects

In the sentences below, underline each prepositional phrase, and draw brackets around the object of the preposition.

EX.   1.   There are many lighthouses <u>along the [coast]</u> <u>of [New England]</u>.

1.   The rescuers searched the water from morning until night.

2.   They were looking for a small boat with three teenagers on board.

3.   The boat had been missing since the afternoon of the previous day.

4.   With luck, they would find the teenagers safe and sound.

5.   They found the boat overturned three miles from the shore.

6.   At dusk they spotted one of the three teenagers.

7.   He was clinging to a life preserver.

8.   Using a cable and a net, the rescuers lifted him from the water and into a helicopter.

9.   The teenager told the rescuers that his friends had swum toward a nearby lighthouse.

10.   The lighthouse stood on a tiny island about a mile away.

11.   The rescuers flew over the island.

12.   They shined the helicopter's searchlights onto the beaches and rocks of the island.

13.   One rescuer spotted two people lying on some rocks near the lighthouse.

14.   The helicopter flew the three teenagers to a hospital, where they were treated for exposure and released.

15.   After their treatment and release, the three teenagers thanked the rescue team at a meeting with reporters.

ADJECTIVE PHRASES AND ADVERB PHRASES

12c **A prepositional phrase that modifies a noun or a pronoun is an** *adjective phrase.*

An adjective phrase follows the noun or pronoun that it modifies. Adjective phrases answer the same questions that adjectives answer: *What kind? Which one? How many?* and *How much?* An adjective phrase may also modify the object of another prepositional phrase.

EXAMPLES   The little book **of poems** sold for ninety-five cents. [The phrase *of poems* modifies the noun *book*. It tells *what kind*.]

All **of the puppies** have been vaccinated. [The phrase *of the puppies* modifies the pronoun *all*. It tells *what kind*.]

The car will seat a group **of six or more**. [The phrase *of six or more* modifies the noun *group*. It tells *how many*.]

Some **of the books on the table** were marked "Half off." [The phrase *of the books* modifies the pronoun *some*. It tells *which ones*. *Books* is the object of the preposition *of*. The phrase *on the table* modifies *books*. It tells *which ones*.]

12d **A prepositional phrase that modifies a verb, an adjective, or** **another adverb is an** *adverb phrase.*

Adverb phrases tell *when, where, why, how,* or *to what extent.* They may come before or after the words they modify.

EXAMPLES   The cougar climbed **up the rocks.** [The phrase *up the rocks* modifies the verb *climbed*. It tells *where*.]

The singers were very popular **with the audience.** [The adverb phrase *with the audience* modifies the adjective *popular*.]

The ball sailed far **over the fence.** [The phrase *over the fence* modifies the adverb *far*. It tells *to what extent*.]

More than one adverb phrase may modify the same word.

EXAMPLES   **In the first act,** Sharon sang **with grace and ease.** [*In the first act* tells *when* Sharon sang, and *with grace and ease* tells *how* she sang.]

EXERCISE 3   Identifying Adjective Phrases

Underline all adjective phrases in the sentences below. Then draw an arrow from each phrase to the word or words it modifies. Some sentences may have more than one phrase.

EX.   1. The houses by the river were all flooded.

1. The scientist was studying communication among chimpanzees.

2. A duck slept under the bridge over the Colorado River.

3. No one in the troop noticed the elk with the big antlers.

4. A charango is a small Latin American guitar from the Andes.

5. A picture in the newspaper showed a man walking thirteen dogs.

6. The flowers along the edge of the lawn included hyacinths and irises.

7. A blanket of snow covered the sleepy little town.

8. The science museum contained a display of a woolly mammoth with large tusks.

9. An alleyway between two large buildings was the site of the street fair.

10. The postcard showed the Arc de Triomphe in Paris.

EXERCISE 4   Identifying Adverb Phrases and the Words They Modify

In each of the sentences below, underline the adverb phrase once and draw an arrow to the word or words it modifies. Several sentences contain more than one adverb phrase.

EX.   1. The geese flew over the marsh, heading south.

1. In 1348, the Black Death raged throughout Europe.

2. Once, after a big storm, we found a robin's nest.

3. Soft as a summer breeze, the music drifted across the park.

4. That building has been standing for over two thousand years.

5. The actor's agent called from New York.

6. Yolanda and her parents traveled by boat down the Amazon River.

7. Michael will arrive from Nova Scotia late in the afternoon.

8. In the United States, more than two thousand dogs are born each hour.

9. The tiny black-and-white kitten strayed far from home.

10. The jeep was parked beside a fire hydrant in a no-parking zone.

VERBALS AND VERB PHRASES

Verbals are forms of verbs that are used as adjectives, nouns, or adverbs. The three kinds of verbals are *participles*, *gerunds*, and *infinitives*.

12e A *participle* is a verb form that can be used as an adjective.

EXAMPLES   The children thought that the carnival rides were **exciting.** [*Exciting*, formed from the verb *excite*, modifies the noun *rides*.]
The **baked** potatoes tasted delicious. [*Baked*, formed from the verb *bake*, modifies the noun *potatoes*.]

(1) *Present participles* end in *–ing*.

EXAMPLES   The movie was **entertaining.** [*Entertaining*, formed from the verb *entertain*, modifies the noun *movie*.]
A wild turkey wandered through the **crackling** stalks of corn. [*Crackling*, formed from the verb *crackle*, modifies the noun *stalks*.]

(2) Most *past participles* usually end in *–d* or *–ed*. A few are formed irregularly.

EXAMPLES   **Dazed** and **confused,** the rider dusted himself off and climbed back onto his horse. [*Dazed* and *confused*, formed from the verbs *daze* and *confuse*, modify the noun *rider*.]
Moths and mosquitoes flew in through the **broken** window. [*Broken*, formed from the verb *break*, modifies the noun *window*.]

Both present and past participles can be used as part of a verb phrase. When used in a verb phrase, a participle is part of the verb. It is not a verbal used as an adjective.

EXAMPLES   The workers **were digging** a tunnel under the river.
The window **was broke**n by the hurricane's strong winds.

EXERCISE 5   **Identifying Participles and the Words They Modify**

Underline the participles used as adjectives in each of the following sentences. Then draw an arrow to the noun or the pronoun that each participle modifies.

EX.   1. The grass around the pond was filled with croaking frogs.

1. The graded papers are on the teacher's desk, next to the roll book.

2. A shooting star streaked across the night sky and then was gone.

3. The Sahara, a burning desert, is the hottest place on our planet.

4. The Sikh men of northern India can be recognized by their turbans, unshaven beards, and long hair.

5. Smiling broadly, Paco accepted the nomination for class president.

6. Bored, Andrea walked to the library to find a good mystery book.

7. A crow sat in a tree in the deepening twilight.

8. "This bicycle is now in good working order," said the mechanic.

9. Satisfied, the diners paid the check and left the restaurant.

10. The telephone poles along the highway were covered with hanging vines of kudzu.

11. Peter liked wearing wrinkled suits.

12. They were looking for a reclining chair, but they bought a sofa instead.

13. The building designed by my uncle won an award.

14. Creeping thyme and roses grow all over our terrace.

15. A hand-pieced quilt is more costly than a quilt that is sewn by machine.

EXERCISE 6   Choosing Appropriate Participles

Complete the paragraph below by writing appropriate participles formed from the verbs given in parentheses. Write your answers on your own paper.

EX.   [1] For English class, Malcolm wrote an (*interest*) story.
   1. interesting

[1] Malcolm's story is about a (*miss*) cat. [2] In the story, a young girl thinks that her cat has crawled through a (*tear*) window screen. [3] (*Worry*), the girl goes outside to search for her pet. [4] For several (*trouble*) hours she searches the alleyways and lawns near her house. [5] She looks everywhere for the cat—in trees, on porches, in drain pipes, and under (*park*) cars. [6] (*Discourage*), she eventually gives up the search and goes back home. [7] Back inside, she notices something (*surprise*). [8] She opens the window shades to let sunlight into her (*darken*) room and sees that the cat's food has been eaten. [9] Then she hears a (*scratch*) sound under her bed. [10] All the time, the cat has been in a secret (*hide*) place, inside the box spring.

PARTICIPIAL PHRASES

12f   A *participial phrase* **consists of a participle and any complements or modifiers it may have. The entire participial phrase acts as an adjective.**

A participial phrase should be placed as close as possible to the word it modifies. Otherwise the sentence may not make sense.

EXAMPLES   **Writing from personal experience,** Thon created a report about life in a small Vietnamese village. [The phrase *Writing from personal experience* modifies the noun *Thon*. The adjective phrase *from personal experience* modifies the participle *Writing*.]

The music **playing over the loudspeakers** was written by the composer Scott Joplin. [The phrase *playing over the loudspeakers* modifies the noun *music*. The adverb phrase *over the loudspeakers* modifies the participle *playing*.]

Completely exhausted by their climb, the hikers stopped to rest and eat some trail mix. [The phrase *Completely exhausted by their climb* modifies the noun *hikers*. The participle *exhausted* is modified by the adverb *completely* and by the adverb phrase *by their climb*.]

REFERENCE NOTE: For information on punctuating sentences that contain participial phrases, see pages 281–283.

EXERCISE 7   Identifying Participles and Participial Phrases

In the following sentences, put brackets around the participles, and underline the participial phrases.

EX.   1.   Have you seen those strange mushrooms [growing] in the cellar?

1. Working around the clock, the farmers saved the orange crop from frostbite.

2. The Somali refugees, weakened by hunger, arrived at an emergency center, where they received food and medical treatment.

3. From the plane we could see Lake Erie, shining brightly below us.

4. Nominated by President Johnson, Thurgood Marshall became the first African American Supreme Court justice.

5. The largest dinosaurs, weighing over 150 tons, were harmless plant-
   eaters.

6. Often costing more than gold or jewels, spices were highly prized in
   the Middle Ages in Europe.

7. Hidden by their markings, tigers are rarely seen in the wild.

8. Zimbabwe is an African country bordered by Zambia, Botswana,
   Mozambique, and South Africa.

9. Known for its hot, wet climate, Papua New Guinea produces coffee,
   coconuts, and cocoa.

10. Nearly destroyed by a great fire, this Midwestern city was rebuilt by its
    mostly immigrant population.

11. Moving forward, backward, and from side to side, the virtual reality
    machine gave us the exciting impression that we were floating in
    space.

12. My grandfather found some ancient tools lying on the floor of a cave.

13. The backpacker loved the haunting sound of wolves howling in the
    distance.

14. Standing skillfully on her toes, the ballerina lifted her arms toward
    the ceiling.

15. Reading alone in his room at night, Grant dreamed of the day when he,
    too, would write books that other people would read.

16. In the center of the room stood a man in a red flannel shirt,
    shoveling coal into the furnace.

17. We admired the stained glass windows of the cathedral.

18. Strengthened by his mother's milk, the colt grew strong and healthy.

19. Through the windows of the preschool, we could see children
    playing happily.

20. The directions included with the videotape player weren't in English.

GERUNDS

12g   A *gerund* is a verb form ending in *–ing* that is used as a noun.

Like nouns, gerunds can be subjects, predicate nominatives, direct objects, or objects of prepositions.

EXAMPLES   **Skiing** is a popular winter sport. [subject]
My favorite activity is **writing.** [predicate nominative]
Marsha loves **skating.** [direct object]
Hector signed up for a class in **cooking.** [object of a preposition]

Do not confuse a gerund with a present participle used as part of a verb phrase or as an adjective.

EXAMPLES   The reporters have finished **taking** pictures, but they **are** still **writing** the story. [*Taking* is a gerund used as the direct object of the verb phrase *have finished. Writing* is a present participle used as part of the verb phrase *are writing.*]
The **cleaning** crew removed the stains by **scrubbing** the carpet with brushes. [*Cleaning* is a present participle used as an adjective to modify the noun *crew. Scrubbing* is a gerund used as the object of the preposition *by.*]

EXERCISE 8   Identifying Gerunds and Their Uses

Underline the gerunds in the following sentences. Then, on the line before each sentence, identify how each gerund is used by writing *s.* for *subject, p.n.* for *predicate nominative, d.o.* for *direct object,* or *o.p.* for *object of a preposition.* Some sentences contain more than one gerund.

EX.   _o.p._ 1. This is an excellent pen for drawing.

_____ 1. Jogging is good exercise but should be done in moderation.

_____ 2. Uncle Ned says that politicians enjoy talking.

_____ 3. One popular activity of the 1980s was break dancing.

_____ 4. The craft center offers classes in weaving.

_____ 5. This shop sells tools and supplies for gardening.

_____ 6. Sara hates cooking, but she loves eating.

_____ 7. One particularly dangerous sport is rock climbing.

_____ 8. Sculpting is easier when done in clay than when done in marble.

_____ 9. These glasses are for reading the tiny print in the dictionary.

_____ 10. A big business in the Pacific Northwest is logging.

_____ 11. Ms. Horowitz studied marketing at a business school.

_____ 12. Harvesting is one of the most difficult jobs on a farm.

_____ 13. A writer must save time for rewriting and for editing.

_____ 14. Darnelle really enjoys skating.

_____ 15. Studying requires a quiet work place and a clear mind.

_____ 16. How dangerous is bungee jumping?

_____ 17. This wide-angle lens is for taking close-ups.

_____ 18. Selling insurance may be the thing for me.

_____ 19. When Lee complained about his grade, I said, "Try studying."

_____ 20. I'm sorry, but I've just never enjoyed cleaning.

EXERCISE 9   Using Gerunds in Sentences

On your own paper, write a sentence for each of the following gerunds. Underline each gerund. At the end of your sentence, identify the gerund's use by writing *s.* for *subject*, *p.n.* for *predicate nominative*, *d.o.* for *direct object*, or *o.p.* for *object of a preposition*. Be sure to vary the uses of the gerunds in your sentences.

EX.   1. flying
    1. A bird needs powerful wings for <u>flying</u>. (o.p.)

1. singing
2. diving
3. shopping
4. reading
5. playing
6. wrestling
7. swimming
8. waltzing
9. harmonizing
10. parking
11. dozing
12. paying
13. driving
14. listening
15. insulting
16. waiting
17. moving
18. wearing
19. dropping
20. noticing

GERUND PHRASES

> **12h** A *gerund phrase* consists of a gerund and any modifiers and complements it may have. The entire gerund phrase acts as a noun.
>
> Like gerunds, gerund phrases can be subjects, predicate nominatives, direct objects, or objects of prepositions.
>
> EXAMPLES   **Working at the teen center** has been fun. [The phrase is the subject of the sentence. The gerund *Working* is modified by the adjective phrase *at the teen center.*]
>
> My favorite pastime is **reading about ancient Egypt**. [The phrase is a predicate nominative. The gerund *reading* is modified by the adjective phrase *about ancient Egypt.*]
>
> I really enjoy **learning mathematics now**. [The phrase is the direct object of the verb *enjoy.* The gerund *learning* has a direct object, *mathematics,* and is modified by the adverb *now.*]
>
> You need special equipment for **skiing across country**. [The phrase is the object of the preposition *for.* The gerund *skiing* is modified by the adverb phrase *across country.*]
>
> When a noun or pronoun comes immediately before a gerund, it is in the possessive form and is considered part of the gerund phrase.
>
> EXAMPLES   **Sandra's singing** woke the neighbors.
> The neighbors don't really appreciate **her singing late at night**.

EXERCISE 10   Identifying Gerund Phrases and Their Uses

Underline the gerund phrases in the following sentences. On the line before each sentence, identify how each gerund phrase is used by writing *s.* for *subject*, *p.n.* for *predicate nominative*, *d.o.* for *direct object*, or *o.p.* for *object of a preposition*.

EX. _**p.n.**_ 1. My dog's favorite activity is <u>chewing on old shoes</u>.

_____ 1. If you see a rattlesnake in the wild, the wisest course of action is staying away from it.

_____ 2. Hosting a live talk show can be quite a challenge.

_____ 3. The people of Bangladesh support themselves by growing rice, tea, sugar cane, and other crops.

_____ 4. The principal considered changing the school dress code.

_____ 5. Washing a car can use a great deal of water.

_____ 6. David Livingstone and Henry Stanley are famous for exploring the interior of Africa.

_____ 7. Picasso disliked artwork that looked like photographs, so he began painting people as simple shapes, such as cubes.

_____ 8. My dream has always been traveling in Latin America.

_____ 9. Zebras, giraffes, wildebeests, and impala live by grazing on grasslands.

_____ 10. One way politicians announce that they will run for office is by holding a press conference.

_____ 11. Many people love Alice Walker's writing about life in the rural South.

_____ 12. Chasing golf balls around a field isn't my idea of a good time.

_____ 13. My brother Sam's hobby is building model airplanes.

_____ 14. By publishing his play, _The Escape_, in 1858, William Wells Brown became the first African American playwright.

_____ 15. Planning an interview takes a great deal of time and thought.

EXERCISE 11   Identifying Gerund Phrases and Their Uses

Underline the gerund phrases in the paragraph below. Then, above each gerund phrase, identify its use by writing _s._ for _subject_, _p.n._ for _predicate nominative_, _d.o._ for _direct object_, or _o.p._ for _object of a preposition_.

EX.   [1] <u>Sewing fabric into useful objects</u> is one of the practical arts.
_s._

[1] The fabric shop in our town offers classes in sewing for pleasure.

[2] I've taken several classes there, but the one I liked most was "Quilting the Old-Fashioned Way." [3] Making a quilt isn't difficult to do, but it does take patience. [4] The hardest parts for me were threading needles and cutting the quilt pieces. [5] You should try making a quilt sometime. It's a great deal of fun.

INFINITIVES AND INFINITIVE PHRASES

12i An *infinitive* is a verb form, usually preceded by *to*, that can be used as a noun, an adjective, or an adverb.

NOUNS   Mariah loves **to dance** and **to sing.** [*To dance* and *to sing* are the direct objects of the verb *loves*.]
To read is **to escape** into another reality. [*To read* is the subject. *To escape* is a predicate nominative.]

ADJECTIVES   The crossing guard is the person **to ask.** [*To ask* modifies the noun *person*.]
The ones **to thank** are your parents. [*To thank* modifies the pronoun *ones*.]

ADVERBS   That horse is certain **to win.** [*To win* modifies the adjective *certain*.]
Daniel has come **to help.** [*To help* modifies the verb *has come*.]

12j An *infinitive phrase* consists of an infinitive together with its modifiers and complements. The entire infinitive phrase can be used as a noun, an adjective, or an adverb.

NOUN   **To swim across the English Channel** must be very difficult. [The phrase is the subject of the sentence.]

ADJECTIVE   The person **to fix your computer** is my friend, Rolf. [The phrase modifies the noun *person*.]

ADVERB   Sometimes it isn't easy **to make new friends.** [The phrase modifies the adjective *easy*.]

 NOTE   An infinitive may have a subject.

EXAMPLE   Chandra wanted **me to help her.** [*Me* is the subject of the infinitive *to help*.]

 NOTE   Sometimes the *to* that is the sign of the infinitive can be left out.

EXAMPLE   The janitor helped us [to] **string** the lights in the auditorium.

EXERCISE 12   Identifying Infinitive Phrases and Their Function

Underline the infinitive phrases in the following sentences. Above each infinitive, identify its use by writing *s.* for *subject, p.n.* for *predicate nominative, d.o.* for *direct object, adj.* for *adjective,* or *adv.* for *adverb.*

EX. 1. The first ship <u>to carry</u> African Americans to the colonies arrived in Jamestown in 1619.
        adj.

1. The first colony to give legal recognition to the institution of slavery was Massachusetts.

2. In another colony, New Netherlands, eleven African Americans petitioned the government to demand their freedom.

3. The first white organization to denounce slavery publicly was a group of Quakers in Germantown, Pennsylvania.

4. Crispus Attucks was killed in the Boston Massacre in 1770, becoming one of the first people to die in the troubles before the Revolutionary War.

5. To fight for freedom was one reason Americans fought and risked their lives.

6. Peter Salem and Salem Poor joined other African Americans to fight in the battles of Bunker Hill and Breed's Hill in 1775.

7. The following year, the Continental Congress approved General Washington's order to enlist free African Americans in the army.

8. In 1777, Vermont became the first American colony to abolish slavery.

9. During the Revolutionary War, African American soldiers helped to win the battles of Rhode Island, Long Island, Red Bank, Savannah, Monmouth, and Fort Griswold.

10. Rhode Island was the first colony in which the slaves were allowed to enlist in its army.

11. To enlist in the British army and to gain their freedom were the reasons thousands of other slaves left their plantations.

12. In 1781, twenty-six people of African descent helped to found the city of Los Angeles, California.

13. A new law to prohibit slavery from the Northwest Territory was passed by the Continental Congress.

14. Many people were unhappy to see that the U.S. Constitution protected slavery.

15. The U.S. Congress refused to accept a legal petition from African Americans in 1797.

REVIEW EXERCISE

A. Identifying and Classifying Prepositional Phrases

Underline the prepositional phrases in the sentences below. Above each phrase, write *adj. phr.* for *adjective phrase* or *adv. phr.* for *adverb phrase*.

EX. 1. Hervé showed us how to use a level.
adv. phr.

1. The meeting of the prom committee lasted late into the evening.

2. A bat flew through the window and landed on the sofa.

3. A house with seven windows stands near the old courthouse.

4. A platypus looks like a prehistoric animal.

5. The antenna on the roof swayed in the wind.

6. The Maoris of New Zealand were fierce warriors who fought with clubs of bone or stone.

7. Singapore is a small country in Southeast Asia.

8. The people with the most packages helped first.

9. The Sears Tower in Chicago and the Empire State Building in New York City are two of the tallest buildings in the world.

10. The capital of West Virginia is Charleston, and the capital of Virginia is Richmond.

B. Identifying Verbals and Verbal Phrases

Underline the verbals and verbal phrases in the following sentences. Then, on the line before each sentence, identify each by writing *part.* for *participle, part. phr.* for *participial phrase, ger.* for *gerund, ger. phr.* for *gerund phrase, inf.* for *infinitive,* or *inf. phr.* for *infinitive phrase.*

EX. *inf. phr.* 1. Carole loves to collect beach glass by the ocean.

_____ 1. Fencing is a popular sport and is an event in the Olympic Games.

_____ 2. The writer was asked to create a screenplay from a contemporary novel.

_____ 3. The clouds looked like a caravan of camels moving across the sky.

_____ 4. Laughing at your troubles can make you feel happier.

_____ 5. To build a fire in a rainstorm, you need shelter and some waterproof matches.

_____ 6. Soledad wants to act, so she studies at night at the school of dramatic arts.

_____ 7. Smiling, the clown handed the child a bright red balloon.

_____ 8. Marc likes playing the infield, but I prefer the outfield.

_____ 9. One of the most unusual of all occupations is operating a dirigible.

_____ 10. Collecting specimens in the Amazon rain forest, the scientist discovered several previously unknown species.

_____ 11. The computer sitting on the table is a color laptop.

_____ 12. Nathan actually enjoys doing the dishes.

_____ 13. Turtles return to land to lay their eggs.

_____ 14. Flowing through a low plain in Ireland, the Shannon is the longest river in all of the British Isles.

_____ 15. The polar bear, captured by park rangers, was released in the wild, far from any towns or cities.

_____ 16. One of the most useful and ancient of all the arts is weaving.

_____ 17. Emilio says that Chicago is a nice place to live.

_____ 18. On our hike we saw an owl sitting quietly on the branches of a spruce.

_____ 19. To build Stonehenge, prehistoric people cut and moved stones that weighed about thirty tons.

_____ 20. In the 1800s and in the early 1900s, women campaigned for the right to vote.

C. Writing a Fax with Verbals and Verbal Phrases

You are part of a research team living underwater in a specially built vessel. You can send a fax to the upper world once a month. However, your fax is limited to ten sentences. On your own paper, write a fax to a friend, telling him or her what you've been doing or what you've seen. In your fax, use at least one participle or participial phrase, one gerund or gerund phrase, and one infinitive or infinitive phrase. Underline each verbal or verbal phrase and label it *part.* for *participle, part. phr.* for *participial phrase, ger.* for *gerund, ger. phr.* for *gerund phrase, inf.* for *infinitive,* or *inf. phr.* for *infinitive phrase.*

                                          inf. phr.
EX.   We've been trying to grow plants in our controlled atmosphere.

APPOSITIVES AND APPOSITIVE PHRASES

12k An *appositive* is a noun or pronoun placed beside another noun or pronoun to identify or explain it.

EXAMPLES   Chris Johnson, the **president,** spoke to the graduating class. [The noun *president* is an appositive that identifies the noun *Chris Johnson.*] We gave it to him, a **writer,** for revising. [The noun *writer* is an appositive that identifies the pronoun *him.*]

12l An *appositive phrase* is made up of an appositive and its modifiers.

EXAMPLES   The slide show was presented by Ms. Vasquez, **the director of the museum.**

The painting, **a work in the style of Mary Cassatt,** hangs in my grandmother's living room.

An appositive phrase usually follows the noun or pronoun it refers to. Sometimes, though, it comes before the noun or pronoun.

EXAMPLE   **A talented magician,** Marc pretended to break an egg and then put it back together again.

NOTE   Appositives and appositive phrases are often set off by commas. Use commas if the appositive or appositive phrase is not needed to identify uniquely the noun or pronoun to which it refers.

EXAMPLES   My brother, **Nathaniel,** is a sculptor. [The writer has only one brother. Therefore, the appositive, *Nathaniel,* is not needed in order to identify the brother.]
My brother **Nathaniel** is a sculptor. [The writer has more than one brother. Therefore, the appositive is needed in order to identify the brother.]

     REFERENCE NOTE: For more information on punctuating sentences with appositives and appositive phrases, see page 285.

EXERCISE 13   Identifying Appositives and Appositive Phrases

Underline the appositives and appositive phrases in the following sentences.

EX.   1.   The winners of the soccer match, the Fifth Street Spikers, celebrated at a local restaurant.

1.   My oldest sister, Susan, is a lawyer in New York City.

2.   Sequoyah, a Cherokee, invented an alphabet for the Cherokee language.

3.   I read Sheila's poem, a ballad, over the public-address system at school.

4. Hector says that he prefers to write in Spanish, his first language.
5. My friend Miguel wants to travel to Australia and New Zealand.
6. We swam in the pool belonging to our neighbors, the Sironises.
7. Denise's father, a tireless worker, volunteers at a shelter for homeless women and children.
8. Across our lawn and into the woods, the fox, a bright orange creature, ran.
9. This brand of cereal, a new product, contains no sugar or fat.
10. In high school, Pilar founded a student newspaper, *The Hamilton High Herald*.
11. This plant, a kind of fern, grows along riverbanks.
12. Have you seen Toshiro's new electric guitar, the one with the sunburst design?
13. Edie, an old friend of mine, now lives in Pennsylvania.
14. In history class we are studying the reign of the Roman emperor Julius Caesar.
15. Beeswax, a material used in candles, can be purchased at a hobby or crafts shop.
16. The storm, a hurricane, spent itself off the coast and caused little damage.
17. Jake is interested in the history of the Hopi, a people of the American Southwest.
18. Outside the United States, cookstoves for camping often require kerosene, a kind of thin oil.
19. Have you written a thank-you note to your cousin Margaret?
20. The car, an antique, was on display in the middle of the shopping mall.

CHAPTER REVIEW

A. Identifying and Classifying Prepositional Phrases

Underline the prepositional phrases in the sentences below. Above each phrase, write *adj. phr.* for *adjective phrase* or *adv. phr.* for *adverb phrase*. Some sentences contain more than one phrase.

EX. 1. The anxious dancer waited <u>in the wings</u>.
adv. phr.

1. The start of the game was delayed by rain.

2. Waste water flows directly into the river.

3. A museum guide showed us some photographs from the 1930s.

4. All the walnuts and chestnuts have fallen from the trees.

5. I spent the morning at my uncle's house.

6. Tina works with small children in a day care center.

7. Mr. Sanchez planted beautiful sunflowers along the back fence.

8. Do you know the nursery rhyme about Mary and the little lamb?

9. Near the park is a small bakery owned by Mr. and Ms. Paulsen.

10. Have you seen the ring around the moon?

11. Some houses are heated with solar energy.

12. Madeleine lived in an old house in Paris.

13. Mr. Johnson slept through the second act.

14. The horse rose on its hind legs and pawed at the sky.

15. Did you attend the powwow in Albuquerque?

B. Identifying Verbal Phrases and Appositive Phrases

Underline the verbal and appositive phrases in the following sentences. Then, on the line before each sentence, identify each by writing *part. phr.* for *participial phrase*, *ger. phr.* for *gerund phrase*, *inf. phr.* for *infinitive phrase*, or *app. phr.* for *appositive phrase*.

EX. _app. phr._ 1. The grizzly, a mother with two cubs, chased some campers away.

_____ 1. My fantasy is writing the perfect one-act play.

_____ 2. To master these techniques, you must have patience.

_____ 3. Waving to the crowd, the queen stepped into the airplane.

_____ 4. Working the early morning shift can be exhausting.

_____ 5. The bird, a bright red cardinal, stood out against the white snow and the black branches of the trees.

_____ 6. The rabbi's message was that we must learn to love others and ourselves.

_____ 7. Did you see those kids coasting down the hill?

_____ 8. Arturo, the new student from Argentina, told us about the gauchos.

_____ 9. Marike likes studying early in the morning.

_____ 10. Totally surprised by the president's announcement, the Congress went into an emergency session.

_____ 11. The maple tree in the back yard grew to be quite tall.

_____ 12. Rolling in from the ocean, a thick fog covered the whole city.

_____ 13. Is Kerry a good driver because she has mastered parallel parking?

_____ 14. Mr. McGregor found a diamond ring lying on the sidewalk.

_____ 15. Going down the rabbit hole led Alice into many strange adventures.

C.   Writing Sentences with Phrases

Write ten sentences, following the directions below. Underline the italicized phrase in each of your sentences.

EX.   1.   Use *along the highway* as an adjective phrase.
1. Have you noticed all the new billboards along the highway?

1. Use *of the house* as an adjective phrase.
2. Use *as a feather* as an adverb phrase.
3. Use *in the hallway* as an adjective phrase.
4. Use *by airplane* as an adverb phrase.
5. Use *lighting his way with a torch* as a participial phrase.
6. Use *learning lines for a play* as a gerund phrase that is the subject of the sentence.
7. Use the infinitive phrase *to study Chinese* as the direct object of the verb.
8. Use the infinitive phrase *to visit Thailand with her parents* as an adverb phrase.
9. Use *a kind of reference work* as an appositive phrase.
10. Use *my youngest sister* as an appositive phrase.

KINDS OF CLAUSES

A *clause* is a group of words that contains a verb and its subject. There are two kinds of clauses, *independent* and *subordinate*.

13a An *independent* (or *main*) *clause* expresses a complete thought and can stand alone as a sentence.

EXAMPLES
          S   V
Roberto Clemente was a great baseball player. [This entire sentence is an independent clause.]

                     S   V   S V
His lifetime batting average was .317 and **he had 3,000 hits.** [This sentence contains two independent clauses.]

         S   V   S   V
Clemente was born in Puerto Rico in 1934; in 1972, he was killed in a plane crash. [This sentence contains two independent clauses.]

         S   V
Clemente helped the Pittsburgh Pirates win the World Series
         S V
in 1971; he got a hit in every single World Series game. [This sentence contains two independent clauses.]

13b A *subordinate* (or *dependent*) *clause* does not express a complete thought and cannot stand alone as a sentence.

Subordinate means "less important." A word such as *who, that, because, if, when, although,* or *since* signals that the clause it introduces is subordinate. The subordinate clause must be joined to an independent clause to make a complete sentence.

SUBORDINATE
  CLAUSES
because I won the election
that I read aloud in class
who loaned me a pen

SENTENCES
Because I won the election, I am now the class president.
The poem **that I read aloud in class** is by Maya Angelou.
I don't know the student **who loaned me a pen**.

As these example sentences show, a subordinate clause may appear at the beginning, the middle, or the end of a sentence.

EXERCISE 1   Identifying Independent and Subordinate Clauses

Identify the italicized clauses in the paragraph below by writing *indep.* for *independent* or *sub.* for *subordinate* on the line before each sentence.

EX   [1]_____ sub _____ *When she died in 1993 at the age of ninety-seven,* Dr. Stella Kramrisch was a world-famous expert on the art and culture of India.

[1] _____ *Stella Kramrisch was born on May 29, 1896, in Mikulov, Moravia.* [2] _____ *When she was a young girl,* she and her parents moved to Vienna, Austria. [3] _____ *When she was a young student,* she discovered her interest in the art and literature of India, something she pursued all her life. [4] _____ *She enrolled at the University of Vienna,* where she studied Indian art and philosophy, Sanskrit, and anthropology. [5] _____ *After she earned her doctorate in 1919,* Dr. Kramrisch traveled to England to give a lecture at Oxford University. [6] _____ Rabindranath Tagore, *who was a great Indian poet,* attended her lecture. [7] _____ He invited Dr. Kramrisch to return to India with him and teach at a university *that he had founded.* [8] _____ She taught in India for almost thirty years; *then she traveled to the United States and became a professor at the University of Pennsylvania.* [9] _____ *While she taught,* she also wrote many books on Indian art and culture. [10] _____ She became the curator of the Philadelphia Museum of Art in 1954. *Today, thanks to Dr. Stella Kramrisch, the museum has one of the most important collections of Indian art.* [11] _____ *Dr. Kramrisch worked at the museum until 1972,* when she retired. [12] _____ *Although she was in her seventies,* she continued to help the museum for nearly twenty more years. [13] _____ *She wrote many important books, including her masterwork, The Hindu Temple.* [14] _____ When she died, *she was at her home.* [15] _____ She will be honored and missed by the museum *because of her great contributions.*

THE ADJECTIVE CLAUSE

13c An *adjective clause* is a subordinate clause that modifies a noun or a pronoun.

An adjective clause always directly follows the word it modifies. If the clause is necessary, or *essential*, to the meaning of the sentence, it is not set off by commas. If the clause simply adds information and is *nonessential* to the meaning of the sentence, commas are used to set it off.

EXAMPLES Men **who are competing in the cooking contest** should know how to make chili. [The clause is necessary to identify *which men*; therefore, it is not set off by commas.]
The cooking contest, **which is open to both male and female cooks**, will be held in the convention hall. [The clause adds nonessential information; therefore, it is set off by commas.]

An adjective clause is usually introduced by a ***relative pronoun*** which *relates* the clause to the word that the clause modifies.

Relative Pronouns				
who	whom	whose	which	that

EXAMPLES I have an uncle **who is a teacher at Tuskegee University**.
[The relative pronoun *who* relates the adjective clause to the noun *uncle*.]
Tuskegee University, **which is in Alabama**, was founded by Booker T. Washington. [The relative pronoun *which* relates the adjective clause to the proper noun *Tuskegee University*.]

Sometimes the relative pronoun may be left out of a sentence. In such cases, the relative pronoun is understood, but it still has a function in the adjective clause.

EXAMPLE Biology is the course **[that] my uncle teaches**. [The understood relative pronoun *that* relates the adjective clause to the noun *course*.]

The relative adverbs *where* and *when* are sometimes used to introduce adjective clauses.

EXAMPLES Here is the classroom **where my uncle teaches biology**.
This is the time **when he holds conferences**.

EXERCISE 2   Identifying Adjective Clauses

In each sentence below, underline the adjective clause once and the relative pronoun or relative adverb twice. Then, on the line before the sentence, write the noun or pronoun that the adjective clause modifies.

EX.   _____artist_____   1. Leonardo da Vinci was the artist who painted the
                                 Mona Lisa.

_____   1. Most people today refer to him as "Leonardo," which
                          was his first name.

_____   2. Besides his famous paintings, Leonardo made many
                          scientific drawings that were ahead of his time.

_____   3. He drew plans for a flying machine that is very similar
                          to a modern helicopter.

_____   4. Leonardo lived in a time when such machines could not
                          be made.

_____   5. Leonardo was born in 1452 near Vinci, which is a village
                          in central Italy.

_____   6. He studied painting with a well-known painter whose
                          name was Andrea del Verrocchio.

_____   7. The painting that made Leonardo most famous is
                          known as the Mona Lisa.

_____   8. The painting shows a woman who has a gentle,
                          mysterious smile.

_____   9. Francis I, who was the king of France, bought the
                          painting from Leonardo.

_____   10. Today, the Louvre in Paris is the place where people
                          may see it.

FRANK AND ERNEST   by Bob Thaves

I'M THE STORE SANTA CLAUS. ERNIE IS, IF YOU WILL EXCUSE THE EXPRESSION, A SUBORDINATE CLAUS.

12-4
THAVES
© 1974 by NEA Inc. T.M. Reg. U.S. Pat. Off.

Frank & Ernest reprinted by permission of NEA, Inc.

THE ADVERB CLAUSE

13d An *adverb clause* is a subordinate clause that modifies a verb, an adjective, or an adverb.

An adverb clause tells *how, where, when, why, to what extent*, or *under what conditions*.

EXAMPLES **Because it was raining,** we came inside. [The adverb clause tells *why* we came inside. It modifies the verb *came*.]

Georgia is taller **than I am**. [The adverb clause tells *to what extent* Georgia is tall. It modifies the adjective *taller*.]

If we hurry, we can catch that bus. [The adverb clause tells *under what conditions* we can catch the bus. It modifies the verb phrase *can catch*.]

NOTE   As the first and third examples above show, an adverb clause at the beginning of a sentence is usually set off by a comma.

An adverb clause is introduced by a *subordinating conjunction*, a word that relates the adverb clause to the word or words that the clause modifies.

Common Subordinating Conjunctions			
after	as though	since	when
although	because	so that	whenever
as	before	than	where
as if	even though	though	wherever
as long as	if	unless	whether
as soon as	in order that	until	while

Some subordinating conjunctions, such as *after, as, before, since*, and *until*, can also be prepositions.

SUBORDINATING   **After we ate lunch,** we went to the museum.
CONJUNCTION

PREPOSITION   **After lunch,** we went to the museum.

EXERCISE 3   Identifying Adverb Clauses and Subordinating Conjunctions

In each sentence below, underline the adverb clause once and the subordinating conjunction twice.

EX. 1. <u>Whenever we climb Mount Katahdin</u>, we are thrilled by the view.

1. I was late this morning because I forgot to set my alarm clock.

2. Please call my uncle Raphael when you arrive in San Juan.

3. As soon as the towels are dry, please fold them and put them away.

4. The hill was steeper than we had expected.

5. Why did the doctor act as if she were worried?

6. He wears a hairpiece, though you wouldn't have guessed.

7. Before I eat dinner, may I have a cup of tea?

8. If you don't clean your room, you'll be grounded.

9. We were worried until we got the message from Chen.

10. I need to know whether your mom can drive us to the concert.

EXERCISE 4   Building Sentences That Have Adverb Clauses

On your own paper, write five sentences. To create your sentences, choose two clauses from the list below. Combine these clauses with subordinating conjunctions from the chart on the previous page. Do not use any subordinating conjunction twice. Underline the adverb clauses in your sentences once and the subordinating conjunctions twice.

EX. 1. she caught the ball   the sun was in her eyes
     1. <u>Although the sun was in her eyes</u>, she caught the ball.

Eleni wrote to me	we missed the bus
someone phoned Barbara	they made the decorations
we went to the concert	you helped
it was raining	we played a game of checkers
she was on vacation	they arrived
we had to reschedule the meeting	we ordered our dinner
she was in Mexico	Delores came to the party
we needed a ride home	she read my poem aloud
I had a cold	he told a funny joke
Jeremy arrived late	I felt unhappy

THE NOUN CLAUSE

13e   A *noun clause* is a subordinate clause used as a noun.

A noun clause may be used as a subject, a predicate nominative, a direct object, an indirect object, or the object of a preposition.

SUBJECT	**Whoever wins the race** will claim the trophy.
PREDICATE NOMINATIVE	His wish is **that he will become a famous singer**.
DIRECT OBJECT	I hope **that you will come to my party**.
INDIRECT OBJECT	He will give **whomever he chooses** the extra ticket.
OBJECT OF A PREPOSITION	We are proud of **what we have accomplished**.

As these examples show, a noun clause is usually introduced by a word such as *that, what, when, where, whether, who, whoever, whom, whomever, whose,* or *why*. Sometimes, however, the word that introduces a noun clause may be omitted.

EXAMPLE   She told me **you won the election**. [The introductory word *that* is understood. The noun clause is the direct object of the verb *told*.]

EXERCISE 5   Identifying and Classifying Noun Clauses

Underline the noun clause in each of the following sentences. Then, on the line before the sentence, tell how the noun clause is used in the sentence. Write *s.* for *subject*, *p.n.* for *predicate nominative*, *d.o.* for *direct object*, *i.o.* for *indirect object*, or *o.p.* for *object of a preposition*.

EX.   _*o.p.*_   1. Waneta has promised a reward to <u>whoever finds her cat</u>.

_____ 1. What we need is an after-school recreation program.

_____ 2. Dr. Donato said that she could meet with us next Tuesday.

_____ 3. That Rita Moreno is a talented actress has been proven by her many great performances.

_____ 4. Would you please give whoever wants one, a ticket to the game?

_____ 5. The art teacher always takes great interest in what we create.

_____ 6. The coach will make whoever scores the most points the "Athlete of the Week."

_____ 7. How you can memorize poems so quickly really amazes me.

_____ 8. My dentist told me I may need a filling.

_____ 9. Will you tell me who sent these roses?

_____ 10. Many people in the group believed that we should serve fried plantains at the dinner.

EXERCISE 6   Creating Sentences by Inserting Noun Clauses

On your own paper, create sentences by inserting noun clauses in the blanks provided. Use the introductory word shown in parentheses.

EX. 1. Eliza told me _____ . (Use *that*.)

  1. Eliza told me that Ramon is going to the carnival tonight.

1. I will loan the money to _____ . (Use *whoever*.)
2. _____ is obvious. (Use *that*.)
3. The best part of the show was _____ . (Use *when*.)
4. _____ will be right. (Use *whatever*.)
5. John told me _____ . (Use *that*.)
6. The teacher will give _____ a free pass to the game. (Use *whoever*.)
7. Did he tell you _____ ? (Use *whether*.)
8. Do you know _____ ? (Use *what*.)
9. The question was, _____ ? (Use *Where*.)
10. _____ is a good question. (Use *whom*.)
11. Martina believes _____ . (Use *that*.)
12. _____ is a secret. (Use *who*.)
13. _____ will love it. (Use *whomever*.)
14. I don't know _____ . (Use *whose*.)
15. She told me _____ . (Use *why*.)

SENTENCE STRUCTURE

The *structure* of a sentence is determined by the number and types of clauses it has.

13f   According to their structure, sentences are classified as *simple*, *compound*, *complex*, or *compound-complex*.

(1) A *simple sentence* has one independent clause and no subordinate clauses. It may have a compound subject, a compound predicate, and any number of phrases.

EXAMPLES   **Kiki** and **Toni came** to my house for dinner last night.

     <small>S   S   V</small>

After dinner, the **three** of us **compared** our notes and **outlined** our report.

     <small>S   V   V</small>

(2) A *compound sentence* has two or more independent clauses and no subordinate clauses.

A compound sentence is actually two or more simple sentences joined by a comma and a coordinating conjunction, by a semicolon, or by a semicolon and a conjunctive adverb such as *therefore, however*, or *consequently*.

EXAMPLES   **Kiki will write** the first draft of the report, and **Toni**

     <small>S   V   S</small>

     will revise it.

     Kiki had some great ideas; **Toni** and **I listened** carefully.

     <small>S   V   S   S   V</small>

     Toni is the best artist in the group; therefore, **she**

     <small>S   V   S</small>

     will illustrate the report.

     <small>V</small>

(3) A *complex sentence* has one independent clause and at least one subordinate clause.

EXAMPLE   After **we discussed** our plans, **I felt** eager to begin writing.

     <small>S   V   S   V</small>

> **(4) A *compound-complex sentence* has two or more independent clauses and at least one subordinate clause.**
>
> EXAMPLE   Because the **report is** due next Tuesday, **we will work** all
> weekend, and **Toni will finish** her illustrations by Monday.

EXERCISE 7   Classifying Sentences According to Structure

Classify the sentences in the following paragraph. On the line before each sentence, write *simp.* for *simple,* *comp.* for *compound,* *cx.* for *complex,* or *cd.-cx.* for *compound-complex.*

EX.   [1] _____cx._____ Although he isn't a sumo wrestler himself,
        Yoshiro Namekata is famous because of the sport.

[1] _____ The sumo wrestlers of Japan wear their hair in special topknots. [2] _____ Because the topknots are difficult to make, the wrestlers must go to expert hairdressers. [3] _____ Yoshiro Namekata is a man who has become one of the sumo wrestlers' most popular hairstylists. [4] _____ As a young man, Namekata didn't plan on a career as a hairdresser; in fact, he wanted to be a sumo wrestler. [5] _____ However, sumo wrestlers must be very large and strong, and Namekata did not grow as large as he needed to be. [6] _____ Nevertheless, with his sumo hairstyling skills, he plays an important role in Japan's traditional sport. [7] _____ There are two basic hairstyles for sumo wrestlers, and Namekata must be an expert at both of them. [8] _____ Top-level wrestlers get their hair styled in a domed knot, which is called an *oicho-mage,* but lower-level wrestlers get a simpler, flatter knot, the *chonmage.* [9] _____ Most knots take Namekata at least thirty minutes to create. [10] _____ He is a very busy man; when they are competing, Japan's top sumo wrestlers ask Namekata to style their hair twice a day.

CHAPTER REVIEW

A. Identifying Independent and Subordinate Clauses

In the sentences below, identify the italicized clauses. On the line before each sentence, write *indep.* if the clause is independent and *sub.* if the clause is subordinate.

EX. _____sub._____ 1. Edna St. Vincent Millay, *who was an American poet*, wrote many beautiful sonnets.

_____ 1. Pierre's uncle Lucien lives in the city of Chartres, *which is an hour's drive from Paris*.

_____ 2. *How hard you study* will affect your test score.

_____ 3. Simone painted a picture of the apple orchard, but *I have misplaced the picture*.

_____ 4. *When he reached his final years*, Leonardo da Vinci lived near the small French village of Amboise; modern visitors can see his house there.

_____ 5. The company *that rebuilt many of Philadelphia's historic row houses* is owned by my neighbor.

_____ 6. He told me *his grandmother came to the United States in 1975*.

_____ 7. The committee will remain *until they reach a decision*.

_____ 8. Julio has repaired many cars; in fact, *he has become extremely successful as a race car mechanic*.

_____ 9. *Gloria Ramírez sent me this postcard* while she was visiting her grandmother in Mexico.

_____ 10. I will call you *as soon as I get home from football practice*.

B. Classifying Clauses in Sentences

Classify the italicized clauses in the following paragraph. On the line before each sentence, write *adj.* for *adjective clause*, *adv.* for *adverb clause*, or *n.* for *noun clause*. Some sentences contain more than one clause.

EX. [1] _____adj._____ Clementine Hunter, *who was an African American folk artist*, was about 101 years old when she died in 1988.

[1] _____ Clementine Hunter's paintings show *what her life was like*. [2] _____ In the 1940s, *when she was middle aged*, she

began painting pictures about life at Melrose Plantation in northern

Louisiana. [3] _____ *While she was a house servant at the plantation,*

she also worked in the fields. [4] _____ Over the next forty-five

years, she created several thousand paintings *that use bright, clear colors.*

[5] _____ *Whatever surfaces she used for her paintings,* including

canvas, cardboard, and paper, did not affect her style.

[6] _____ With vivid colors, she painted scenes *that show the many*

activities of the farm workers at Melrose. [7] _____ There are

pictures of workers *who are tending animals or gardens,* and there are

others *that show the workers at dances and picnics.* [8] _____ The

African American Museum, *which is located in Dallas, Texas,* has

organized a show of almost one hundred of Clementine Hunter's

paintings. [9] _____ *That Hunter was a talented painter and*

storyteller is clearly seen in the many different paintings in the collection.

[10] _____ *The great popularity of the traveling exhibit* is what artists

everywhere dream of achieving.

C. Writing Sentences with Varied Structures

Follow each set of directions to create your own sentences. Write your
sentences on your own paper.

EX. 1. a complex sentence with a noun clause used as the subject
1. What I need is a new notebook.

1. a simple sentence with a compound subject
2. a simple sentence with a compound verb
3. a compound sentence with two independent clauses joined by the
   conjunction *and*
4. a compound sentence with two independent clauses joined by a
   semicolon
5. a compound sentence with two independent clauses joined by a
   semicolon and the conjunctive adverb *therefore*

NUMBER

Number is the form of a word that indicates whether the word is singular or plural.

14a **When a word refers to one person or thing, it is *singular* in number. When a word refers to more than one, it is *plural* in number.**

Singular	stereo	woman	he	wolf	myself
Plural	stereos	women	they	wolves	ourselves

In general, nouns ending in –*s* are plural (*shirts, reports, horses, valleys*); verbs ending in –*s* are singular (*brings, makes, goes, has, is*).

 REFERENCE NOTE: For more information on the plural forms of nouns, see page 315.

EXERCISE   **Identifying Words as Singular or Plural in Number**

On the line before each of the following words, write *sing.* for *singular* or *pl.* for *plural*.

EX. ___*pl.*___ 1. mice

_____ 1. I

_____ 2. country

_____ 3. them

_____ 4. goes

_____ 5. she

_____ 6. children

_____ 7. crews

_____ 8. two

_____ 9. himself

_____ 10. programmer

_____ 11. yourselves

_____ 12. knives

_____ 13. laughs

_____ 14. geese

_____ 15. were

_____ 16. newspaper

_____ 17. men

_____ 18. dishes

_____ 19. tastes

_____ 20. us

_____ 21. people

_____ 22. night

_____ 23. intermission

_____ 24. handrails

_____ 25. prizes

_____ 26. breakfast

_____ 27. winners

_____ 28. thunderstorms

_____ 29. month

_____ 30. tides

_____ 31. developments

_____ 32. history

_____ 33. cities

_____ 34. airplane

_____ 35. conversation

_____ 36. planets

_____ 37. mice

_____ 38. she

_____ 39. recipe

_____ 40. feet

_____ 41. summer

_____ 42. myself

_____ 43. holds

_____ 44. grapefruits

_____ 45. waterfront

_____ 46. tugboat

_____ 47. detailers

_____ 48. follows

_____ 49. their

_____ 50. excitement

EXERCISE 2   Using Singular Subjects and Plural Subjects in Sentences

Rewrite each sentence below on your own paper. Change the singular subjects to plural and the plural subjects to singular. Be sure to make each verb agree with its subject.

EX.   1. The dog barks.
      1. The dogs bark.

1. The actor dances.
2. Lloyd's brother cooks dinner.
3. Is the door closed?
4. The chickens supply us with eggs.
5. The vegetable gardens are planted.
6. The barn belongs to his family.
7. The turquoise stone is beautiful to see.
8. Victor's friends wait for him.
9. The mountain bikes are two-wheeled vehicles.
10. Does the meeting start tomorrow?

SUBJECT-VERB AGREEMENT

14b   A verb should agree with its subject in number.

(1) Singular subjects take singular verbs.

EXAMPLE   The peach **seems** ripe. [The singular verb *seems* agrees with the singular subject *peach*.]

(2) Plural subjects take plural verbs.

EXAMPLE   The peaches **seem** ripe. [The plural verb *seem* agrees with the plural subject *peaches*.]

Verb phrases also agree in number with their subjects. In a verb phrase, only the first auxiliary (helping) verb changes form to agree with the subject.

SINGULAR   The swimmer **is diving** into the pool.
  PLURAL   The swimmers **are diving** into the pool.
SINGULAR   **Has** the swimmer **started** the race?
  PLURAL   **Have** the swimmers **started** the race?

The form *were* is plural except when used with the singular *you* and in sentences that are contrary to fact.

EXAMPLES   **You were** the best player on the team. [*You* is the singular subject.]

If he were captain, we would be a stronger team. [The statement is contrary to fact, for he is not the captain.]

EXERCISE 3   **Selecting Verbs That Agree in Number with Their Subjects**

For each of the following phrases, underline the verb or verb phrase in parentheses that agrees in number with the subject given.

  EX.   1. they (*needs, _need_*)

1. Joan (*says, say*)

2. apartment (*seems, seem*)

3. bread (*tastes, taste*)

4. men (*hopes, hope*)

5. cat (*jumps, jump*)

6. we (*wishes, wish*)

7. children (*plays, play*)

8. horse (*eats, eat*)

9. dishes (*breaks, break*)

10. class (*has started, have started*)

11. you (*was, were*)

12. geese (*is flying, are flying*)

13. wax (*has dried, have dried*)

14. we (*is riding, are riding*)

15. boxes (*is packed, are packed*)

16. team members (*was voting, were voting*)

17. benches (*has been built, have been built*)

18. George (*has finished, have finished*)

19. he (*has been sleeping, have been sleeping*)

20. mice (*has been nibbling, have been nibbling*)

EXERCISE 4 Identifying Verbs That Agree in Number with Their Subjects

For each sentence below, underline the verb or verb phrase in parentheses that agrees in number with the subject.

EX. 1. The houses (*needs, need*) new roofs.

1. Laura Pausini (*is, are*) a popular singer.

2. The car (*has, have*) a flat tire.

3. Ella Mae and Julio (*is playing, are playing*) the piano.

4. She (*enjoys, enjoy*) fast-pitch softball.

5. (*Was, Were*) Willie Mays a fantastic baseball player?

6. They (*has begun, have begun*) a new project.

7. You (*was asking, were asking*) interesting questions.

8. The children (*was skating, were skating*) at the rink.

9. If I (*was, were*) president, I'd reorganize the club.

10. Somebody (*has borrowed, have borrowed*) my tennis racket.

11. (*Has, Have*) you ever heard of the tennis player Roger Federer?

12. While Donald (*is reading, are reading*), we should listen.

13. Because she (*was, were*) my best friend, I helped her.

14. The Taj Mahal (*stands, stand*) like a jewel in the sun.

15. (*Do, Does*) morning walks make you feel better?

INTERVENING PHRASES

14c **The number of the subject is not changed by a phrase following the subject.**

The subject of a sentence is never part of a prepositional phrase.

EXAMPLES   The **man** with the dark glasses **is** a famous singer. *[man is]*
            The **women** on that team **are** great players. *[women are]*

Prepositional phrases may begin with compound prepositions such as *together with, in addition to, as well as,* and *along with.* These phrases do not affect the number of the verb. A verb agrees in number with its subject.

EXAMPLES   **Rafael,** as well as Jim and Tony, **is** a fantastic soccer player. *[Rafael is]*

            My **suitcases,** along with my duffel bag, **were** loaded onto the plane. *[suitcases were]*

A negative construction following the subject does not change the number of the subject.

EXAMPLES   **Ellen,** not Peter and Julio, **has made** the posters. *[Ellen has made]*

            The **chickens,** not his prize ram, **have won** the blue ribbon. *[chickens have won]*

EXERCISE 5   **Identifying Verbs That Agree in Number with Their Subjects**

For each of the following sentences, underline the verb or verb phrase in parentheses that agrees in number with the subject.

EX.   1.   A bag of groceries (*has fallen, have fallen*) off the kitchen counter.

1. The girls on the tennis team (*is playing, are playing*) in a tournament.

2. Members of the music club (*is having, are having*) a concert tonight.

3. My dog, as well as my two cats, (*needs, need*) a rabies shot every year.

4. For me, the best poems in the entire book (*was written, were written*) by Maya Angelou.

5. The new exhibit by the Puerto Rican artists (*has been, have been*) well attended.

6. Those comedians we saw last week at that theater in the city (*was, were*) really funny.

7. The platter, along with the plates and glasses, (*was, were*) clean.

8. The horses, not the sheep or the cow, (*has been fed, have been fed*).

9. Thunder, as well as lightning and dark clouds, (*means, mean*) a storm is gathering.

10. Vivian, not her sisters, (*is, are*) making Uncle Remo's birthday cake.

EXERCISE 6   Proofreading a Paragraph for Correct Subject-Verb Agreement

In the paragraph below, draw a line through each verb or verb phrase that does not agree with its subject. Write the correct form of the verb or verb phrase in the space above the incorrect word or phrase. Some sentences may contain no agreement errors.

EX.   [1] Elizabeth Yastrzemski, not her cousins, ~~teach~~ *teaches* in-line skating.

[1] A family of athletes live in Long Island, New York. [2] The name of the family is Yastrzemski. [3] One of the most famous of this large group of cousins are Carl Yastrzemski. [4] Carl, for many years, were a great baseball player and a member of the Boston Red Sox. [5] Each of the other cousins enjoy sports, too. [6] The youngest cousin of the group are Elizabeth Yastrzemski. [7] She, unlike her older cousins, have chosen in-line skating as her sport. [8] Use of helmets and pads on the knees, wrists, and elbows are important in this sport, as Elizabeth knows well. [9] In-line skating, together with roller-skating and street hockey, are sports accomplished on cement. [10] This kind of skating, like many other sports, require practice.

AGREEMENT WITH INDEFINITE PRONOUNS

An *indefinite pronoun* is a pronoun that refers to a person, place, or thing not specifically named. When used as the subject of a sentence, an indefinite pronoun must agree with its verb in number.

14d A singular indefinite pronoun must take a singular verb. The following indefinite pronouns are singular: *each, either, neither, one, everyone, everybody, no one, nobody, anyone, anybody, someone,* **and** *somebody.*

Notice that a phrase or a clause following one of these pronouns does not affect the number of the verb.

EXAMPLES   **Everybody** on this project **is** working hard.
Neither of them **has** finished.
Someone who wears glasses **has** left them on the bus.

14e A plural indefinite pronoun must take a plural verb. The following indefinite pronouns are plural: *several, few, both,* **and** *many.*

EXAMPLES   **Many** of my friends **have** seen that movie.
A **few** in the room **have** finished the test.

14f The indefinite pronouns *some, all, any, most,* **and** *none* **may be either singular or plural, depending on the words they refer to.**

These pronouns are singular when they refer to a singular word and plural when they refer to a plural word.

SINGULAR   **Most** of the milk **has** been drunk. [*Most* refers to *milk.*]
PLURAL   **Most** of the women **have** arrived. [*Most* refers to *women.*]
SINGULAR   **None** of the wood **is** wet. [*None* refers to *wood.*]
PLURAL   **None** of the bicycles **have** been sold. [*None* refers to *bicycles.*]

EXERCISE 7 Writing Sentences with Verbs That Agree with Their Subjects

On the lines provided, rewrite each of the following sentences. Follow the directions that appear in parentheses. If necessary, change the number of the verb to agree with the subject.

EX.   1. Everyone on the team plays well. (Change *everyone* to *all of the players.*)

All of the players on the team play well.

1. No one in my class knows the answer. (Change *No one* to *Everybody.*)

_____

2. All of the juice is sour. (Change *All* to *Most.*)

   _____

3. Nobody needs a ride. (Change *Nobody* to *Some of my friends.*) _____

   _____

4. One of the puppies has black ears. (Change *One* to *Many.*) _____

   _____

5. Several of the actors are talented and ambitious. (Change *Several* to *Each.*)

   _____

6. Most of the water is gone. (Change *water* to *strawberries.*) _____

   _____

7. Both of the dancers have learned the new steps. (Change *Both* to *None.*)

   _____

8. Are any of the papers torn? (Change *papers* to *paper.*) _____

   _____

9. Some of the bread tastes delicious. (Change *bread* to *pears.*) _____

   _____

10. Have all of the candidates spoken? (Change *all* to *either.*) _____

    _____

11. Is one of the bikes a twelve-speed? (Change *one* to *many.*) _____

    _____

12. Several of our players are over six feet tall. (Change *Several* to *Each.*)

    _____

13. All of the houses have been painted. (Change *houses* to *house.*)_____

    _____

14. Few in my family like skiing. (Change *Few* to *All.*) _____

    _____

15. Did anybody eat my casserole? (Change *anybody* to *somebody.*) _____

    _____

COMPOUND SUBJECTS

A *compound subject* consists of two or more nouns or pronouns that are joined by a conjunction and have the same verb.

14g   Subjects joined by *and* usually take a plural verb.

Compound subjects joined by *and* that name more than one person or thing always take plural verbs.

EXAMPLES   **TomCruise** and **Charlize Theron** have been in many movies.
Corn, tomatoes, and **green peppers grow** in my garden.

Compound subjects that name only one person or one thing take a singular verb.

EXAMPLES   My favorite **singer and dancer is** Ben Vereen. [one person]
Macaroni and cheese is a terrific meatless meal. [one thing]

14h   Singular subjects joined by *or* or *nor* take a singular verb.

EXAMPLES   **Roberto** or **Eleanora has** been elected.
Has neither your **brother** nor your **sister** arrived?

14i   When a singular subject and a plural subject are joined by *or* or *nor*, the verb agrees with the subject nearer the verb.

EXAMPLES   Neither my parents nor my **sister is** in the audience tonight.
Either Emma or her **parents are** baby-sitting for Dr. Aquino tonight.

EXERCISE 8   Selecting Verbs That Agree in Number with Their Subjects

In each of the following sentences, underline the verb or verb phrase in parentheses that agrees in number with its subject.

EX.   1.   Brazil and Argentina (*is*, *are*) South American nations.

1.   Either Katya or Marie (*is leading*, *are leading*) the parade tomorrow.
2.   Both Sandy Koufax and Nolan Ryan (*has set*, *have set*) pitching records.
3.   Neither the fruit nor the vegetables (*seems*, *seem*) ripe.
4.   Either Robert De Niro or Sean Connery (*is playing*, *are playing*) the role.
5.   (*Is*, *Are*) beans or corn being served as a side dish?

6. Willie Nelson and she (*has recorded, have recorded*) a duet.

7. Either Japan or China (*is, are*) the site of the chess tournament finals.

8. (*Was, Were*) the director and star of the movie Mel Gibson?

9. Either the lead singer or all of the band members (*is, are*) accepting the award.

10. Neither the spark plugs nor the starter (*appears, appear*) damaged.

EXERCISE 9   Working With a Partner to Write Sentences Using Correct Subject-Verb Agreement

Working with a partner, make complete sentences of the compound subjects below. On your own paper, add correct verbs and any other words you might need.

EX.   1.   Either the laser beam or the x-rays

1.   Either the laser beam or X-rays were among the greatest discoveries.

1. Radar and sonar

2. Either penicillin or aspirin

3. Neither Saturn nor Pluto

4. Both fire and atomic energy

5. Science and industry

6. Neither a missile nor several rockets

7. The sliced tomatoes and the baked squash

8. Not only the computer disks but also the display terminals

9. Neither our science project nor theirs

10. Either the players or the captain

COLLECTIVE NOUNS

14j   Collective nouns may be either singular or plural.

A *collective noun* is singular in form, but it names a group of persons or things.

Collective Nouns			
army	club	group	series
assembly	committee	herd	squad
audience	crowd	jury	staff
band	faculty	majority	swarm
choir	family	number	team
class	flock	public	troop

Use a singular verb with a collective noun when you mean the group as a unit. Use a plural verb when you mean the members of the group as individuals.

EXAMPLES   The choir **is** singing at today's assembly.[the choir as a unit]
The choir **are** helping each other to learn the new music.[the choir members as individuals]

EXERCISE 10   Writing Sentences with Collective Nouns

From the list above, select ten collective nouns. On your own paper, use each in a pair of sentences. Each pair of sentences should show how the collective noun may be singular and plural.

EX.   1.   a.   The faculty meets every Thursday afternoon.

b.   The faculty are comparing their different class schedules.

Shoe, by Jeff MacNelly, reprinted by permission: Tribune Media Services.

REVIEW EXERCISE 1

A. Selecting Verbs That Agree with Their Subjects

In each sentence below, underline the verb or verb phrase in parentheses that agrees in number with its subject.

EX. 1. Someone who has made many great movies (*is*, *are*) Al Pacino.

1. My aunt Kamaria often (*goes, go*) back to her birthplace in Africa.

2. Lima, along with Buenos Aires, (*has, have*) many beautiful buildings.

3. (*Does, Do*) the sandwiches in the picnic basket need to be refrigerated?

4. The cost of wool coats (*has risen, have risen*) recently.

5. Suzanne Vega's ability as a musician, as well as her beautiful song lyrics, (*has made, have made*) her very popular.   .

6. Neither of the doctors (*is seeing, are seeing*) any patients today.

7. (*Has, Have*) most of the birds flown south for the winter?

8. None of the ink (*has stained, have stained*) the rug.

9. Either Sheila or Bart and Alan (*is holding, are holding*) a cast party.

10. The songwriter and singer whom I respect most (*is, are*) Stevie Wonder.

B. Proofreading For Subject-Verb Agreement

In each sentence below, underline any verbs that do not agree in number with their subjects. Then, on the line before the sentence, write the correct form of the verb. If a sentence contains no errors in subject-verb agreement, write *C* on the line.

EX. _____is_____ 1. All of the paint in this store are on sale.

_____ 1. Most of the action scenes in the movie was exciting.

_____ 2. Has any of the bread turned stale?

_____ 3. The goat, along with the horses and sheep, have been in the pasture all day.

_____ 4. Volunteer jobs at the local hospital is plentiful.

_____ 5. Do either of your parents work in a factory?

OTHER PROBLEMS IN AGREEMENT

14k **A verb agrees with its subject, not with its predicate nominative.**

SINGULAR   My favorite **vegetable is peas**.

  PLURAL   **Peas are** my favorite **vegetable**.

14l **When the subject follows the verb, make sure that the verb agrees with it.**

In sentences beginning with *here* or *there* and in questions, the subject follows the verb.

SINGULAR   Here **is** the **box** of napkins.   PLURAL   Here **are** the **napkins**.
SINGULAR   Where **is** that **pair** of socks?   PLURAL   Where **are** those **socks**?

NOTE   Contractions such as *here's*, *there's*, *how's*, and *what's* include the singular verb *is*. Use one of these contractions only if a singular subject follows it.

  INCORRECT   There's many cars on the road. [plural subject, singular verb]
   SINGULAR   **There's** a lot of **traffic** on the road.
    PLURAL   There **are** many **cars** on the road.

14m **Words stating amounts usually take singular verbs.**

EXAMPLES   Two weeks **makes** a great vacation.
       Five dollars **is** the price of a movie ticket.

14n **The verb in a clause following the phrase *one of those* should be plural.**

EXAMPLE   *Aladdin* is **one of those** movies that **remain** popular for years.

14o *Every* **or** *many a/an* **before a subject takes a singular verb.**

EXAMPLES   **Every** man and woman **is voting** today.
       Many an athlete **improves** with the help of a coach.

14p **Some nouns, although plural in form, take singular verbs. Such nouns may include the titles of works of art, literature, or music.**

EXAMPLES   **News** of the hurricane **has been reported** on television.
       Trees **is** a poem by the American author Joyce Kilmer.

A few nouns ending in *–ics* may be singular or plural.

EXAMPLES   **Politics is** an interesting subject.
       Your **politics were** the cause of the argument.

EXERCISE 11 Selecting Verbs That Agree in Number with Their Subjects

In each sentence below, underline the verb, phrase, or contraction in parentheses that agrees in number with its subject.

EX. 1. Velma is one of those singers who (*has, have*) natural talent.

1. Five years (*seems, seem*) a long time to be away from home.

2. Here (*is, are*) my collection of stamps.

3. The main ingredient in borscht, a Russian soup, (*is, are*) beets.

4. (*Where's, Where are*) the public swimming pool?

5. Every dog and cat at the city pound (*is, are*) available for adoption.

6. *The Three Sisters* (*is, are*) a play by the Russian playwright Anton Chekhov.

7. (*There's, There are*) nine planets in our solar system.

8. Many a young reader (*has, have*) enjoyed the books by Katherine Paterson.

9. Of all the local musical groups, Grupo Fantasma (*seems, seem*) the best, in my opinion.

10. Old Yeller was one of those fictional dogs that (*was, were*) always getting into trouble but still remained lovable.

11. An apple (*is, are*) one of those fruits that (*tastes, taste*) good raw.

12. Every plate in that cupboard (*has, have*) a chip on it.

13. My uncle's pumpkins (*win, wins*) a ribbon every year at the county fair.

14. Two cars (*fill, fills*) the work area in Mr. Kristan's garage.

15. (*How's, How are*) the weather in Florida?

16. (*Is, Are*) civics a good course to take?

17. This chain of stores (*sells, sell*) the best bread.

18. My favorite place (*is, are*) the mountains.

19. That sack of potatoes (*contain, contains*) the russet type of potatoes.

20. I am on a train that (*has, have*) two cabooses.

REVIEW EXERCISE 2

A.   Selecting Verbs That Agree in Number with Their Subjects

In each sentence below, underline the verb or phrase that agrees in number with its subject.

EX.   1.   (*Here's*, *Here are*) a collection of poems by Gwendolyn Brooks.

1.   *The Woman and the Men* (*is, are*) a book of poems by Nikki Giovanni.

2.   News about the flood (*makes, make*) us very concerned.

3.   Twenty dollars (*seems, seem*) too high a price for a CD.

4.   Where (*does, do*) your parents shop for fresh vegetables?

5.   (*There's, There are*) many pieces of broken glass on the sidewalk.

6.   A popular German dish (*is, are*) sauerbraten and noodles.

7.   *More Cricket Songs* (*is, are*) a collection of Japanese haiku poems translated and edited by Harry Behn.

8.   (*Has, Have*) all of the firewood been burned?

9.   Every singer and dancer in the production (*rehearses, rehearse*) in this hall.

10. *Hunted Mammals of the Sea* is one of those valuable books that (*describes, describe*) the problem of endangered animals.

B.   Proofreading a Paragraph for Errors in Subject-Verb Agreement

In the following paragraph, draw a line through any verb that does not agree in number with its subject. Write the correct form of the verb in the space above the incorrect word. Some sentences may contain no errors in agreement.

EX.   [1] Many a young tennis player ~~enjoy~~ *enjoys* watching professional tennis matches.

[1] Gabriela Sabatini was one of those tennis players who played a strong game. [2] Her match against Steffi Graf in the U. S. Open proved her greatness as a competitor. [3] Sabatini, who is from Argentina, were giving Steffi Graf, the German tennis star, a hard match. [4] Here's

the details from that match. [5] In the middle of the second set, Graf, as well as most of the spectators, were sure that Sabatini would lose.

[6] However, one of Sabatini's greatest strengths were volleys at the net.

[7] Suddenly, Sabatini, not Graf, were playing very aggressive tennis.

[8] What was the results of her aggressive playing? [9] She were successful in winning the last four games of the set! [10] Friendship and respect was evident between these two great players; and although Graf finally won the match in the third set, she was full of compliments for her talented rival.

C. Reporting on School Activities

You are the reporting secretary for the tenth grade at your school. You have been asked to report to the class president on the plans for the upcoming school talent show. Several clubs and organizations in the school have volunteered to help. On your own paper, write your report to the class president. Base your report on the details and notes listed below. Feel free to add your own ideas as well. Your report should contain ten sentences. Make sure that your report contains no errors in subject-verb agreement.

NOTES:

Ushers:	varsity cheerleaders and student council representatives
Music:	the honor band or the concert orchestra
Ticket sales:	Vocational Club or Spanish Club
Advertising:	school newspaper staff or Literary Club
Staging:	Drama Club or Debate Team
Master of ceremonies:	member of the Speech Club

EX.   1.   The varsity cheerleaders and three student council representatives
have volunteered to be ushers for the performance.

PRONOUN AGREEMENT

The word that a pronoun refers to is called its *antecedent*.

14q   A pronoun should agree with its antecedent in gender and number.

Only the third-person singular pronouns indicate the gender of their antecedents. Masculine pronouns (*he, him, his*) refer to males; feminine pronouns (*she, her, hers*) refer to females; and neuter pronouns (*it, its*) refer to things and, often, to animals.

EXAMPLES   Has **Cheryl** finished **her** report?
The **horse** was hungry, so I filled **its** bucket with oats.

When the antecedent of a personal pronoun is another kind of pronoun, determine the gender to use by looking at the phrase that follows the antecedent.

EXAMPLES   **Neither** of the **men** has finished **his** work.
Each of the **girls** has brought **her** lunch.

When the antecedent could be either masculine or feminine, use both the masculine and feminine forms.

EXAMPLE   **Each** of the **students** has finished **his or her** report.

 NOTE   You can often avoid the *his or her* construction by revising the sentence to use the plural form of the pronoun.

EXAMPLE   **All** of the **students** have finished **their** reports.

(1) Use a singular pronoun to refer to the antecedent *each, either, neither, one, everyone, everybody, no one, nobody, anyone, anybody, someone,* **or** *somebody.* **The use of a clause or phrase after the antecedent does not change the number of the antecedent.**

EXAMPLES   **Each** of the **birds** has made **its** nest.
Everyone who plays on the **girls'** tennis team has **her** own racket.

(2) Use a singular pronoun to refer to two or more singular antecedents joined by *or* **or** *nor.*

EXAMPLE   Either **Jonas** or **William** will make **his** presentation next.

(3) Use a plural pronoun to refer to two or more antecedents joined by *and.*

EXAMPLE   The **director** and the **stage manager** made the sets **themselves.**

EXERCISE 12   Selecting Pronouns That Agree with Their Antecedents

In each sentence below, fill in the blank with a pronoun or a pair of pronouns that agrees with the antecedent.

EX.   1. Each of the orchestra members has practiced ___his or her___ part.

1. Students who want to join the skating team should turn in

    _____ registration forms.

2. Do both of the boys need _____ schedules changed?

3. Marilyn and Sue designed the costumes _____ .

4. Has everyone in the apartment building put out _____ trash?

5. Neither Phil nor Roberto has eaten _____ lunch yet.

6. One calf had strayed from _____ herd.

7. Two of the singers in the men's chorus have misplaced

    _____ sheet music.

8. Nobody in my class rides _____ bike to school anymore.

9. One of the men who works with us has gotten _____ pay raise.

10. The treasurer and the secretary have filed _____ reports.

11. Someone in the girls' school has called _____ parents.

12. Each of my sisters has _____ own workshop.

13. When she closed the door, it fell off _____ hinges.

14. Both of her uncles brought _____ presents to the wedding.

15. Either Mr. Petrakis or Mr. Villeré will read _____ family history.

16. The bull got _____ horns caught in a fence.

17. My mother washed _____ car last Saturday.

18. All my uncles knit _____ own sweaters.

19. The pig and the stallion escaped from _____ pens.

20. Did you see the statue of Miss Lila Ogletree, the founder of our school?

    There's a pigeon sitting on _____ nose.

CHAPTER REVIEW

A. Proofreading Sentences for Subject-Verb and Pronoun-Antecedent Agreement

Proofread the sentences below for errors in subject-verb agreement and pronoun-antecedent agreement. Draw a line through any errors. Then, on the line before the sentence, write your correction. If a sentence contains no errors, write C on the line.

EX. _has_ 1. Many a wild horse ~~have~~ been trained to accept a saddle.

_____ 1. Each of the clubs has their own rules.

_____ 2. The coach and leading player were Gordie Howe.

_____ 3. All of the sportscasters have written their stories.

_____ 4. Sixty dollars seem too much to pay for a team jacket.

_____ 5. None of the fruit in the orchard were ripe.

_____ 6. Most of our neighbors grows flowers around their mailboxes.

_____ 7. Tanya, together with her sisters, were planning a party.

_____ 8. Every citizen must protect their civil rights.

_____ 9. Matt, not Cora and I, always wash the dishes after Sunday dinner.

_____ 10. Here's the directions to the Museum of African Culture.

B. Proofreading a Paragraph for Errors in Subject-Verb and Pronoun-Antecedent Agreement

In the following paragraph, draw a line through any errors in subject-verb agreement or pronoun-antecedent agreement. Write your correction in the space above the incorrect word. Some sentences may contain no agreement errors.

EX. [1] Joni Phelps, along with her sons Mike and Marty, ~~have~~ _has_ climbed to the top of Mount McKinley.

[1] Joni Phelps is one of those women who knows what courage is all

about. [2] Phelps, throughout her life, have enjoyed hikes and adventures.

199

[3] However, Phelps lost their eyesight almost twenty-five years ago.

[4] She has relied on a guide dog and his sense of sight ever since. [5] One winter, Phelps, together with her two grown sons, were preparing for a dream come true. [6] They began lifting weights and practicing his rock-climbing skills. [7] All of the work were worth it. [8] Phelps, accompanied by her sons, were the first woman who is visually impaired to climb Mount McKinley, the tallest mountain in North America. [9] Anyone who has climbed Mount McKinley has had their own hardships with the sheer, rocky cliffs and the sudden snowstorms. [10] Many a climber have been forced to turn back, but not Joni, Mike, and Marty Phelps.

C.   Creating a Time Capsule

You and your classmates are creating a time capsule to show people of the future what life was like during your time. Choose ten items you would like to leave in the time capsule. In the space below, identify each item, and explain why you chose it. Create two or more sentences for each item. Be sure to check your sentences for subject-verb agreement and pronoun-antecedent agreement.

EX.   A pennant from the team that won the last World Series seems like
  ·   an interesting item for the time capsule. To many people I know,
      baseball is very important.

_____

_____

_____

_____

_____

_____

_____

_____

_____

CASE OF PRONOUNS

Case is the form of a noun or pronoun that shows how the word is used in a sentence. There are three cases: *nominative*, *objective*, and *possessive*.

Nouns have the same form in both the nominative and the objective case. For example, a noun used as a subject (nominative case) will have the same form when it is used as the object of a preposition (objective case). Nouns usually add an apostrophe and an *s* to form the possessive case.

NOMINATIVE CASE	The **girl** dropped her book.	[subject]
OBJECTIVE CASE	Give the **girl** her book.	[indirect object]
POSSESSIVE CASE	This is the **girl's** book.	[ownership]

 REFERENCE NOTE: See page 301 for information on forming the possessives of nouns.

Personal pronouns change form in the different cases.

CASE FORMS OF PERSONAL PRONOUNS		
Singular		
Nominative Case	**Objective Case**	**Possessive Case**
I	me	my, mine
you	you	your, yours
he, she, it	him, her, it	his, her, hers, its
Plural		
Nominative Case	**Objective Case**	**Possessive Case**
we	us	our, ours
you	you	your, yours
they	them	their, theirs

Notice that only *you* and *it* have the same form in the nominative and the objective case.

 Some teachers prefer to call possessive pronouns, such as *my*, adjectives. Follow your teacher's directions in labeling possessive forms.

EXERCISE 1   Identifying Personal Pronouns and Their Cases

Identify the case of the italicized pronoun by writing *nom.* for *nominative*, *obj.* for *objective*, or *poss.* for *possessive* on the line before each sentence below.

EX.   _poss._ 1. Stephen Hawking was in Seattle to talk about *his* new book.

_____   1.   Because of an illness, *he* communicates through a computer.

_____   2.   Stephen Hawking, one of the most famous scientists in the world, gave *his* speech from a wheelchair.

_____   3.   Several teenagers in his audience were sitting in *their* own wheelchairs.

_____   4.   Although Hawking has Lou Gehrig's disease, *he* continues to work both as a scientist and as an author.

_____   5.   His book, *A Brief History of Time,* has sold more thant five million copies even though *its* topic is highly scientific.

_____   6.   Sean and *I*, as some of those Seattle teenagers, have read the book.

_____   7.   Hawking may be more familiar to *them* from an appearance on the television program *Star Trek: The Next Generation.*

_____   8.   *They* would also have seen Albert Einstein and Sir Isaac Newton, famous scientists from the past, on that show.

_____   9.   The rerun of that episode was on last week and we watched *it.*

_____ 10.   If that episode comes on again, please tell *us.*

_____ 11.   Hawking's book is about *his* theories of black holes and new universes.

_____ 12.   The book also gives information about *him* and his personal life.

_____ 13.   Someone asked *him* why he wrote a book.

_____ 14.   Using a computer voice, *he* said that he did it because he had to pay for his nurses.

_____ 15.   What an amazing man *he* is!

_____ 16.   The Seattle teenagers asked Hawking many questions about *his* daily life.

_____ 17.   They wanted *him* to explain how he is able to communicate.

_____ 18.   How does the computer screen that is attached to *his* wheelchair work?

_____ 19.   Does *it* operate like an ordinary computer?

_____ 20.   How much work on the keyboard does *he* have to do?

THE NOMINATIVE CASE

15a   The subject of a verb is in the nominative case.

EXAMPLES   **I** read the magazine. [*I* is the subject of *read*.]
Anne and **he** sang together. [*Anne* and *he* are the two parts of the compound subject of the verb *sang*.]
We hoped that **they** would win the contest. [*We* is the subject of *hoped*, and *they* is the subject of *would win*.]

If you are not sure which form of the pronoun to use in a compound subject, try each pronoun separately with the verb.

EXAMPLE   (*Him, He*) and (*me, I*) waited for the bus.
Him waited for the bus. [incorrect use of objective case]
He waited for the bus. [correct use of nominative case]
Me waited for the bus. [incorrect use of objective case]
I waited for the bus. [correct use of nominative case]

ANSWER   **He** and **I** waited for the bus.

15b   A predicate nominative is in the nominative case.

A *predicate nominative* is a noun or pronoun that follows a linking verb and explains or identifies the subject of the sentence. A pronoun used as a predicate nominative always follows a form of the verb *be* or a verb phrase ending in *be* or *been*.

EXAMPLES   The writer of that essay is **she**. [*She* follows the linking verb *is* and identifies the subject *writer*.]
The artist could have been **he**. [*He* follows the linking verb *could have been* and identifies the subject *artist*.]
The cocaptains of the team will be **she** and **I**. [*She* and *I* follow the linking verb *will be* and identify the subject *co-captains*.]

NOTE   In casual conversation, expressions such as *It's me* and *That's her* are acceptable. Avoid them in more formal speaking situations, such as job interviews. In your written work, don't use them unless you are creating casual conversation in dialogue.

EXERCISE 2   Identifying Nominative Case Pronouns

For each of the following sentences, underline the correct personal pronoun in parentheses.

EX.   1. It may be (*she, her*) at the door.

1. The ride was long and boring, and (*I, me*) soon fell asleep.

2. Mrs. Olivero and (*her, she*) enjoy jogging together.

3. Mom thought that (*us, we*) should learn how to cook authentic Mexican dishes.

4. Ray suggested that he and (*I, me*) study together after school.

5. The person in charge of the project is (*he, him*).

6. Gloria and (*them, they*) signed up to work at the recycling center.

7. The winners of the tournament could be that team or (*we, us*).

8. Would you and (*she, her*) like to stay for dinner?

9. I think that you and (*me, I*) will be chosen to represent our class.

10. The last two people to sign up to learn Korean in the adult education class were my mother and (*her, she*).

EXERCISE 3 **Proofreading for Correct Use of Nominative Case Pronouns**

In the paragraph below, draw a line through each incorrect pronoun form. Write the correct pronoun in the space above the word. Some sentences are correct.

EX.   [1] Karina and ~~me~~ wanted to learn how to make pottery.

[1] Her and I signed up for a pottery-making class at the Borden Crafts Center. [2] Every Saturday morning, she and me bike over to the center. [3] Sylvia Chin is a well-known local potter, and it is her who teaches the class. [4] She and her husband also own a small pottery shop. [5] She makes the clay pottery; the sculptor of the porcelain is him. [6] Sylvia says Karina and me will soon be making beautiful bowls and cups. [7] Karina learns quickly and, in fact, the star of the class is her. [8] The one to worry about doing well should be me. [9] Ms. Chin says, "I think that you and me have something in common. [10] The first vase I ever made was mistaken for a cereal bowl."

THE OBJECTIVE CASE

15c   Direct objects and indirect objects are in the objective case.

A *direct object* is a noun or pronoun that receives the action of the verb or shows the result of the action.

EXAMPLES   The neighbor's dog followed **us** home. [*Us* tells *whom* the dog followed.]
Earline described **it** in perfect detail. [*It* tells *what* Earline described.]

An *indirect object* is a noun or pronoun that tells *to whom* or *for whom* the action of the verb is done.

EXAMPLES   Miss Acosta gave **them** free passes to the science museum. [*Them* tells *to whom* Miss Acosta gave the passes.]
Hillary bought **her** the video. [*Her* tells *for whom* Hillary bought the video.]

To choose the correct pronoun in a compound direct object or compound indirect object, try each form of the pronoun separately in the sentence.

EXAMPLE   The artist drew a sketch of her and (*me, I*).
The aritist drew *I*. [incorrect use of nominative case]
The artist drew *me*. [correct use of objective case]

ANSWER   The artist drew a sketch of her and **me**.

EXAMPLE   Julian sent them and (*we, us*) postcards.
Julian sent *we* postcards. [incorrect use of nominative case]
Julian sent *us* postcards. [correct use of objective case]

ANSWER   Julian sent them and **us** postcards.

EXERCISE 4   Using Objective Case Pronouns

In each of the following sentences, write a personal pronoun on the line provided. Use a variety of pronouns. Do not use *you* or *it*.

EX.   1. The teacher gave _____them_____ a surprise quiz.

1. Have you asked _____ about the math assignment?

2. The committee will award _____ an honorary prize.

3. After the auditions were over, the director picked _____ to play the part of the shopkeeper.

4. Carlotta's mother offered _____ and _____ some helpful advice.

5. Tell _____ three causes for the beginning of the Civil War.

6. The fire alarm startled _____ .

7. Don't forget to mail Janine and _____ their concert tickets.

8. Tranh showed _____ and _____ how to make a Vietnamese dessert called *banhit*.

9. Watching horror movies before bed sometimes gives _____ nightmares.

10. A crowd of people pushed _____ through the open doors.

EXERCISE 5   Proofreading Sentences for Correct Pronoun Case

In each of the sentences below, draw a line through any incorrect pronouns. On the line before the sentence, write the correct form of each pronoun. If a sentence contains no error in pronoun usage, write C.

EX.   _____him_____   1. I showed Dad and ~~he~~ photographs from the trip.

_____ 1. Because of heavy traffic, the ride from the airport took Francie and I over an hour.

_____ 2. My uncle who lives in San Juan, Puerto Rico, invited us to spend part of the summer with him.

_____ 3. If this explanation confuses you and he, I'll repeat it in simpler terms.

_____ 4. The ending surprised he and I.

_____ 5. Who told you and she about what happened in science lab?

_____ 6. The reporter asked the other witnesses and I what had happened.

_____ 7. Dolores read he and me an excerpt from a book by one of her favorite writers, Amy Tan.

_____ 8. We waved when we spotted Maurice and they a few rows back.

_____ 9. Mrs. Barry paid me generously for baby-sitting the twins.

_____ 10. A monorail carried our parents and we across the amusement park.

OBJECTS OF PREPOSITIONS

15d The object of a preposition is in the objective case.

A prepositional phrase is a group of words consisting of a preposition, a noun or pronoun that serves as the object of the preposition, and any modifiers of that object.

EXAMPLES   from the **governor**   near **us**   behind the **door**
               to Tekla and **her**   in front of **them**   next to **him**

When the object of a preposition is compound, try each pronoun separately in the prepositional phrase.

EXAMPLE   The report was prepared by (*he, him*) and (*I, me*).
            The report was prepared by *he.* [incorrect use of nominative case]
            The report was prepared by *him.* [correct use of objective case]
            The report was prepared by *I.* [incorrect use of nominative case]
            The report was prepared by *me.* [correct use of objective case]
ANSWER   The report was prepared by **him** and **me.**

NOTE   Using incorrect pronoun forms after the prepositions *between* and *for* is a common error. The pronouns should be in the objective case.

INCORRECT   between you and *I*; for *he* and *they*
CORRECT   between **you** and **me**; for **him** and **them**

   REFERENCE NOTE: For a list of commonly used prepositions, see page 123.

EXERCISE 6 Choosing Correct Pronouns as Objects of Prepositions

In each of the following sentences, underline the correct pronoun in parentheses.

EX.   1. The photograph was of (*she, <u>her</u>*) and (*I, <u>me</u>*).

1. The director lost his temper and yelled at (*they, them*).

2. These letters just arrived for Shanti and (*I, me*).

3. According to (*he, him*), this is the way to Becky's house.

4. The dog jumped on the couch and squeezed between Lenny and (*he, him*).

5. After Val finished his biographical sketch of Harriet Tubman, he gave copies of it to (*we, us*) and (*he, him*).

6. The kite soared high above (*she, her*) and (*I, me*).

7. Six others are coming to the movie in addition to you and (*I, me*).

8. They were unaware that a giant snapping turtle was crawling behind (*he, him*) and (*she, her*).

9. Tómas handed a bowl of the paella that he had made for Spanish class to (*they, them*) and (*I, me*).

10. Who is standing in front of (*they, them*) and (*we, us*)?

11. Pilar wanted to know what her boss had said about (*she, her*).

12. During the earthquake, we heard the tinkling of glasses knocking together all around (*we, us*).

13. Ask Namka and (*he, him*) if they can wash the dishes today for Ben and (*I, me*).

14. The rabbit tried to make herself small when she saw the hawk hovering over (*she, her*).

15. What made you pour water onto (*they, them*) and (*we, us*)?

EXERCISE 7   Writing Sentences Using Pronouns as Objects of Prepositions

Write twenty sentences on your own paper, using each of the following prepositions with a personal pronoun as the object of the preposition. Include compound objects in at least four of your sentences. [Hint: You may want to refer to the charts of personal pronouns on page 201.]

EX.   1. without

    1. We left for school without James and her.

1. with	11. against
2. behind	12. over
3. for	13. near
4. instead of	14. in addition to
5. except	15. past
6. according to	16. underneath
7. between	17. on account of
8. toward	18. through
9. concerning	19. without
10. because of	20. beside

REVIEW EXERCISE

A. Identifying Correct Pronoun Forms

In each of the sentences below, underline the correct pronoun in parentheses. On the line before the sentence, identify the pronoun's use in the sentence. Write *s.* for *subject,* *p.n.* for *predicate nominative,* *d.o.* for *direct object,* *i.o.* for *indirect object,* or *o.p.* for *object of the preposition.*

EX. _____*s.*_____ 1. Will Maria and (*she, her*) leave early?

_____ 1. The teacher assigned (*we, us*) a report on the poetry of Gwendolyn Brooks.

_____ 2. Cynthia and (*she, her*) have been friends since kindergarten.

_____ 3. Is there any mail for (*he, him*) and (*I, me*)?

_____ 4. Olympic silver medal winner Sasha Cohen inspired João and (*she, her*) to take up ice-skating.

_____ 5. Are your sisters and (*they, them*) coming home for Thanksgiving?

_____ 6. It's (*he, him*) or (*she, her*) at the door.

_____ 7. The referee seemed to be against (*we, us*).

_____ 8. Did you send (*she, her*) and (*he, him*) invitations to the awards ceremony?

_____ 9. When Spanish explorers came to the Americas, (*they, them*) came in search of the legendary kingdom of Quivira.

_____ 10. The caller could have been Sadie or (*she, her*).

_____ 11. Brenda said, "I'll give (*she, her*) a piece of my mind."

_____ 12. Native Americans in the Northeast made birch canoes and used (*they, them*) for fishing.

_____ 13. I looked up Fred Gipson in a biographical dictionary and found it was (*he, him*) who wrote *Old Yeller.*

_____ 14. Marco thought the book on chess would turn (*he, him*) into a champion player.

_____ 15. The archaeologists at the Cahokia site in East St. Louis gave permission for (*we, us*) to visit the excavations.

B. Proofreading for Correct Pronouns

In the paragraph below, draw a line through each pronoun used incorrectly. In the space above it, write the correct form of the pronoun. Some sentences contain no errors.

EX.   [1] She and ~~me~~ were discussing the portrayal of teenagers in the media.

[1] Often, newspaper stories and television programs show we to be selfish and lazy. [2] Here is a true story that her and I heard that presents teenagers in a different light. [3] Six-year-old Hung Ho was on his way home from school in Modesto, California, when a German shepherd began chasing him. [4] The boy was so frightened that him screamed and ran out into the street. [5] Coming down the street and aimed right at he was an automobile. [6] At the time, fourteen-year-old Poeuth Pann was at his post as school crossing guard. [7] Without thinking about his own safety, Poeuth ran to Hung, and him grabbed the boy from the car's path. [8] It was him that also comforted Hung until the young boy stopped crying. [9] As a result of his actions, the American Automobile Association presented Poeuth with one of its highest awards, the School Safety Patrol Lifesaving Medal. [10] I don't know if I could have been so brave if that had been me.

C. Collaborating to Write a Space Log Entry

For the last few months, you and three partners have been stationed at the outpost on planet Dima. Working with two or three partners, create an update for your space log describing what the four of you have done during the past week. On your own paper, write twenty sentences that tell about your daily schedules, your food sources and living quarters, the plant and animal life on Dima, or any other features of your life at this outpost. Use five nominative case and five objective case pronouns in your sentences. Underline and label the pronouns *nom.* for *nominative* or *obj.* for *objective.*

EX.   Day 45. Yesterday, Charles joined me [obj.] to check out Sector 421. We [nom.] took our lunches with us [obj.], because we [nom.] weren't sure the people along our route would have food that they [nom.] could share with us [obj.].

WHO *AND* WHOM

15e **The use of *who* and *whom* in a subordinate clause depends on how the pronoun functions in the clause.**

Nominative Case	who, whoever
Objective Case	whom, whomever

NOTE In spoken English, the use of *whom* is gradually dying out. These days, it is acceptable to begin any spoken question with *who* regardless of whether the nominative or objective form is grammatically correct. In writing, though, it is still important to distinguish between *who* and *whom*.

When you are deciding whether to use *who* or *whom* in a subordinate clause, follow these steps.

Step 1: Find the subordinate clause.
Step 2: Decide how the pronoun is used in the clause—as a subject, predicate nominative, direct object, indirect object, or object of a preposition.
Step 3: Determine the case of the pronoun according to the rules of standard English.
Step 4: Select the correct form of the pronoun.

EXAMPLE Did you know that Julio is the one (*who, whom*) saved seats for us?
Step 1: The subordinate clause is (*who, whom*) *saved seats for us.*
Step 2: In this clause, the pronoun is the subject of the verb *saved*.
Step 3: As a subject, the pronoun should be in the nominative case.
Step 4: The nominative form is *who*.
ANSWER Did you know that Julio is the one **who** saved the seats for us?

EXAMPLE Rosie is the one (*who, whom*) the judges selected.
Step 1: The subordinate clause is (*who, whom*) *the judges selected.*
Step 2: In this clause, the pronoun is the direct object of the verb *selected: The judges selected* (*who, whom*)?
Step 3: As a direct object, the pronoun should be in the objective case.
Step 4: The objective form is *whom*.
ANSWER Rosie is the one **whom** the judges selected.

Remember that no words outside the subordinate clause affect the case of the pronoun.

> Frequently, *whom* is left out of a subordinate clause, but its function is understood.
>
> EXAMPLE   The woman (whom) I spoke to is my aunt. [*Whom* is understood to be the object of the preposition *to*.]

EXERCISE 8   Identifying the Use of *Who* and *Whom* in Subordinate Clauses

In each sentence below, underline the subordinate clause containing *who* or *whom*. On the line before each sentence, write how the relative pronoun (*who* or *whom*) is used in its own clause. Write *s.* for *subject*, *p.n.* for *predicate nominative*, *d.o.* for *direct object*, *i.o.* for *indirect object*, or *o.p.* for *object of the preposition*.

EX. _p. n._ 1. Do we know who the members are?

_____ 1. The people whom I read about are scientists.

_____ 2. These scientists, who belong to the Rapid Assessment Program, study specific areas of the world's rain forests.

_____ 3. Do you know who the leader of the group is?

_____ 4. The team leader is Ted Parker, who likes studying birds.

_____ 5. Do you know to whom the study of mammals is most interesting?

_____ 6. Louise Emmons, who spent her childhood in such places as Malaysia and Spain, studies mammals.

_____ 7. Team members gather the information for whoever needs it.

_____ 8. Some of the information is used to prove to those who live near the rain forest that laws should be passed to preserve the forest.

_____ 9. Those people take this information to lawmakers whom they trust to make new laws.

_____ 10. This action benefits everyone, especially those people for whom the forest is home.

OTHER PRONOUN PROBLEMS

15f   Pronouns used as appositives should be in the same case as the word they refer to.

An *appositive* is a noun or pronoun used with another noun or pronoun to identify or explain it.

EXAMPLES   The program speakers, **he** and **she**, should sit up front. [The pronouns are in the nominative case because they are in apposition with the subject *speakers*.]

He cooked enough food for three people, **her, him,** and **me**. [The pronouns are in the objective case because they are in apposition with the object of the preposition *people*.]

To figure out the correct form of a pronoun used as an appositive or with an appositive, read the sentence with only the pronoun.

EXAMPLES   The woman offered the two boys, Paul and (*he, him*), a reward.
The woman offered he a reward. [incorrect]
The woman offered him a reward. [correct]
The woman offered the two boys, Paul and **him,** a reward.

(*We, Us*) friends went camping together.
Us went camping together. [incorrect]
We went camping together. [correct]
We friends went camping together.

EXERCISE 9   Identifying the Correct Pronouns

In each of the following sentences, underline the correct pronoun in parentheses.

EX.   1. Mom called (*we, us*) girls in to dinner.

1. Have you met the new students, Denise and (*they, them*)?

2. Her best friends, Miki and (*she, her*), are her most loyal companions.

3. The band dedicated their final song to the music teachers, Ms. Enzio and (*she, her*).

4. The dance academy sent two applicants, you and (*I, me*), acceptance letters.

5. Two people, Karl and (*he, him*), missed the bus.

6. James Berry's children's short story "Ajeemah and His Son" is a favorite of my younger sister Odessa and (*she, her*).

7. (*We, Us*) yearbook workers meet every Wednesday before school.

8. The magician demonstrated for (*we, us*) members of the audience how the trick was done.

9. Dad heard the three opera singers, Plácido Domingo, José Carreras and (*he, him*), in concert.

10. Last Sunday evening, (*we, us*) photo club members gathered to look at slides of Anna's trip to Guatemala.

15g   After *than* or *as* introducing an incomplete construction, use the pronoun form that would be used if the construction were completed.

EXAMPLES   I understand French better than **she** (understands French).
I understand French better than (I understand) **her**.
We visit the city as often as **they** (visit the city).
We visit the city as often as (we visit) **them**.

EXERCISE 10   Selecting Pronouns for Incomplete Constructions in Sentences

On your own paper, write the correct pronoun in parentheses for each of the following sentences. Also, write in parentheses the missing part of the incomplete construction. If a sentence may be completed in two different ways, write both completions.

EX.   1. I know Janet better than (*she, her*).
    1. she (knows Janet); (I know) her

1. We argued about the answer more loudly than (*they, them*).
2. Did they talk about the incident as much as (*we, us*)?
3. I understood the meaning of the poem better than (*he, him*).
4. She watched the Native American dance exhibition longer than (*I, me*).
5. Joe ate more lunch than (*we, us*).
6. Ms. Belindo offered to pay Nancy more than (*we, us*).
7. Did Kai hand in her paper sooner than (*I, me*)?
8. I traveled to see Grandfather as often as (*they, them*).
9. Koko liked Mr. Hirata even less than (*she, her*).
10. Not many gardeners are as careful as (*she, her*).

INEXACT PRONOUN REFERENCE

15h A pronoun should always refer clearly to its antecedent.

(1) Avoid an ambiguous reference.

In an *ambiguous reference*, a pronoun can refer to more than one antecedent.

AMBIGUOUS   Bob saw Andy on his way home. **[Who was on his way home, Bob or Andy?]**

   CLEAR   While Bob was on **his** way home, **he** saw Andy.

or

   CLEAR   While Andy was on **his** way home, Bob saw **him**.

(2) Be sure that each pronoun you use has a specific, stated antecedent.

Sometimes a writer will suggest a particular word or idea without stating it. A pronoun that refers to this unstated word or idea is said to have a *weak reference* to the antecedent.

WEAK   When I'm ready to eat, I cook it quickly in the microwave. [*It* **may refer to breakfast, lunch, dinner, or a snack. The writer suggests, but does not state, which one.**]

CLEAR   When I'm ready to eat **lunch**, I cook **it** quickly in the microwave.

WEAK   Joy loves playing the piano and wants to study it in college. [*It* **may refer to the unstated noun** *music.*]

CLEAR   Joy loves playing the **piano**, and she wants to study **music** in college.

In conversation, people often use the pronouns *it*, *they*, and *you* unnecessarily. In writing, be sure to avoid such *indefinite reference* errors.

INDEFINITE   On the postcard, it has a place for your return address. **[The pronoun** *it* **is not necessary to the meaning of the sentence.]**

   CLEAR   The postcard has a place for your return address.

INDEFINITE   On the television news program, they warned that there would be a severe thunderstorm. **[The pronoun** *they* **is not necessary to the meaning of the sentence.]**

   CLEAR   The television news program issued a severe thunderstorm warning.

NOTE   Familiar expressions such as *it is raining*, *it's early*, and *it seems like* are correct even though they contain inexact pronoun references. The antecedents to these pronouns are commonly understood to be the weather, time, and so forth.

EXERCISE 11   Correcting Inexact Pronoun References

On your own paper, rewrite each of the following sentences, correcting the inexact pronoun reference.

EX.   1. Michael talked to Max while he was in the cafeteria.

    1. While Michael was in the cafeteria, he talked to Max.

1. Sue saw Aretha while she was waiting at the bus stop.
2. After reading Rob's poem and Earl's essay, Ms. Cowens commended it.
3. Whenever I see a play, I want to be like that.
4. In the article about professional basketball player Dikembe Mutombo, they talk about his childhood in Zaire.
5. Fish were jumping all over the lake, but I didn't catch it.

EXERCISE 12   Proofreading for Inexact Pronoun References

On your own paper, revise the paragraph below, correcting the inexact pronoun references. If a sentence contains no errors, make no changes.

EX.   [1] The surgeon general advises the president on federal health policies, which is his main responsibility.

    1. The surgeon general's main responsibility is to advise the president on federal health policies.

[1] In 1993, President Bill Clinton appointed a new surgeon general, and it was confirmed by the United States Senate. [2] Dr. Joycelyn Elders succeeded Dr. Antonia Novello, and she was this country's fifteenth surgeon general. [3] In her career as a medical doctor, she concentrated on children's diseases, studying their causes and why they got them. [4] Because Dr. Elders was especially interested in health issues related to children, as surgeon general she focused on it. [5] In this article about Dr. Elders, they say that Dr. Elders oversaw the 6,500 people who work for the Public Health Service. [6] The Public Health Service was originally created in 1798 to provide health benefits for merchant marines, which helps explain why today they wear the Navy-type uniforms. [7] Public Health Service workers also hold Navy ranks because of it. [8] One of the most famous surgeon generals was Dr. C. Everett Koop. [9] Dr. Koop was appointed by President Ronald Reagan, and he really enjoyed wearing his admiral's uniform. [10] Dr. Koop worked hard to educate Americans about the dangers of smoking, and it declined because of this.

CHAPTER REVIEW

A. Correcting Pronoun Forms in Sentences

In each sentence below, draw a line through the incorrect pronoun form. On the line before the sentence, write the correct form of the pronoun. If the sentence contains no errors, write C.

EX. ___*she*___ 1. Ben and ~~her~~ went to the movies together.

_____ 1. We asked whom the stranger was.

_____ 2. Can you make up song lyrics as well as him?

_____ 3. Halfway through the race, the leaders were Angie, Marty, and her.

_____ 4. Sitting right in front of Josh and I was the actor Denzel Washington.

_____ 5. Do you and her disagree about everything?

_____ 6. Aki demonstrated her karate skills to Melissa, Paula, and I.

_____ 7. The coach asked her and me to work with the new players.

_____ 8. This year, there will be two band leaders, Elena and him.

_____ 9. Who do you think will be elected mayor next month?

_____ 10. Karla is a good artist, and no one draws better than her.

B. Proofreading a Paragraph for Correct Pronoun Forms

In the following paragraph, draw a line through each incorrect pronoun form. In the space above it, write the correct form of the pronoun. Some sentences may contain no errors.

EX. [1] *We*
~~Us~~ students believed we could make things better.

[1] On our way home from school every day, a group of we students would walk past a vacant lot that was overgrown with weeds and littered with bottles, cans, and other trash. [2] Tanya and me would always comment about how awful the place looked and how someone should clean it up. [3] One day Nat, who likes to tease me, said, "You two, her and you, should clean it up if it bothers you so much." [4] At first I just

gave him one of my looks that said, "Who do you think you're talking

to?" [5] Then Tanya said that maybe Nat was actually talking smarter than

us for a change. [6] So, for the next six weeks, her and I showed up at the

vacant lot every Saturday morning in our work clothes. [7] Nat came, too,

with his older brother, and you wouldn't believe what hard workers they

were. [8] Our parents gave us some trash bags and rubber gloves.

[9] Before us kids knew it, the weeds and litter were gone, and the place

was cleaned up. [10] The neighbors, all of who were happy about the

change, discussed how to keep the lot clean. [11] Whomever suggested

that it be used for community gardens had a good idea, I thought. [12] But

Mr. Itoh said nothing uses more water than them, and the lot doesn't have

running water. [13] Then, some local merchants who we are friendly with

donated trees and bushes, some grass seed, two park benches, and lights.

[14] Of course, the gifts meant more work for we kids. [15] That vacant lot

is now a pretty park, and no one could be prouder than us.

C.   Writing a Report on a Music Video

You are the director of a music video for the new song called "Life on the
Edge." You have been asked to write a report to the producer to explain
your ideas for the video.

Decide which singers, dancers, and musicians you will cast in your
video. Their names may be fictitious or real. On your own paper, write
fifteen sentences about the performers and the set. Include information
about the performers' roles in the video. In ten of the sentences, use a
different pronoun. Be sure all pronouns have clear, definite antecedents.

EX.   Video Report: Ziggy Marley would use his talent in Jamaican music to set
the rhythm. I think we should light the set to make it look like the sun is
shining.

REGULAR VERBS

16a The four principal parts of a verb are the *base form*, the *present participle*, the *past*, and the *past participle*.

Base Form	Present Participle	Past	Past Participle
start	(is) starting	started	(have) started
use	(is) using	used	(have) used

 NOTE When the present participle and past participle forms are used as main verbs in sentences, they always require helping verbs.

16b A *regular verb* forms its past and past participle by adding *–d* or *–ed* to the base form.

Base Form	Present Participle	Past	Past Participle
cook	(is) cooking	cooked	(have) cooked
share	(is) sharing	shared	(have) shared
offer	(is) offering	offered	(have) offered
slip	(is) slipping	slipped	(have) slipped

 NOTE A few regular verbs have an alternate past form ending in *–t*. For example, the past form of *dream* is *dreamed* or *dreamt*.

EXERCISE 1   Using Correct Verb Forms

In each of the following sentences, write the correct form of the verb given.

EX. 1. *learn*   Most people have ____learned____ new computer skills.

1. *call*   Have you _____ the doctor?

2. *praise*   Critics are _____ the new book.

3. *risk*   Julio _____ losing the race when he tripped.

4. *carry*   She is _____ a heavy load in her backpack.

5. *advertise*   We usually _____ our fall crafts show on the radio.

6. *play*   The band is _____ my favorite song.

7. *burn*   The old house _____ to the ground.

8. *recycle* The Fosters always _____ their newspapers.

9. *cook*   He has_____ Vietnamese food for us several times.

10. *decide* After a long time, the judges _____ on the winner of the debate.

11. *jump*   Everyone_____ into the pool when the whistle blew.

12. *watch*   At the International Dance Festival, we _____ the dancers from Mexico.

13. *drown*   Several people_____ in the flood.

14. *dream*   Lee is _____ of visiting his grandparents in Hong Kong.

15. *attack* We were _____ by mosquitoes.

16. *play*   Sam and Robin have been _____ tennis for three hours.

17. *walk*   Last Sunday afternoon we _____ around Monument Valley.

18. *happen* What _____ to the rest of the visitors?

19. *climb*   The team from Korea is _____ the highest peak in South America.

20. *hope*   I _____ my aunt will show us the musical instruments she brought back from Africa.

21. *sell*   Today, records and cassettes do not usually_____ as well as compact discs.

22. *include* This state park _____ ponds, campsites, and an excellent bicycle path.

23. *offer*   In the past, the book club_____ a fifteen-percent discount to all its members.

24. *march*   After we ate a picnic lunch, we _____ in the Thanksgiving Day parade.

25. *boil*   Eric, is the soup still _____ ?

IRREGULAR VERBS

16c An *irregular verb* forms its past and past participle in some other way than by adding *–d* or *–ed* to the base form.

Base Form	Past	Past Participle
break	broke	(have) broken
begin	began	(have) begun

NOTE When you are not sure whether a verb is regular or irregular, check a dictionary that lists the principal parts of irregular verbs.

COMMON IRREGULAR VERBS

Base Form	Present Participle	Past	Past Participle
begin	(is) beginning	began	(have) begun
bite	(is) biting	bit	(have) bitten *or* bit
blow	(is) blowing	blew	(have) blown
break	(is) breaking	broke	(have) broken
bring	(is) bringing	brought	(have) brought
build	(is) building	built	(have) built
burst	(is) bursting	burst	(have) burst
catch	(is) catching	caught	(have) caught
choose	(is) choosing	chose	(have) chosen
come	(is) coming	came	(have) come
cost	(is) costing	cost	(have) cost
do	(is) doing	did	(have) done
draw	(is) drawing	drew	(have) drawn
drink	(is) drinking	drank	(have) drunk
drive	(is) driving	drove	(have) driven
eat	(is) eating	ate	(have) eaten
fall	(is) falling	fell	(have) fallen
feel	(is) feeling	felt	(have) felt
freeze	(is) freezing	froze	(have) frozen
get	(is) getting	got	(have) gotten *or* got

COMMON IRREGULAR VERBS

Base Form	Present Participle	Past	Past Participle
give	(is) giving	gave	(have) given
go	(is) going	went	(have) gone
grow	(is) growing	grew	(have) grown
hurt	(is) hurting	hurt	(have) hurt
know	(is) knowing	knew	(have) known
lead	(is) leading	led	(have) led
lend	(is) lending	lent	(have) lent
lose	(is) losing	lost	(have) lost
make	(is) making	made	(have) made
meet	(is) meeting	met	(have) met
put	(is) putting	put	(have) put
ride	(is) riding	rode	(have) ridden
ring	(is) ringing	rang	(have) rung
run	(is) running	ran	(have) run
say	(is) saying	said	(have) said
see	(is) seeing	saw	(have) seen
sell	(is) selling	sold	(have) sold
send	(is) sending	sent	(have) sent
shrink	(is) shrinking	shrank	(have) shrunk
sing	(is) singing	sang	(have) sung
sink	(is) sinking	sank	(have) sunk
speak	(is) speaking	spoke	(have) spoken
stand	(is) standing	stood	(have) stood
steal	(is) stealing	stole	(have) stolen
swim	(is) swimming	swam	(have) swum
swing	(is) swinging	swung	(have) swung
take	(is) taking	took	(have) taken
tell	(is) telling	told	(have) told
throw	(is) throwing	threw	(have) thrown
wear	(is) wearing	wore	(have) worn
win	(is) winning	won	(have) won
write	(is) writing	wrote	(have) written

EXERCISE 2   Using the Correct Past and Past Participle Forms of Verbs

For each of the sentences below, write the correct form of the verb given.

EX. 1. *say*   Lily __*said*__ she is going to the folk-dancing class.

1. *sing*   Before the game started, the players _____ the National Anthem.

2. *write*   My neighbor has _____ a book about American Indian crafts.

3. *see*   We _____ the exhibit of moon rocks at the Museum of Science.

4. *steal*   The runner just _____ second base.

5. *freeze*   The pond hasn't _____ yet this winter.

6. *go*   Manuel _____ to Mexico to visit his aunt.

7. *make*   Have you _____ your costume for the parade?

8. *eat*   Yoshi said that when he lived in Japan they _____ a lot of fish.

9. *blow*   The wind has _____ down several power lines.

10. *sink*   The *Titanic*_____ after it hit an iceberg.

11. *take*   We _____ our boat out today for the first time this season.

12. *win*   Do you know who _____ the 2007 World Series?

13. *sell*   Dexter has _____ his old guitar so that he can buy a new one.

14. *wear*   Last night, we had a good laugh looking at the pictures of the clothes my parents _____ when they were young.

15. *tell*   Dad _____ everyone that dinner was ready.

16. *lend*   Six weeks ago, Craig _____ me his skis.

17. *ring*   Last night, the church bells _____ for five minutes.

18. *stand*   The tourists have _____ in line for hours, waiting to enter the museum.

19. *drink*   The children _____ all the cider.

20. *grow*   These yellow roses are the most fragrant we have ever _____.

EXERCISE 3   Using the Correct Past or Past Participle Forms of Verbs

In each of the sentences below, underline the correct form of the verb in parentheses.

EX.   1.   Last night we (<u>*went*</u>, *gone*) to the State Fair.

1.   Have you (*chose, chosen*) a topic for your report?

2.   The Ashanti woman (*wore, worn*) a cloth called "kente."

3.   Lani (*broke, broken*) open the coconut to drink the milk.

4.   People have (*swam, swum*) in that lake for many years.

5.   In Mali, farmers have (*build, built*) stone walls on the sides of mountains to hold the soil in place where they grew their crops.

6.   Sarah had never (*drank, drunk*) Japanese green tea.

7.   The carolers (*rang, rung*) bells as they sang.

8.   Congresswoman Peters has (*rode, ridden*) in that parade every year.

9.   Every year for the last ten years, Mr. Goldstein has (*ran, run*) in the Boston Marathon.

10.   As a result of whaling, the number of whales in the ocean has (*shrank, shrunk*).

11.   I (*saw, seen*) a copy of that poster at the museum store.

12.   Because he was late getting home, Joe has not yet (*began, begun*) his homework.

13.   During the heavy wind last night, the old maple tree (*fell, fallen*).

14.   "This year on my birthday, I (*gave, given*) a new book to the library," Sharell said.

15.   The one act-play (*wrote, written*) by my drama teacher drew a large audience at the festival.

16.   The movie was the best science-fiction film we have (*saw, seen*).

17.   On her trip to Utah, Elaine (*took, taken*) more than thirty pictures.

18.   "The juice is sweet," said Paul, after he (*bit, bitten*) into the orange.

19.   After the architect has (*drew, drawn*) the plans for the new house, the contractor will begin.

20.   We cannot skate on the pond until the ice has (*froze, frozen*).

VERB TENSE

16d The *tense* of a verb indicates the time of the action or state of being expressed by the verb.

(1) The *present tense* is used to express an action or a state of being occurring now, at the present time.

EXAMPLES   She **runs** every day.
              Are we **working** together? [progressive form]

The present tense is also used to express a general truth—something that is true all the time.

EXAMPLES   Peace **walks** with freedom.   The early bird **gets** the worm.

The present tense is often used in discussing literary works, particularly to summarize the plot or subject of a work. This use of the present tense is called the *literary present*.

EXAMPLE   In *Jane Eyre*, a poor orphan **takes** a job as a governess in a mysterious house.

(2) The *past tense* is used to express an action or a state of being that occurred in the past but does not continue into the present.

EXAMPLES   He **opened** the door.
              Was Herbert **working** with you? [progressive form]

(3) The *future tense* is used to express an action or a state of being that will occur in the future. It is formed with *will* or *shall*.

EXAMPLES She **will work** harder.   **Shall** I **answer** the phone?

(4) The *present perfect tense* is used to express an action or a state of being that occurred at an indefinite time in the past. It is formed with *have* or *has*.

EXAMPLE   Johnette **has** not **visited** us recently.

(5) The *past perfect tense* is used to express an action or a state of being that was completed before some other past action or event took place. It is formed with *had*.

EXAMPLE   After they **had eaten** supper, they washed the dishes.

(6) The *future perfect tense* is used to express an action or a state of being that will be completed before some future action or event takes place. It is formed with *shall have* or *will have*.

EXAMPLE   By the end of the year, I **will have run** in seventeen races.

For each tense another form, the *progressive form*, may be used to show continuing action. The progressive form is made up of a form of *be* plus the verb's present participle.

Form	Examples
Present Progressive	am, are, is running
Past Progressive	was, were running
Future Progressive	will (shall) be running
Present Perfect Progressive	has, have been running
Past Perfect Progressive	had been running
Future Perfect Progressive	will (shall) have been running

EXERCISE 4   Identifying Verb Tenses

In each sentence below, identify the tense and form of the verb. Write the answers on your own paper.

EX. 1. In the lecture series, American Indians are sharing their ideas on political issues.
     1. present progressive

1. Julia discovered the game of baseball at age eight.
2. Within hours, Caroline was boarding a plane to Washington, D.C.
3. The German shepherd and its owner rescue people in trouble.
4. Don has been broadcasting the news for the past five years.
5. How long will you remain in major league baseball?
6. By the end of this trip, we will have been traveling for six weeks straight.
7. Jocelyn had been planning to spend the weekend at Elaine's.
8. The train is running late this morning.
9. All the pipes in the neighborhood had frozen in the night.
10. Chicago and his brother are riding their horses today.
11. A robin has made a nest outside my window.
12. All this month, our class will be studying the South Pacific.
13. I write in my journal every night.
14. According to reports, the rain will have stopped by morning.
15. Had they been waiting long?

EXERCISE 5 **Using the Different Tenses and Forms of Verbs in Sentences**

In each of the following sentences, change the tense and form of the verb according to the directions given after the sentence.

EX. 1. She visited Chicago. (Change to present perfect.)

     She has visited Chicago.

1. Elena lived in Costa Rica for a year. (Change to present perfect.)

_____

2. After he revised his research paper, he typed it. (Change *revised* to past perfect.)

_____

3. We rehearsed the play. (Change to present progressive.)

_____

4. What happened in the story? (Change to present perfect progressive.)

_____

5. After five o'clock, the mariachi band will play for an hour. (Change to future perfect progressive.)

_____

6. The Apache performers were preparing for the Sunrise Dance. (Change to present perfect progressive.)

_____

7. The plane arrives on time. (Change to future.)

_____

8. The Inuit people developed ways to survive in the frozen Arctic regions. (Change to present perfect.)

_____

9. Martha will start her science project by this afternoon. (Change to future perfect.)

_____

10. Julian studies Spanish. (Change to past.)

_____

11. We talked about the Aztec civilization. (Change to past perfect progressive.)

_____

12. I read a book about African traditions, called *Ashanti to Zulu*. (Change to past progressive.)

_____

13. Josie has been practicing every day. (Change to present.)

_____

14. The tourists will visit Mesa Verde first. (Change to future progressive.)

_____

15. Joseph Campbell collected myths from all over the world. (Change to present perfect.)

_____

16. Toni Morrison wrote a new book. (Change to past perfect.)

_____

17. We invited Inga to sing at the program. (Change to present perfect progressive.)

_____

18. Before the day is over, I will have found my keys. (Change *will have found* to future.)

_____

19. Cecilia will leave for Guatemala this week. (Change to future progressive.)

_____

20. Have they gone to the Harvest Festival? (Change to future.)

_____

CONSISTENCY OF TENSE

16e   Do not change needlessly from one tense to another.

NONSTANDARD   Kam puts on her glasses and read the letter while everyone watched her.

STANDARD   Kam **put** on her glasses and **read** the letter while everyone **watched** her. [The verbs are all in past tense.]

STANDARD   Kam **puts** on her glasses and **reads** the letter while everyone **watches** her. [The verbs are all in present tense.]

NOTE   Sometimes, to show a sequence of events, you will need to mix verb tenses.

EXAMPLE   Before the class was over, we had heard several wonderful legends from the storyteller and now we will begin writing our own stories.

EXERCISE 6   Proofreading Paragraphs for Consistent Verb Tenses

In the following paragraphs, draw a line through each incorrect verb form. In the space above the verb, write the form of the verb that will make the verbs in the paragraph consistent in tense. Some sentences may be correct.

EX.   [1] Rachel Carson was a marine biologist who ~~writes~~ *wrote* in a poetic manner about the world around her.

[1] Rachel Carson, who was an important figure in the movement to protect the environment, first become known for her books about the sea. [2] It must have surprised some people that she wrote about the ocean, because she grows up in western Pennsylvania, hundreds of miles from the sea. [3] As a girl, she showed a talent for writing and is interested in exploring the outdoors. [4] She wins a scholarship to the Pennsylvania College for Women, and there she struggled to decide whether to be a writer or a biologist. [5] She said she didn't realize that she could combine her two interests.

[6] She plans to become a college teacher. [7] Then she has decided to do some advanced studies. [8] She spends two summers working at the Woods Hole Marine Biological Laboratory on Cape Cod in Massachusetts. [9] This is where Ms. Carson has come to know the sea. [10] She has decided her future work must involve the ocean.

[11] When she has finished her studies, she tried writing short pieces about the ocean for newspapers. [12] She needed, however, a reliable source of income to support her mother and her two orphaned nieces. [13] She finds a job writing about the ocean for a U.S. government radio program planned by the Bureau of Fisheries, part of the Department of the Interior. [14] The program is called "Romance Under the Waters," and Ms. Carson was paid $19.25 a week to write for it. [15] After she had been working several years for the government, she publishes an essay called "Undersea." [16] Her vivid descriptions of the ocean had caught the attention of the public. [17] She goes on to write a book, *Under the Sea Wind*. [18] It has been published during World War II and was, for the most part, unnoticed. [19] During the war, she continues to write for the government, working long hours as an editor in chief of publications. [20] When the war is over, she published a second book about the ocean, *The Sea Around Us*. [21] This book has been a best seller. [22] Perhaps her most important book, *Silent Spring* is published in 1962. [23] In it, Ms. Carson has warned about the effects of DDT, a chemical that was being widely used then to kill mosquitoes and other insects. [24] DDT is discovered to be harmful to humans and the environment. [25] At this time, people are not as concerned about protecting the environment, and *Silent Spring* help inspire new efforts to protect the earth.

ACTIVE VOICE AND PASSIVE VOICE

16f . **A verb in the *active voice* expresses an action performed *by* its subject. A verb in the *passive voice* expresses an action done *to* its subject.**

ACTIVE VOICE   The tornado **uprooted** several large trees. [The subject, *tornado*, performs the action.]

PASSIVE VOICE   Several large trees **were uprooted** by the tornado. [The subject, *trees*, receives the action.]

NOTE   In a passive sentence, the verb phrase always includes a form of *be* and the past participle of the main verb. Other helping verbs may also be included.

    ACTIVE VOICE   She **raises** cattle on her farm.
    PASSIVE VOICE   Cattle **are being raised** on her farm.

The passive voice emphasizes the person or thing receiving the action rather than the person or thing performing the action. The passive voice is useful when the performer is difficult to identify, when you don't know who performed an action, or when you don't want to give away the performer's identity.

EXAMPLES   The plan **was endorsed** both by public officials and local residents. [The performer is difficult to identify.]
            She **was sent** an anonymous letter. [The performer is unknown.]
            The flowers **were put** on Ms. Ortega's desk when she wasn't looking. [The performer is deliberately concealed.]

NOTE   In most cases, you should avoid the passive voice. The active voice will make your writing much more direct and forceful.

EXERCISE 7   Identifying Sentences in the Active or Passive Voice

Identify each of the following sentences as *active* or *passive*. On the line before each sentence, write *act.* for *active* or *pass.* for *passive*.

EX. _____act._____ 1. Ruth is lighting the candles.

_____ 1. The tapes have been erased.

_____ 2. Many buildings in Los Angeles were damaged by the earthquake.

_____ 3. Lin wrote a skit for the program.

_____ 4. In Ghana, the people celebrate a Yam Festival to mark the beginning of their new year.

_____ 5. The generous contributions to the relief fund were appreciated.

_____ 6. The Hopi dancers performed their traditional Snake Dance.

_____ 7. A huge storm is forming off the coast of Alaska.

_____ 8. The votes were recounted carefully.

_____ 9. Raoul is going to the market.

_____ 10. Cecilia has been named captain of the team.

_____ 11. The band performed in the half-time show.

_____ 12. The refreshments were provided by volunteers.

_____ 13. Tomás is giving guitar lessons on Tuesdays.

_____ 14. Annie Oakley was born in 1860.

_____ 15. The earth is orbited by the moon.

EXERCISE 8   Using Verbs in the Active Voice and the Passive Voice

Study this illustration of an invention designed to help you wake up in the morning. Then write five sentences to describe the invention. Use both the active voice and the passive voice. After each sentence, write *act.* for *active* or *pass.* for *passive*.

EX.   1.   The sleeping person is being wakened by a ringing bell. (pass.)

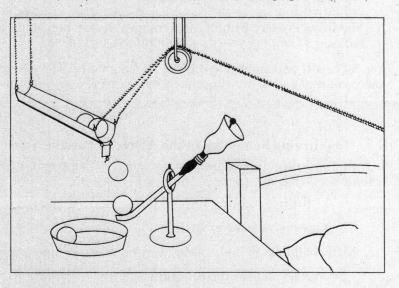

LIE *AND* LAY

16g **The verb *lie* means "to rest," "to recline," or "to remain in a lying position." *Lie* never takes an object. The verb *lay* means "to put (something) in a place." *Lay* usually takes an object.**

Base Form	Present Participle	Past	Past Participle
lie (to rest)	(is) lying	lay	(have) lain
lay (to put)	(is) laying	laid	(have) laid

To decide whether to use *lie* or *lay*, ask yourself two questions:

Question 1: What do I want to say? Is the meaning "to be in a lying position" or "to put something down"?

Question 2: What time does the verb express, and which principal part accurately shows this time?

EXAMPLE   The puppy has (*laid, lain*) there for an hour.

Question 1: **Meaning?** The meaning here is "to be in a lying position." Therefore, the verb should be *lie*.

Question 2: **Principal part?** The time is past, and the sentence requires the past participle with *have*. The past participle of *lie* is *lain*.

ANSWER   The puppy **has lain** there for an hour.

EXAMPLE   Maria (*lay, laid*) her books on the table.

Question 1: **Meaning?** The meaning here is "to put." Therefore, the verb should be *lay*.

Question 2: **Principal part?** The time is past and requires the past form, which is *laid*.

ANSWER   Maria **laid** her books on the table.

EXERCISE 9   Identifying the Correct Forms of *Lie* and *Lay*

In each of the following sentences, underline the correct form of *lie* or *lay*.

EX.   1. The cat is (<u>lying</u>, *laying*) in the sun.

1. Israel (*lies, lays*) between Egypt and Jordan.

2. Akio (*lay, laid*) his shoes outside the door.

3. She didn't answer the doorbell because she was (*lying, laying*) down.

4. They have had to (*lie, lay*) a new floor in the library because of the flood.

5. That street sign has (*lain, laid*) on its side all day.

6. The newspaper is (*lying, laying*) in a puddle.

7. Please (*lie, lay*) the parcel on the table.

8. On the table, they (*lay, laid*) the food for the Harvest Festival.

9. The Khyber Pass (*lies, lays*) in rugged territory in Afghanistan.

10. The workers (*lay, laid*) down in the shade for a rest.

EXERCISE 10   Proofreading for the Correct Use of *Lie* and *Lay*

For each sentence below, underline the error. Then, on the line before each sentence, write the form of *lie* or *lay* that should appear in the sentence. If a sentence contains no errors, write C on the line.

EX. _____lain_____ 1. The children have <u>laid</u> down for a nap.

_____ 1. The old books have laid in the attic for many years.

_____ 2. Will you lie the package on the counter?

_____ 3. Carmen couldn't tell from the map where the entrance to the cave lay.

_____ 4. In the afternoon, everyone laid down for a siesta.

_____ 5. The peddler lay his wares on a carpet by the roadside.

_____ 6. The dog is laying in the warmest spot in the house.

_____ 7. The Andes lay in South America.

_____ 8. We chose the route that laid to the west.

_____ 9. Olga has laid the cups all around the samovar.

_____ 10. His thoughts laid miles away.

_____ 11. Lori said, "Please lay the baby in his crib."

_____ 12. The carpenter has lain the hammer on the bench.

_____ 13. Thick fog laid over the harbor.

_____ 14. Why did you lie in bed so long?

_____ 15. Dust was laying everywhere in the room.

SIT *AND* SET *AND* RISE *AND* RAISE

SIT AND *SET*

16h The verb *sit* means "to rest in a seated position." *Sit* almost never takes an object. The meaning of the verb *set* is "to place" or "to put (something)." *Set* usually takes an object. Notice that *set* does not change form in the past or the past participle.

Base Form	Present Participle	Past	Past Participle
sit (to rest)	(is) sitting	sat	(have) sat
set (to put)	(is) setting	set	(have) set

EXAMPLES   I'll **sit** in the front row. [*Sit* takes no object.]
I'll **set** your papers here. [*Set* what? *Papers* is the object.]

EXERCISE 11   Writing the Forms of *Sit* and *Set*

In each sentence below, write the correct form of *sit* or *set* on the line provided.

EX.   1. Please _____*sit*_____ here, Ms. Garcia.

1. Isabel _____ in the second balcony.

2. My aunt _____ the appetizers on the table.

3. That bird has been _____ on the windowsill for hours.

4. We _____ around the campfire, telling stories.

5. David _____ the lit menorah in the window.

6. Felicity has _____ out the plants in her garden.

7. They had to _____ their experiment in the sunlight.

8. Lillian has _____ here for an hour.

9. The Hopi participants _____ out the gifts that are an important part of the Niman Dance.

10. Did you know there is a package _____ on the steps?

RISE AND *RAISE*

16i   The verb *rise* means "to go up" or "to get up." *Rise* never takes an object. The verb *raise* means "to lift up (something)" or "to cause (something) to raise." *Raise* usually takes an object.

Base Form	Present Participle	Past	Past Participle
rise (to get up)	(is) rising	rose	(have) risen
raise (to lift up)	(is) raising	raised	(have) raised

EXAMPLES   Please **rise** from your seats to greet your guest. [*Rise* takes no object.]
Please **raise** your hand if you have a question. [*Raise* what? *Hand* is the object.]

EXERCISE 12   **Writing the Forms of *Rise* and *Raise***

In each sentence below, write the correct form of *rise* or *raise* on the line provided.

EX.   1.   The full moon is ____rising____ .

1.   The temperature _____ in the afternoon.

2.   The Himalayas_____ between the plateau of Tibet and the plains of India.

3.   Matthew's job is to _____ the curtain before each set.

4.   Tanya _____ to ask a question.

5.   To make piroshki, you need to let the dough _____ .

6.   The woman walked to the window and _____ the blinds.

7.   The price of gasoline has _____ this summer.

8.   The audience _____ to applaud the speaker.

9.   We are trying to _____ money to build an animal rescue center.

10.   The students' interest in Mary McLeod Bethune has _____ since we started studying her life.

CHAPTER REVIEW

A. Writing Sentences Using the Correct Forms of Verbs

On your own paper, rewrite the following sentences. Correct verbs that are in the wrong tense or that use an awkward voice. If a sentence is correct, write C.

> EX. 1. My friend Vernon, an Ojibwe, has several poems written by him.
>   My friend Vernon, an Ojibwe, wrote several poems.

1. Another name for the Ojibwe, a large group of American Indians living north of Mexico, will be the Chippewa.

2. Vernon says that the name *Chippewa* was given to them by the U.S. government but that the name *Ojibwe* is preferred by his people.

3. The word *Ojibwe* is meaning "original people" or "spontaneous people."

4. Many Ojibwe now live in an area surrounding the Great Lakes.

5. From Vernon, I learned that the Ojibwe have felt a strong relationship with nature, even if they are now living in a city or town.

6. Before the arrival of Europeans, the Ojibwe believed in taking from nature only what they need for food, clothing, and shelter.

7. The Ojibwe will lose many of their traditions and beliefs when they were put on reservations and sent away to schools run by missionaries.

8. Now, Vernon tells me, the Ojibwe are trying to preserve their culture, and he will have been writing down stories he hears from elders in his tribe.

9. Powwows are held by the Ojibwe, and at these powwows, people join in ceremonial dancing, singing, games, and feasts.

10. Storytelling will also be an important Ojibwe tradition, and this tradition is being carried on by Vernon.

B. Proofreading a Paragraph for the Correct Forms of Verbs

Read the following paragraph. If a sentence contains an error in verb form, draw a line through the incorrect form and write the correct form on the line before the sentence. If the sentence is correct, write C.

> EX. [1] _____*came*_____ My family ~~come~~ to the United States from Greece when I was two years old.

  [1] _____ I want to learn as much as I could about Greece.

[2] _____ I knew it has a famous history. [3] _____ About 2,500 years ago is a time called the Golden Age of Greece. [4] _____ Plays that were wrote then are still performed today. [5] _____ The style of buildings that were builded then has been copied for many centuries. [6] _____ I also had read stories about the ancient Greek gods and goddesses. [7] _____ My favorite stories are about Artemis, the goddess of the moon. [8] _____ Someday I hope I will have gone to Greece. [9] _____ I regularly write to my cousins who still lived in Greece. [10] _____They are telling me that they will be very happy if I can come visit them.

C.   Using Verbs to Express Time Relationships

The time line below shows several key events from world history. On your own paper, write ten sentences that show time relationships between two or more of the events named. In your sentences, use at least three different tenses.

EX.   1.   The French Revolution began after the Revolutionary War in the United States had started.

1707 Moguls rule India.	1815 Napoleon is defeated at Waterloo.	1909 Robert Peary and Matthew Henderson reach the North Pole.
1728 Vitus Bering discovers a passage between America and Asia.	1851 David Livingston explores Africa.	1911 Amundsen and Scott reach the South Pole.
1750 Industrial Revolution begins in Britain.	1857 Indians mutiny against British presence in India.	1914–1918 World War I
1775 American Revolutionary War	1861 American Civil War begins.	1914 Panama Canal Opens.
1789 French Revolution begins.	1861 Russia abolishes serfdom.	1936 Spanish Civil War
		1939–1945 World War II
		1947 Gandhi leads India to independence from Britain.

```
|———————————+————————————————+————————————————+——————————|
          1700             1800             1900
```

COMPARISON OF MODIFERS

17a Modifiers change form to show comparison. The three degrees of comparison are *positive, comparative,* and *superlative.*

Positive	Comparative	Superlative
high	higher	highest
tearful	more tearful	most tearful
promptly	more promptly	most promptly

(1) One-syllable modifiers form their comparative and superlative degrees by adding *–er* and *–est.*

Positive	Comparative	Superlative
thick	thicker	thickest
dry	drier	driest

(2) Some two-syllable modifiers form their comparative and superlative degrees by adding *–er* and *–est.* Other two-syllable modifiers form their comparative and superlative degrees with *more* and *most.*

Positive	Comparative	Superlative
lovely	lovelier	loveliest
sticky	stickier	stickiest
awkward	more awkward	most awkward

(3) Modifiers that have more than two syllables form their comparative and superlative degrees with *more* and *most.*

Positive	Comparative	Superlative
generous	more generous	most generous
believably	more believably	most believably

NOTE A few two-syllable modifiers may use either *–er, –est* (*able, abler, ablest*) or *more, most* (*more able, most able*).

(4) Modifiers indicate less or least of a quality with the words *less* and *least*.

Positive	Comparative	Superlative
frequent	less frequent	least frequent
painfully	less painfully	least painfully

Some modifiers do not follow the regular methods of forming the comparative and superlative degrees.

Positive	Comparative	Superlative
bad	worse	worst
good	better	best
well	better	best
many	more	most

EXERCISE 1   Forming the Degrees of Comparison of Modifiers

On your own paper, write the forms for the comparative and superlative degrees of the modifiers below. Write the comparative and superlative degrees with *less* and *least*, too.

EX.   1. original   *more original; less original   most original; least original*
2. fast   *faster; less fast   fastest; least fast*

1. fragile
2. quiet
3. comfortable
4. friendly
5. silly
6. exciting
7. loudly
8. humid
9. wisely
10. happily
11. courageous
12. lively
13. brief
14. crunchy
15. proud

EXERCISE 2   Using Comparison Forms

On your own paper, write five sentences comparing the items in each of the following pairs. Use the comparative forms of modifiers in your sentences.

EX.   1. china dishes and paper plates
1. *China dishes are stronger than paper plates.*

1. spring and fall
2. books and movies
3. personal computers and typewriters
4. basketball and baseball
5. pens and pencils

USES OF COMPARATIVE AND SUPERLATIVE FORMS

17b **Use the comparative degree when comparing two things. Use the superlative degree when comparing more than two.**

COMPARATIVE   This sweater is **heavier** than that one.
Of the two cats, Muffin was the **more active.**
This month is **less rainy** than last month was.

SUPERLATIVE   This sweater is the **heaviest** of all.
Of the three cats, Muffin was the **most active.**
This month was the **least rainy** I can remember.

 NOTE   In everyday conversation, people sometimes use the superlative degree when comparing two things: *Put your best foot forward.* In writing, however, you should always use the comparative degree when comparing two things.

17c **Include the word *other* or *else* when comparing one thing with others in the same group.**

NONSTANDARD   Hector can draw better than anyone in art class.
[As a member of the art class, Hector cannot draw better than himself.]

STANDARD   Hector can draw better than anyone **else** in art class.

17d **Avoid double comparisons. A double comparison is incorrect because it contains both *–er* and *more* or *–est* and *most.***

NONSTANDARD   The second exercise was more harder than the first one.
STANDARD   The second exercise was **harder** than the first one.

NONSTANDARD   Which bird has the most smallest beak?
STANDARD   Which bird has the **smallest** beak?

17e **Be sure your comparisons are clear.**

UNCLEAR   Tamara would rather read books than television.
CLEAR   Tamara would rather read books than **watch** television.

EXERCISE 3   Revising Sentences by Correcting Modifiers

Draw a line through the incorrect modifier in each of the following sentences. Write the correct comparative or superlative form above the sentence. Some sentences may be correct.

EX.   1. Some people consider trust a ~~more fine~~ quality than loyalty. *finer*

1. Of my two closest friends, Carlos is the most trustworthy.

2. Isaac is the most smartest person I know.

3. My friend Saki is funnier than Clement.

4. I think Emilie has the prettier name of anyone in my class.

5. Which of the two baseball leagues do you like best?

6. W. E. B. Du Bois was one of the more important leaders of the civil rights movement in the United States.

7. Amelia Earhart's flight from Hawaii to California was longer than her flight from the United States to Europe.

8. Of all the artist's paintings, the one in Washington, D.C., is the more widely known.

9. The damage from this year's flood was worser than the damage from last year's drought.

10. Skipper is the gentlest dog I've ever known.

11. Regarding wool and flannel, which is warmest?

12. My grandmother's later quilts are lesser detailed than her earlier ones.

13. In China, the most important visual art is calligraphy.

14. Of the two pairs of scissors, this one is the most sharpest.

15. Ben's speech about Chief Joseph was the more powerful of all the speeches in the class.

16. The Library of Congress is the largest library in the world.

17. Centuries ago, the spice cinnamon was valuabler than gold.

18. Janell thinks couscous is more tastier than oatmeal.

19. The kitchen is the brighter of all the rooms.

20. The sky is more cloudier today than it was yesterday.

FRANK & ERNEST® by Bob Thaves

Frank & Ernest reprinted by permission of NEA, Inc.

DANGLING MODIFIERS

17f **A modifying phrase or clause that does not clearly and sensibly modify a word in the same sentence is a *dangling modifier*.**

NOTE When a sentence begins with a verbal phrase, the phrase is followed by a comma. The word that the phrase modifies should come immediately after that comma. To correct a dangling modifier, rearrange the words in the sentence, and add or change words to make the meaning logical and clear.

UNCLEAR Weeding the garden, a cabbageworm crawled across my arm.

CLEAR Weeding the garden, **I** felt a cabbageworm crawl across my arm.

NOTE A sentence may appear to have a dangling modifier when *you* is the understood subject. In such cases, the modifier is not dangling; it is modifying the understood subject.

EXAMPLE To take a photograph, **(you)** first focus the lens.

 REFERENCE NOTE: For more information on verbals and verbal phrases, see pages 153–162.

EXERCISE 4 Revising Sentences by Eliminating Dangling Modifiers

On your own paper, revise each of the following sentences to eliminate the dangling modifier. You will have to supply some words to complete the sentences properly.

EX. 1. While standing on the beach, the bay looked misty and cold.
   1. *While we were standing on the beach, the bay looked misty and cold.*

1. During yesterday's trail hike, deer grazed in an open field.
2. While resting from our hike, the flock of sea gulls was a soothing sight.
3. Having never lived in the country, seeing deer was a surprise.
4. Watching the deer, a marvelous feeling came over me.
5. To become a naturalist, natural history should be studied.
6. After hiking back to camp, a crisp apple was refreshing.
7. Preparing the campfire and then cooking and eating dinner, the evening passed quietly.
8. To see the stars at their brightest, we suggest getting away from city lights.

9. After waking up in the chilly morning air, a breakfast of steaming oatmeal is warming.

10. To cross the bay, the ferry at the peninsula dock should be taken.

EXERCISE 5   Writing Sentences with Introductory Modifiers

On the lines below, write complete sentences using the introductory modifiers given. Be sure that the word modified by the introduction immediately follows the comma.

EX.   1. **To understand the experiment,**
<u>To understand the experiment, Kathleen reviewed her chemistry chapter.</u>

1. To prepare for class, _____

_____

2. To make sure she wouldn't oversleep, _____

_____

3. Having arrived early, _____

_____

4. Quietly voicing his opinion, _____

_____

5. Setting the table, _____

_____

6. Hopping from leaf to leaf, _____

_____

7. While making his breakfast, _____

_____

8. To avoid the crowd, _____

_____

9. Writing her first term paper, _____

_____

10. Performing before the large audience, _____

_____

MISPLACED MODIFIERS

17g A modifying phrase or clause that makes a sentence awkward or unclear because it seems to modify the wrong word or group of words is a *misplaced modifier.*

Modifying phrases should be placed as near as possible to the words they modify.

MISPLACED   Mr. Ogata noticed rotting wood painting his house trim.
CORRECTED   **Painting his house trim,** Mr. Ogata noticed rotting wood.

17h Adjective clauses and adverb clauses should be placed where they are clearly linked to the words they modify.

To correct a misplaced clause, place the modifying clause as close as possible to the word or words that it modifies.

MISPLACED   The tennis racket is still in my car that I meant to return to you.
CORRECTED   The tennis racket **that I meant to return to you** is still in my car.

EXERCISE 6   Revising Sentences by Correcting Misplaced Modifiers

Revise each of the following sentences by moving the misplaced phrase or clause near the word or words it modifies.

EX.   1. Felicia saw the shooting stars in the sky with her brother.
      With her brother, Felicia saw the shooting stars in the sky.

1. Mr. Fitzgerald entertained us with stories about sea monsters in his living room. _____

_____

2. Jorge poured the milk for the kitten in a bowl. _____

_____

3. Turning cartwheels, the audience applauded as Vanessa left the stage.

_____

_____

4. Mateo and Betsy could see the ants climbing the hill with their magnifying glasses. _____

_____

5. Blue and yellow, Alex was amazed by the colors of the butterfly. _____

_____

6. A board game was discovered by an archaeologist, thought to be the

oldest in the world. _____

_____

7. There are several people in our office waiting for the doctor, which has

just been repainted. _____

_____

8. An old piece of cheddar cheese sat in the refrigerator that was covered

with mold. _____

_____

9. Frank crossed the street on his bicycle, which was busy with rush-hour

traffic. _____

_____

10. A tenth-century Chinese cook invented fireworks in his kitchen that

exploded with sparks. _____

_____

11. He ate a pear and two apples baby-sitting Tony and Jessica._____

_____

12. My sister and I could see the dark funnel cloud approaching from the

bedroom window. _____

_____

13. I gave a dozen cucumbers to my next-door neighbor that I had picked

from the garden. _____

_____

14. Jacqueline showed the rocking chair to her friends that she had

refinished. _____

_____

15. As a child, my mother taught me how to swim. _____

_____

CHAPTER REVIEW

A. Revising Sentences by Correcting Modifiers

In each sentence below, underline any error in the use of modifiers. Write the correct form in the space above the sentence.

EX. 1. Finding the brightest star in tonight's sky was ~~difficulter~~ *more difficult* than finding it in last night's sky.

1. Which constellation do you see most often, Leo Minor or Pegasus?

2. Since the most earliest times, groups of stars have been named after mythical characters and objects.

3. Astronomers found it least difficult to identify groups of stars rather than individual ones.

4. The ancient astronomer Ptolemy is more interesting to me than any astronomer.

5. With fewer exceptions, the names of the constellations in Ptolemy's catalog are still used today.

6. Ptolemy believed that of all the planets, Earth was nearer to the center of the universe.

7. The most brightest "stars" in the sky are not true stars at all, but planets.

8. The planet most close to the sun is Mercury.

9. The most smallest and most distant planet, Pluto was not discovered until 1930.

10. To me the dry Martian riverbeds are more interesting than any planetary feature.

B. Writing Sentences Using the Comparative and Superlative Forms of Modifiers

At the beginning of the twentieth century, teenagers thought a ride on an elaborate, hand-carved carousel was exciting. Today, as we approach the year 2000, young people are more likely to be interested in a wild roller-coaster ride! Picture a carousel of horses painted in fanciful colors, ridden by women in large hats and long skirts and by men wearing top hats. Now, picture a roller coaster, cars filled with screaming teenagers. Write five sentences using comparative forms of adverbs and adjectives to compare the two rides. Then write five sentences comparing three rides—the carousel, the roller coaster, and a ride you imagine will be a favorite at the turn of the twenty-second century.

After you use at least two modifers from each box, you may use any other modifiers that you wish.

bright	happy	good	intense	exciting
simple	high	many	colorful	stressful
young	pretty	little	expensive	thrilling
scary	fast	much	compelling	mature
safe	long	bad	enjoyable	romantic

EX.   1. The carousel is more romantic but less thrilling than the roller coaster.

C. Using Modifiers Correctly in a Paragraph

On your own paper, correct the misplaced or incorrect modifiers in the paragraph below.

EX.   [1] Two students enjoy bird-watching in our class.
       1. Two students in our class enjoy bird-watching.

[1] Pedro has a better knowledge of birds than anyone I know.

[2] However, Leah thinks her sister Sara knows more about grosbeaks and finches than Pedro. [3] Sara said that the grosbeak's song is softer than the purple finch. [4] Smaller than the grosbeak, Pedro once saw a white-winged crossbill. [5] Pedro and Sara agree that the grosbeak is the larger of all northern finches. [6] Known for their well-hidden nests, Sara has patiently watched for winter wrens. [7] Sara explained how the winter wren moves like a mouse in a class presentation. [8] More shyer than the song sparrow, Pedro told us about the features of the Lincoln's sparrow in his presentation. [9] Walking in a bog, the shy sparrow sings its rich, bubbling song. [10] After completing their presentations, the applause lasted until the class bell rang.

ACCEPT, EXCEPT / AT

This chapter contains an alphabetical list of common problems in English usage. Throughout the chapter, examples are labeled *standard* or *nonstandard*. **Standard English** is the most widely accepted form of English. **Nonstandard English** is language that does not follow the rules and guidelines of standard English.

accept, except   *Accept* is a verb that means "to receive." *Except* may be either a verb or a preposition. As a verb, *except* means "to leave out" or "to exclude"; as a preposition, *except* means "other than" or "excluding."

EXAMPLES   Please **accept** this award.
Please do not **except** Peter from the team. [verb]
I practice piano every day **except** Saturday. [preposition]

affect, effect   *Affect* is a verb meaning "to influence." *Effect* used as a verb means "to bring about." Used as a noun, *effect* means "the result of some action."

EXAMPLES   The heavy flooding **affected** the crops.
The mayor **effected** many changes in the government. [verb]
The scarecrow had no **effect** on the birds. [noun]

all the farther, all the faster   These expressions are used informally in some parts of the country to mean "as far as" and "as fast as."

NONSTANDARD   This is all the farther we can go.
STANDARD   This is **as far as** we can go.

allusion, illusion   An *allusion* is a reference to something. An *illusion* is a mistaken idea or a misleading appearance.

EXAMPLES   Her speech made an **allusion** to the stories of Edgar Allan Poe.
The documentary shattered **illusions** about the war.
The magician was a master of **illusion.**

among, between   Use *among* when referring to all members of a group rather than to separate individuals in the group. Use *between* when you are referring to two things at a time, even if they are part of a larger group.

EXAMPLES   We distributed the toys **among** the children.
There is a strong bond **between** England and the United States.

and etc.   *Etc.* is an abbreviation of the Latin *et cetera*, which means "and other things." Thus, *etc.* includes *and*.

EXAMPLE   I earn money by baby-sitting, mowing lawns, **etc.** [not *and etc.*]

---

anywheres, everywheres, nowheres, somewheres   Use these words without the *s* at the end.

EXAMPLE   **Anywhere** you travel, you can find the same hotel chains.

as   See **like, as.**

at   Do not use *at* after *where.*

EXAMPLE   Where did you see them?[not *see them at*]

EXERCISE 1   Identifying Correct Usage

For each sentence below, underline the correct word in parentheses.

EX.   1. Her sister lives (*somewheres, somewhere*) in Europe.

1. The audience was deeply (*affected, effected*) by her piano solo.

2. You can choose from (*among, between*) many national parks in the United States for a camping vacation.

3. The full moon was so bright that it gave the (*allusion, illusion*) of daylight.

4. Did everyone (*accept, except*) Julian arrive on time?

5. Some people believe that painting a room blue gives it a soothing (*affect, effect*).

EXERCISE 2   Proofreading a Paragraph to Correct Errors in Usage

In each sentence in the paragraph below, draw a line through the error in usage. Then write the correct usage in the space above the word. Some sentences may contain no errors.

EX.   [1] The artist stood up to ~~except~~ *accept* the award.

[1] He spoke about the many years he had spent traveling anywheres he could to find subjects for his paintings. [2] He lived in Tanzania, between villagers in the Masai country. [3] The audience laughed when he described how he tried to climb Mount Kilimanjaro: The base of the mountain was all the farther he could get. [4] He also painted the wildlife and the countryside, and etc. [5] His talk was short, but it had a powerful affect on the people listening; everyone was eager to see his award-winning paintings and drawings.

BEING AS, BEING THAT / INVENT, DISCOVER

being as, being that   Avoid using these expressions. Use *because* or *since* instead.

NONSTANDARD	Being as her grades were so high, she got a scholarship.
STANDARD	**Because** her grades were so high, she got a scholarship.
NONSTANDARD	Being that he was late, he missed the beginning of the play.
STANDARD	**Since** he was late, he missed the beginning of the play.

between, among   See **among.**

bust, busted   Avoid using these words as verbs. Use a form of *break* or *burst* instead.

EXAMPLE   I **broke** the chain on my bicycle. [not *busted*]

could of   Do not use *of* with the helping verb *could*. Use *could have* instead. Also avoid *had of, ought to of, should of, would of, might of,* and *must of.*

EXAMPLE   Sam **could have** gone with us. [not *could of*]

discover, invent   *Discover* means "to find, see, or learn about something that already exists." *Invent* means "to be the first to make or do something."

EXAMPLES   William Herschel **discovered** the planet Uranus.
The game of checkers was **invented** in ancient Egypt.

effect   See **affect, effect.**

See **anywheres**, etc.

fewer, less   *Fewer* is used with plural nouns. It tells "how many." *Less* is used with singular nouns. It tells "how much."

EXAMPLES   We saw **fewer** whales this summer.
This fruit punch contains **less** sugar than that one does.

good, well   *Good* is an adjective. Do not use it to modify a verb. Use *well* instead.

NONSTANDARD	She skis good.
STANDARD	She skis **well.**

had of   See **could of.**

illusion   See **allusion, illusion.**

invent, discover   See **discover.**

EXERCISE 3   Identifying Correct Usage

For each sentence below, underline the correct word in parentheses.

EX.   1.   We (*should of, should have*) turned off the lights.

1.   The game *Parcheesi* was (*discovered, invented*) in India.

2.   The (*affect, effect*) of the food was to make them ill.

3.   We saw (*fewer, less*) hawks this year on our bird-watching trip.

4.   Tranh plays the piano (*good, well*).

5.   Do you know who (*invented, discovered*) the cave?

6.   Jason (*broke, busted*) the lamp during the experiment.

7.   I wish I (*could of, could have*) gone to the concert.

8.   Anders thought the play was very (*good, well*) done.

9.   Her test scores were (*good, well*).

10.   The next time I make bread I will use (*fewer, less*) yeast.

EXERCISE 4   Proofreading a Paragraph to Correct Errors in Usage

In the paragraph below, draw a line through each error in usage. Then write the correct usage in the space above each word. Some sentences may contain no errors.

EX.   [1]   Scott owns no ~~less~~ than three umbrellas.
                         fewer

[1] The umbrella originated in Mesopotamia around 1400 B.C. [2] The reason that the umbrella was discovered was not to keep out rain. [3] Instead, the early umbrella was a protection from the affects of the sun. [4] Along with fans, people used umbrellas everywheres to keep cool. [5] Before this invention, no one would of thought anything could work as good as the fan. [6] Later in Egypt, the umbrella had religious meaning. [7] Being as Egyptians believed that there was a goddess of the heavens, they thought the umbrella represented her. [8] Therefore, only kings and queens could have umbrellas held over their heads. [9] It was considered a special privilege between royal families to stand under an umbrella. [10] These customs endured good for many centuries.

KIND, SORT, TYPE / SHOULD OF

kind, sort, type These words should always agree in number with the words *this* and *that* (singular) or *these* and *those* (plural).

EXAMPLE   Those **kinds** of flowers grow wild; however, this **type** is a garden flower.

kind of a, sort of a The *a* (or *an*) is unnecessary. Omit it.

EXAMPLE   This motor needs a special **kind of** filter [not *kind of a*]

learn, teach *Learn* means "to acquire information." *Teach* means "to instruct" or "to show."

EXAMPLES   Maya **taught** me Spanish.
She **learned** to speak Spanish in Mexico.

let, leave *Leave* means "to go away." *Let* means "to allow or permit."

NONSTANDARD   Leave them go.
STANDARD   **Let** them go.

less, fewer See **fewer, less.**

like, as, as if *Like* is usually a preposition. In informal English, *like* is often used in place of the conjunctions *as, as if,* or *as though.* Formal English calls for one of these conjunctions to introduce a subordinate clause.

EXAMPLES   The shadow looked **like** a shark in the water. [*Like* introduces the prepositional phrase *like a shark.*]
It had a fin **as** a shark does. [The conjunction *as* introduces the subordinate clause.]
It looked **as if** (or **as though**) it might swim by us.

nowheres See **anywheres.**

of Do not use *of* with prepositions such as *inside, off,* and *outside.*

EXAMPLES   The diver jumped **off** the diving board. [not *off of*]
Outside the restaurant was a garden. [not *outside of*]

off of See **of.**

ought to of See **could of.**

should of See **could of.**

EXERCISE 5   Identifying Correct Usage

For each sentence below, underline the correct word or words in parentheses.

EX.   1.   Please (*let*, *leave*) the dog stay in the house.

1.   It looked (*like*, *as*) a spider on the wall.

2.   Out of (*nowhere*, *nowheres*) came a baseball.

3.   I'm looking for a certain (*kind of*, *kind of a*) button.

4.   (*Let*, *Leave*) Carlos tell about the Mayans.

5.   We sold (*fewer*, *less*) tickets than we expected.

6.   Does it shed its skin (*like*, *as*) a lizard does?

7.   Tanya frightened the bird (*off*, *off of*) the rock.

8.   His grandmother tried to (*learn*, *teach*) us how to sing the song.

9.   Yusef (*ought to*, *ought to of*) enter his photographs in the contest.

10.   Andreas usually wins (*this*, *these*) type of game.

EXERCISE 6   Proofreading a Paragraph to Correct Errors in Usage

In the paragraph below, draw a line through each error in usage. Then write the correct usage in the space above the word. Some sentences may contain no errors.

EX.   [1] The small ball of fur meowed ~~like~~ *as* a kitten does.

[1] I ought to of known better, but I never can resist kittens. [2] This kitten seemed to have come out of nowheres. [3] I found it sitting just outside the fence. [4] It looked like a tiny kind of a tiger. [5] It looked hungry and cold, too. [6] Since a blizzard was coming, I let the cat come inside of my house. [7] I thought it would be all right to leave the cat stay for a night. [8] It found the most comfortable place in the house, like a cat always does. [9] I moved it a few times off of the chair by the fireplace before I gave up and let it sleep there. [10] I guess we will get along pretty well—if only I can learn it to share my favorite chair with me.

SOME, SOMEWHAT / WOULD OF

some, somewhat   Do not use *some* as an adverb in place of *somewhat*.

EXAMPLE   This medicine should help your allergy **somewhat**. [not *some*]

sort   See **kind, sort, type.**

sort of   See **kind of, sort of.**

teach   See **learn, teach.**

than, then   *Than* is a conjunction used in comparisons. *Then* is an adverb telling "when."

EXAMPLES   He is shorter **than** I.
I did my homework; **then** I went for a run.

them   Do not use *them* as an adjective. Use *those* instead.

EXAMPLE   It's one of **those** surprise endings. [not *them*]

this here, this there   *Here* and *there* are unnecessary after *this* and *that*.

EXAMPLE   Let's try **this** trail. [not *this here*]

try and   The correct expression is *try to*.

EXAMPLE   When you play this game, **try to** concentrate. [not *try and*]

type   See **kind, sort, type.**

way, ways   Use *way*, not *ways*, in referring to a distance.

EXAMPLE   The school is quite a **way** from here. [not *ways*]

well   See **good, well.**

what   Do not use *what* in place of *that* to introduce a subordinate clause.

EXAMPLE   This is the article **that** I told you about. [not *what*]

when, where   Do not use *when* or *where* incorrectly in writing a definition.

NONSTANDARD   A debate is where people present different opinions about issues.
STANDARD   A debate is a presentation of differing viewpoints.

where   Do not use *where* for *that*.

EXAMPLE   I read **that** November 20 is a holiday in Thailand. [not *where*]

---

which, that, who   *Which* refers only to things. *That* refers to either people or things. *Who* refers only to people.

EXAMPLES   The Louvre Museum, **which** is quite famous, is in Paris.
This is the part **that** I need for the engine.
Is she the one **that** you are waiting for?
He is the one **who** called earlier.

would of · See **could of.**

EXERCISE 7   Correcting Errors in Usage

In the sentences below, draw a line through each error in usage. Then write the correct usage in the space above the word.

EX.   1.   This book is one of ~~them~~ *those* bestsellers.

1.   This here book is really funny.

2.   My brother is younger then I am.

3.   A dispute is when two people can't agree.

4.   The quarterback threw quite a long ways for a touchdown.

5.   A tornado is where you have a violent, whirling wind

accompanied by a funnel-shaped cloud.

6.   Ruth is the one which won the race.

7.   I am going to try and find a job.

8.   This lotion relieves the itch of poison ivy some.

9.   It's one of them dress-up parties.

10.   I read where there is a celebration in Mexico called *La Fiesta de las Posadas*.

11.   First the strawberries become ripe, than the raspberries.

12.   In sailing, a regatta is where several boats meet to race.

13.   Dena likes basketball better then baseball.

14.   We decided to try this here beach for a change.

15.   Where did you find them flowers?

THE DOUBLE NEGATIVE

A *double negative* is the use of two negative words when one is enough.

NONSTANDARD   She did not have no time to finish her work.
STANDARD   She **did not have time** to finish her work.

hardly, scarcely   Do not use the words *hardly* or *scarcely* with another negative word.

NONSTANDARD   There are scarcely no more blue whales left in the ocean.
STANDARD   There are **scarcely** any blue whales left in the ocean.

no, none, nothing   Do not use any of these negative words with another negative word.

NONSTANDARD   There isn't no reason to be worried.
STANDARD   There **is no** reason to be worried.   .
NONSTANDARD   I didn't hear nothing.
STANDARD   I **didn't hear anything.** or I **heard nothing.**

EXERCISE 8   Correcting Errors in Usage

In each of the following sentences, underline the error in usage. Write the correct form above the error.

EX.   1.   I've never seen *anything* <u>nothing</u> as beautiful as Yosemite National Park.

1.   It was so foggy you couldn't hardly see the road.

2.   Elena didn't have no pictures of her hometown in Costa Rica.

3.   Don't you cook no vegetables?

4.   We didn't have no more time.

5.   They hadn't hardly started walking when Joshua said his feet hurt.

6.   I didn't have nothing to read while I waited for the train to arrive.

7.   Lee asked for a map of the Navajo reservation, but they didn't have none.

8.   There weren't no seats left for the concert.

9. We hadn't scarcely enough room for all the people who came to see the dancers from the South Pacific.

10. After her gerbil got loose in the house, Sofia said she didn't want no more pets.

11. I hadn't seen no eclipse before!

12. Wyatt looked for the missing socks but didn't find none.

13. Cecilia hadn't never been to the Chinese New Year's parade.

14. Before we went to visit her, our neighbor hadn't never told anyone about her homeland, which is Vietnam.

15. Didn't you hear nothing?

16. There isn't no easy way to the top of Mount Everest.

17. He doesn't know nothing about fixing cars.

18. Mimi couldn't hardly go to the city all alone.

19. Before I went to Mexico, I hadn't never tasted spicy foods.

20. I heard a sound outside, but I didn't see nothing.

EXERCISE 9   Using Negatives Correctly in Sentences

You are the Safety Officer on Space Station IV. You have been asked to create a list of safety tips to give to all new workers coming from Earth. On your own paper, create ten safety tips. Write each safety tip as a sentence, using a negative in at least five of your tips.

EX.   1.   Do not enter the space lock without your spacesuit.

CHAPTER REVIEW

A. Correcting Errors in Usage

In each sentence below, draw a line through the error in usage. Then write the correct usage in the space above the word. Some sentences may contain no errors.

EX. 1. We didn't get ~~no~~ *any* rain this summer.

1. The Iroquois discovered the game of lacrosse.

2. There are scarcely no more wolves left in the United States, except for in Alaska.

3. Why are these sorts of games really complicated to play?

4. Place a mirror on that wall to give the allusion of a bigger room.

5. We saw fewer wildflowers this year then last year.

6. This low-cholesterol recipe calls for less egg yolks.

7. Have you ever read this here book called *Of Mice and Men*?

8. I knew I'd left my homework somewheres.

9. Marie and Pierre Curie invented radium.

10. We searched for clues but didn't find nothing.

11. Reindeer and others of these hardy type of animal live in the Arctic.

12. Did you hear where the town wants to build a public swimming pool?

13. It was hard to choose between all of the fine entries in the science contest.

14. Shirley Chisholm was the first African American woman which was elected to Congress.

15. Jordan said he would let us go to the museum.

16. Her powerful speech about the rights of working people really effected the audience.

17. Vanda's story made an allusion to Tokyo's Kabuki Theater.

18. The Tour de France is a bicycle race that goes quite a long ways around France.

19. We were lucky we didn't have no hurricanes this year.

20. I must of left my books on the bus.

B.   Correcting Errors in Usage

In the paragraph below, underline the errors in usage. Then write the correct usage in the space above the word. Some sentences contain no errors.

EX.   [1]   All of these tribes <u>accept</u> the Cherokee belonged to the Iroquois

       except

       Confederacy.

[1] Being as the five nations of the Iroquois were tired of fighting, they formed a peace pact between the tribes. [2] They called themselves the *Ongwanonhsioni*, which means "people of the long house," because their lands lay next to each other just as the long houses they built. [3] They held council meetings that were attended by leaders from everywheres in the Iroquois territory. [4] Nothing could never be decided at these councils unless all fifty leaders, or sachems, agreed.

[5] To keep records of these meetings, the Iroquois used wampum. [6] Wampum was where they arranged beads in meaningful patterns. [7] The beads, who were made of seashells, were strung together and sewn into leather belts. [8] At the end of the council meetings, wampum was exchanged. [9] If the leaders didn't agree, sometimes they didn't exchange no wampum. [10] Today people try and read the wampum belts; but the belts are so old, no one living knows their meaning.

C.   Writing a Newspaper Article

You are a reporter who has been assigned to write an article for the "Lifestyle" section of your newspaper. The article is about a special celebration that takes place in your community. In at least ten sentences, describe this event, and discuss its origins or its meaning to the community. In this article, use at least five of the expressions that are covered in this chapter. Underline these expressions. Double-check to make sure you are using the correct form.

EX.   Let me tell you about the street fair in our town. <u>This</u> fair, <u>which</u> raises

      money for a local church, is held in the middle of the summer.

PEOPLE AND PLACES

19a Capitalize the names of persons.

EXAMPLES   Igor Stravinsky, Alice Walker, Ms. Nicole Arzola

The abbreviations *Jr.* (*junior*) and *Sr.* (*senior*) should always be capitalized.

EXAMPLES   Jerome W. Wilson, **Jr.**   Simon L. Snyder, **Sr.**

19b Capitalize geographical names.

Type of Name	Examples
towns, cities	Houston, Albany, Jackson, Bridgeport
counties, states	Ocean County, Penobscot County, Utah
countries	India, Russia, Belize, Japan, Kenya
islands	Nantucket, Sicily, Puerto Rico, Sri Lanka
bodies of water	Amazon River, Boston Harbor, Gulf of Mexico
forests, parks	Sherwood Forest, Shenandoah National Park
streets, highways	Jewett Street, Massachusetts Turnpike, Route 81
mountains	Mount Everest, Appalachian Mountains
continents	Africa, North America, Australia, Asia
regions	the Midwest, Lake Region, the North

NOTE   Words such as *east, west, north,* and *south* are not capitalized when they indicate direction.

EXAMPLES   We drove south on the parkway.
Sula's town is east of my town.

NOTE   In a hyphenated street number, the second part of the number is not capitalized.

EXAMPLE   West Sixty-eighth Street

EXERCISE 1   Correcting Errors in Capitalization

For the sentences below, correct the errors in capitalization by drawing a line through each incorrect letter and writing the correct form above it.

EX.   1.   We will be traveling west on essex avenue.
            (E over e in essex, A over a in avenue)

1.   With my friend alma, I watched the sun rise from cadillac mountain.

2.   My favorite writer, maya angelou, lived in stamps, arkansas.

3.   Reeds have been used to make roofs on structures in africa and north america.

4.   Did you know that henry david thoreau lived by walden pond in concord, massachusetts?

5.   We traveled South on route 95 and then took washington street to get to brooklyn botanic garden.

6.   My school is located on west seventy-eighth street in apple ridge county.

7.   The lowest point in the united states is death valley.

8.   Our friends, the chens, visited king's canyon national park.

9.   The country of vietnam is located in southeast asia.

10. My teacher, mr. bill james, sr., has lived in the south all his life.

EXERCISE 2   Proofreading Sentences for Correct Capitalization

In the sentences below, underline the words that should be capitalized. Write the correct form in the space above the word. Some sentences may be correct.

EX.   1.   We swam in the <u>caribbean</u> <u>sea</u> on a trip to <u>cancún</u>.
            Caribbean Sea   Cancún

1.   My friend jane won a scuba-diving trip to the florida keys.

2.   Dale is moving to helena, which is the capital of montana.

3.   I stayed with my aunt, irisa Mendoza, in san juan, puerto rico.

4.   States in the Northeast experienced cooler temperatures last night.

5.   Our house in newark county is right off the garden state parkway.

SCHOOL SUBJECTS, FIRST WORDS, PROPER ADJECTIVES

19c **Capitalize the first word in every sentence.**

EXAMPLES The red panda eats plants. It is related to the raccoon.

The first word of a sentence that is a direct quotation is capitalized even if the quotation begins within a sentence.

EXAMPLE Shelby answered, "**W**e were just rehearsing with our band."

Traditionally, the first word in a line of poetry is capitalized.

EXAMPLES **W**ind was rough that winter night.
It tossed the boats with all its might,
But we stayed warm by the firelight.

The pronoun *I* and the interjection *O* are capitalized whether or not they are the first words of a sentence. The common interjection *oh* is capitalized only when it begins a sentence or is part of a title.

EXAMPLES Sam and **I** won the race, and, **oh**, was **I** tired.
The story began, "Help me, **O** Great One, for **I** am lost."

19d **Capitalize proper nouns and proper adjectives.**

A *proper adjective* is formed from a proper noun.

 REFERENCE NOTE: For more about proper nouns and proper adjectives, see pages 101 and 109.

Proper Nouns	Proper Adjectives
Mexico	Mexican blanket
Louis Braille	Braille alphabet
Shakespeare	Shakespearean drama

NOTE Proper nouns and adjectives may lose their capitals through frequent use.

EXAMPLES bologna   pasteurized   diesel

19e **Do *not* capitalize the names of school subjects, except for names of languages and course names followed by a number.**

EXAMPLE This semester, Chantel is taking English, Latin, earth science, art, and Geometry II.

EXERCISE 3   Using Capital Letters Correctly

For the sentences below, correct the errors in capitalization by drawing a line through each incorrect letter and writing the correct form above it.

EX.   1. $\overset{W}{\text{w}}$e walked to the corner market and bought bread.

1.   I'm taking a spanish class this year.

2.   My sister said, "read my essay, please."

3.   Karuna's favorite subjects are Algebra and German.

4.   Anne wrote, "if we cannot attend, i will call you."

5.   My cousin has a recipe for irish soda bread.

6.   Give Misha a copy of our latin vocabulary list.

7.   Have you ever tried brazil nuts?

8.   my favorite poet of the Harlem renaissance is Countee Cullen.

9.   We worked with a Bunsen burner today in our Science class.

10.   "please tell Angelo about my birthday party," Luna said.

11.   The parade began in the morning. we saw some beautiful floats.

12.   The best line in Azi's poem is "oh, the moon was a glowing pearl."

13.   My grandmother told us about lithuanian traditions.

14.   The principal walked onstage and said, "welcome, everyone."

15.   Our apartment is in a beautiful victorian house.

16.   She said, "guide me, o wondrous stars."

17.   I want to learn more about dolphins because i find them interesting.

18.   that beautiful branched candleholder is a menorah.

19.   A poem started, "puppies with floppy ears and sloppy tongues."

20.   Clea signed up for chemistry II.

21.   Please ask for extra rice when you order the chinese food.

22.   Ten burmese musicians will present a concert tonight.

23.   All at once, Lainie shouted, "oh, no! the cake is burning!"

24.   main Street in our town is lined with old brick buildings and ends at a white-spired church.

25.   would you please make me a Bologna sandwich?

GROUPS, ORGANIZATIONS, AND RELIGIONS

19f **Capitalize the names of teams, organizations, businesses, institutions, buildings, and government bodies.**

Type of Name	Examples
teams	Chicago White Sox, Philadelphia Flyers, Los Angeles Dodgers
organizations	International Red Cross World Health Organization
businesses	Jalapeño's Mexican Restaurant Caboose Travel Service
institutions	Florida State University, Boston Latin School, Emerson College
buildings	Allen Theater, Eiffel Tower
government bodies	Department of Health and Human Services, United States Congress

Do not capitalize words such as *democratic, republican,* and *socialist* when they refer to principles or forms of government. Capitalize these words only when they refer to a specific political party.

EXAMPLES   We used a **d**emocratic process to elect club officers.
The **R**epublicans are having their convention.

The word *party* in the name of a political party may or may not be capitalized; either way is correct.

EXAMPLES   the **D**emocratic **p**arty (*or* **P**arty)

    REFERENCE NOTE: Do not capitalize words such as *building, hotel, theater, college, high school, post office,* and *courthouse* unless they are part of a proper name. For more discussion about the differences between common and proper nouns, see page 101.

19g   **Capitalize the names of specific nationalities and peoples.**

EXAMPLES   African American, Caucasian, Asian, Hispanic, Cherokee,
Korean, Romanian

> **19h Capitalize the names of religions and their followers, holy days and celebrations, sacred writings, and specific deities.**
>
> EXAMPLES   Buddhism, Christianity, Taoist, Mormon, Yom Kippur,
>   Epiphany, New Testament, Koran, Torah, God, Allah, Buddha

EXERCISE 4   Identifying Correct Capitalization

Write the letter C on the line before each phrase that is capitalized correctly.

EX. _____ 1. a. the minnesota twins
     __C__   b. the Minnesota Twins

_____ 1. a. the Republican Party

_____   b. the republican party

_____ 2. a. Roxbury Community
              College

_____   b. roxbury community
              college

_____ 3. a. Department of Energy

_____   b. department of energy

_____ 4. a. the Humane society

_____   b. the Humane Society

_____ 5. a. the Iroquois

_____   b. the iroquois

_____ 6. a. International Court
              of Justice

_____   b. International Court
              of justice

_____ 7. a. Dragon Light Restaurant

_____   b. dragon light restaurant

_____ 8. a. farm creek construction

_____   b. Farm Creek Construction

_____ 9. a. U.S. Coast Guard

_____   b. U.S. coast guard

_____10. a. San Diego padres

_____   b. San Diego Padres

EXERCISE 5   Proofreading Sentences for Correct Capitalization

For each sentence below, correct the errors in capitalization by drawing a line through each incorrect letter and writing the correct form above it.

EX.   1. Do you know many Hanukkah songs?

1. My canadian relatives visited for easter.

2. My sister works for new england telephone.

3. I gave money to save the children, an international organization.

4. We learned about the muslim fast of ramadan.

5. That store sells items made by haitian artists.

OBJECTS, EVENTS, AND AWARDS

19i **Capitalize the brand names of business products.**

EXAMPLES   Apple computer, Minute Maid juice, Noxzema skin cream

NOTE   The word showing the type of product is not capitalized.

19j **Capitalize the names of historical events and periods, special events and holidays, and other calendar items.**

EXAMPLES   Louisiana Purchase, Harlem Renaissance, Tony Awards, Feast of St. Anthony, Tuesday, Chinese New Year

19k **Capitalize the names of ships, monuments, awards, planets, and any other particular places, things, or events.**

Type of Name	Examples
ships, trains	USS *Chesapeake*, Burlington *Zephyr*
aircraft, spacecraft, missiles	*Spruce Goose, Apollo I,* Gemini-Titan
monuments, memorials	Lincoln Memorial, Ether Monument
awards	National Merit Scholarship
planets, stars	Jupiter, Polaris

EXERCISE 6   Proofreading Sentences for Correct Capitalization

Each of the following sentences contains errors in capitalization. Write your corrections on the lines provided, and separate your answers with a semicolon. Write *C* if the sentence is correct.

EX.   1.   At johnson space center, I saw pictures of the *apollo I* taking off.
           Johnson Space Center; Apollo I

1.   On a dark night we can see the constellation orion.

_____

2.   The *Monitor* was an armored ship built during the Civil War.

_____

3. Have you been inside the statue of liberty?

    _____

4. The writer Toni Morrison won the nobel prize in 1993.

    _____

5. We went to the dentist on the monday just after new year's day.

    _____

6. It was bastille day, so we learned about French customs.

    _____

7. The downtown area is a busy place from monday to friday.

    _____

8. Sheena did a report on the war of 1812.

    _____

9. In 1666, London, England, experienced a tragic event called the Great Fire.

    _____

10. The beautiful taj mahal is a famous marble structure in India.

    _____

11. We bought Dial soap and Comet cleanser for the bathroom.

    _____

12. Did you read the book about our galaxy, the milky way?

    _____

13. That wonderful documentary won an emmy award last september.

    _____

14. The uss *constitution* is open to tourists.

    _____

15. My father bought a box of gorton's fish for our memorial day picnic.

    _____

TITLES

19l   Capitalize titles.

(1) Capitalize the title of a person when the title comes before the name.

EXAMPLES   The university honored **Dr.** Chatterjee last night.
She saw **President** Clinton when he toured the country.

(2) Capitalize a word showing family relationship when the word is used before or in place of a person's name, but not when preceded by a possessive pronoun.

EXAMPLES   We went to the lake with **D**ad and **A**unt Luisa.
We went to the lake with my **d**ad and my **a**unt Luisa.

(3) Capitalize the first and last words and all important words in titles of books, magazines, newspapers, poems, short stories, historical documents, movies, television programs, works of art, and musical compositions.

Unimportant words in titles include articles (*a, an, the*), coordinating conjunctions (*and, but, for, nor, or, so, yet*), and prepositions of fewer than five letters (*at, for, from, with and so on*).

NOTE   The article *the* preceeding a title is not capitalized unless it is the first word of the title.

EXAMPLE   Devon enjoys reading the *Georgetown Weekly*.

Type of Title	Exampless
books	*The Red Pony, Native Son*
newspapers	*Detroit Free Press, The Oakland Tribune*
magazines	*Newsweek, Ebony, Seventeen*
poems	"*The Fish,*" "*Morning Song*"
short stories	"Sonny's Blues," "Everyday Use"
historical documents	Emancipation Proclamation
movies	*Sound of Music, Superman Returns*
television programs	*60 Minutes, The Apprentice, Late Show*
works of art	*Moon River, Mona Lisa*
musical compositions	"Ebony and Ivory," *The Mikado*

EXERCISE 7   Proofreading for Correct Capitalization

For the sentences below, correct the errors in capitalization by drawing a line through each capitalization error and writing the correct form above it.

EX.   1.   Write a letter to ~~senator~~ Senator Kennedy about that issue.

1. I've heard a lot about Ralph Ellison's book, *invisible man*.

2. Cassandra still has that issue of *essence*.

3. Give mom that message from aunt Clarice.

4. I enjoy Langston Hughes's poetry, especially a poem called "dream variations."

5. We all wrote a letter to the editor of the *des moines register*.

6. I know that uncle Pat has learned many new recipes from the TV show *great chefs of the east*.

7. My favorite book used to be E. B. White's *charlotte's web*.

8. We took Shayla to dr. Ron Serrano when she had the flu.

9. My little brother often watches the show *reading rainbow*.

10. The painting style called Impressionism began with Claude Monet's painting *impression: sunrise*.

11. I went with cousin Al to see the declaration of independence.

12. We recently rented the movie *hamlet*, starring Mel Gibson.

13. My sister bought grandpa the book *among schoolchildren*.

14. Has professor Goldstein written another book lately?

15. My teacher read us an article from the *los angeles times*.

16. King John of England signed the magna carta in 1215.

17. My family gave my great aunt bonita a surprise party.

18. R. K. Narayan's story "naga" is very well written.

19. I have enjoyed stories by William Faulkner, especially "spotted horses."

20. I saw a dog growl at his reflection on the television show *america's funniest home videos*.

CHAPTER REVIEW

A.   Correcting Errors in Capitalization

Each of the following sentences contains errors in capitalization. Write your corrections on the lines provided, and separate your answers with a semicolon.

> EX.   1.   That woman, dr. olivera, gave a speech on tuesday.
> Dr. Olivera; Tuesday

1.   sheila said, "my favorite team is the new york mets."

2.   We ate indian dishes at the restaurant called aroma on route 1.

3.   The headquarters of the society for ecology restoration is at 1207 seminole highway in madison, wisconsin.

4.   Did you know cousin keisha wanted to work for the u.s. secret service someday?

5.   My family traveled on the subway, called the mbta, when we visited the museum of fine arts in boston.

6.   The Book *a guide to enjoying wildflowers* was given to me by my uncle jerome.

7.   I had a coupon for tropicana orange juice, so I went to stop & shop on Route 127.

8.   what was the best part of your labor day trip to yosemite national park?

9.   The book *the bluest eye* by african american writer toni morrison is in the Boston public library.

10. Alberto ríos wrote a poem called "madre sofía," which I recited at the brown high school talent show.

B. Proofreading for Correct Capitalization

For the sentences below, correct the errors in capitalization by drawing a line through each error and writing the correct form above it.

EX.   [1] On ~~friday mr.~~ *Friday Mr.* Nguyen gave us interesting news.

[1] He said, "this british literature class will plan a medieval banquet."

[2] *Medieval* is another name for the middle ages, a period in european

history. [3] The banquet will take place in the pérez high school cafeteria,

on valentine's day, and we will dress as characters from works we read

in class. [4] I have decided to go as sir gawain, from the poem *sir gawain*

and the green knight, and my friend nico will go as king Arthur from Sir

Thomas Malory's story *Le Morte D'Arthur*. [5] I have invited aunt pearl,

who is a photographer for the *neighborhood gazette*, for she thinks our

banquet will make a good feature story for the saturday edition.

C.   Working Cooperatively to Write a Guidebook

At a recent town meeting, you were elected to prepare a guidebook for newcomers to your neighborhood. Working with a partner, give two specific items that fit into each category below. Explain where they are located, when they are open, and why they are worth knowing about. Write your sentences on your own paper, and be creative and thorough. You don't want people to miss any of the hot spots!

theaters   places to shop
libraries   museums
entertainment areas   historical sites
good places to eat   recreational sites
scenic areas   schools

EX.   **Panda Garden.** Enjoy the best Chinese food in the area in an elegantly decorated dining room. Prices are moderate; complete dinner specials include beverages and dessert. Be sure to sample the award-winning spring rolls and lo mein dishes. Panda Garden is located at 223 School Street, just one block from the Loomis Public Library. It is open seven days a week, 11:00 A.M. to 10:00 P.M.

END MARKS

An *end mark* is a mark of punctuation placed at the end of a sentence. The three kinds of end marks are the period, the question mark, and the exclamation point.

20a A statement (*or* declarative sentence) is followed by a period.

EXAMPLES I have been studying for the algebra quiz all evening**.**
　　　　　For our party, Georgia brought latkes, and Lea brought
　　　　　　　empanadas**.**

20b A question (*or* interrogative sentence) is followed by a question mark.

EXAMPLES May I borrow that book when you are through**?**
　　　　　Shouldn't we leave early, since the weather is bad**?**

NOTE Be sure to distinguish between a declarative sentence that contains an indirect question and an interrogative sentence, which asks a direct question.

　　INDIRECT QUESTION She asked me to join the team. [declarative]
　　　DIRECT QUESTION Will you join the team? [interrogative]

20c An exclamation is followed by an exclamation point.

EXAMPLES Wow**!** What a beautiful sunset**!**
　　　　　Oh**!** We would love to go to the game with you**!**

Instead of a period or question mark, use an exclamation point after declarative and interrogative sentences that express strong emotion.

EXAMPLES Jake is finally here**!**
　　　　　Why won't this rain stop**!**

20d An imperative sentence is followed by either a period or an exclamation point.

EXAMPLES Please clean this room**.**
　　　　　Clean this room now**!**

An imperative sentence may be stated in the form of a question. However, since its purpose is to give a command or make a request, it should be followed by a period or an exclamation point.

EXAMPLES May I have your undivided attention**.**
　　　　　Will you give me your undivided attention**!**

EXERCISE 1   Correcting Sentences by Adding End Marks

Add the correct end mark to each of the following sentences. [Note: There may be more than one correct way to punctuate a sentence.]

EX. 1. Would you like any help?

1. Students in Giorgio's cooking class made a delicious guacamole dip for their final project

2. Please move the red bicycle into our garage before the rain begins

3. Avery asked if I would please teach him how to do that funny dance

4. What an incredible idea that was

5. Watch where you're going

6. When does Renata begin her paper route

7. That red kimono in the hall closet belonged to my great-grandmother

8. Call the country music station, and request Esperanza's favorite song

9. How surprised you must have been

10. Does your diving watch need a new battery

11. Watch your step

12. She asked you to quiet down

13. Mia will be joining us later in the evening for dinner and for a game of charades

14. Do any of the art projects that are hanging in the school cafeteria belong to you

15. Stop that bus

16. The International Club asked if they could plan a party

17. Could we attend the festival this weekend

18. Ask Mr. Olivera to be a chaperone

19. My cousin just learned how to drive

20. It is disappointing that the town pool will be closed next week

21. How do you expect me to do that

22. Join the choir

23. I asked if I could help with any of the plans

24. Are you bringing Oliver

25. My goodness, you scared me

ABBREVIATIONS

20e   Use periods after most abbreviations.

Abbreviations with Periods	
Personal Names	Susan B. Anthony, W. C. Fields
Titles Used with Names	Dr., Jr., Sr., Mr., Mrs., Ms.
States	N. Mex., Ga., Conn., Wash.
Organizations and Companies	Co., Inc., Corp., Assn.
Addresses	St., Rd., Ave., P.O. Box, Blvd.
Times	A.M., P.M., A.D., B.C.

Some common abbreviations are often written without periods.

EXAMPLES   FBI, TV, FDA, oz, ft, lb, cm, kg, ml, VCR, PTA, NAACP

NOTE   Two-letter state codes are used only when the ZIP Code is included. Two-letter state codes are **not** followed by periods.

EXAMPLE   Austin, TX 78729

When an abbreviation that ends with a period comes at the end of a sentence, do not add another period as an end mark. *Do* add a question mark or an exclamation point if one is needed.

EXAMPLES   The artifact was dated 3500 B.C.
Why did he move to St. Louis, Mo.**?**

NOTE   *Inch(es)* is abbreviated *in.* to avoid confusing it with *in,* the preposition. If you are not sure whether to use periods with an abbreviation, look in a dictionary.

EXERCISE 2   Using Punctuation Correctly in Abbreviations

On your own paper, rewrite the phrases below, using the correct punctuation. If the abbreviation is correct, write *C.*

EX.   1. Dr E Hilario
       1. Dr. E. Hilario

1. 1 oz of cheddar cheese
2. 54 Hanover St
3. The news program on MTV
4. Ms Feona S Doyle
5. the nature program on PBS at 5:00 P M
6. Rockport Art Assn
7. Anchorage, AK 99502
8. 8 mi to the FBI building
9. Rufus Thompson, Jr
10. PO Box 245

REVIEW EXERCISE

A. Correcting Punctuation in Sentences

In the sentences below, insert any missing punctuation, and draw a line through any punctuation that is not needed. [Note: There may be more than one correct way to punctuate a sentence.]

EX. 1. I'm so excited to see Ms. Rego again!

1. May I have your attention, please

2. We met about 6:00 P M at Monticello St and Rivera Ave

3. Dr Montel said that our new baby sister weighs 7 lbs and 5 oz

4. That's an amazing C.D.

5. Did you know that Cousin Fernando was joining the Peace Corps

6. Quiet down immediately

7. My family moved to St. Paul, Minn, from Hartford, Conn

8. The measuring tape uses ft on one side and m and c.m. on the other

9. My business is called Child Inc, and it is a popular baby-sitting service

10. I mailed a package to my best friend, Angela, whose address is 1819 Elm Street, Austin, TX 78746

11. Is Mount Caubvick in Labrador more than 15,000 ft high

12. I remember seeing a T.V. show about the F.B.I.

13. Did W E B Du Bois found the NAACP

14. The grocery store moved from Washington St to Jefferson Ave

15. Frank didn't know whether 1 kg. equaled 2.2 lb

B. Working Cooperatively to Write an Advertising Description

Work with a partner to create an idea for an educational board game. Base it on a specific subject, choose a name, and decide on the object of your game. Then with your partner, write an advertising description for your board game. The description, written on your own paper, should include ten sentences that use three of the five punctuation rules on pages 273 and 275.

EX. Name: PROFESSOR SCIENCE

Object: to answer correctly ten questions from three science areas—animals, plants, earth

Sentence: Wow! This is a game every kid will love!

COMMAS IN A SERIES

20f   Use commas to separate items in a series.

EXAMPLES   My sisters and I collect baseball cards, coins, hats, rocks, and stamps. [words]

We found information in reference books, in magazine articles, and in newspaper articles. [phrases]

The school dance will be a success if Sergio sets up a refreshment table, if Maya hires a good band, and if plenty of students attend. [clauses]

NOTE   Some words—such as *macaroni and cheese, law and order,* and *peace and quiet*—are paired so often that they may be considered one item in a series.

EXAMPLE   My father prepared a delicious meal of steamed broccoli, macaroni and cheese, and apple crisp.

If all items in a series are joined by *and, or,* or *nor,* do not use commas to separate them.

EXAMPLES   Neither my brother **nor** my friend **nor** I could coax the puppy from under the bed after the thunderstorm.

On vacation I jogged **and** read books **and** wrote in the journal I had started.

20g   Use a comma to separate two or more adjectives preceding a noun, but not after the last adjective before the noun.

EXAMPLE   Running that road race was a fun, challenging, exhausting experience.

EXERCISE 3   Correcting Sentences by Adding Commas

Add commas where they belong in the following sentences. If a sentence is correct, write *C* on the line before the sentence.

EX.   _____ 1. Doreen has played shortstop, third base, and left field for her baseball team.

_____ 1. You can help that organization by donating money by volunteering your time or by attending fund-raising events.

_____ 2. Marty adopted a large beautiful affectionate cat from the animal shelter.

_____ 3. We packed food canteens blankets flashlights and a tent for our one-night camping trip.

_____ 4. We are looking forward to some fun some adventure and some peace and quiet.

_____ 5. Tell Mercedes she can visit on Tuesday or on Friday or on Sunday afternoon.

_____ 6. I hid the children's prizes in the bushes under some lawn chairs and behind big rocks.

_____ 7. That bakery sells French bread sourdough rolls Portuguese rolls and challah.

_____ 8. Wasn't my apartment humid hot and terribly uncomfortable yesterday afternoon?

_____ 9. I would like some advice about putting up wallpaper painting shutters and repairing cabinet doors.

_____ 10. People swim hike and jog at the park on West Street.

_____ 11. Do you expect many friends family members and neighbors to attend the church bazaar?

_____ 12. Feta cheese tastes wonderful on sandwiches in salads or crumbled on crackers.

_____ 13. The town hired three more police officers so that people could enjoy more protection more peace of mind and more quiet.

_____ 14. It was decided that Martina Sarah and Erin would be in charge of organizing the track-and-field events.

_____ 15. "My favorite magazines are _National Geographic Seventeen_ and _Ebony_," Danielle said.

_____ 16. The spaghetti dinner was sponsored by the Fire Department the Ambulance Association and a local bank.

_____ 17. The map is in the glove compartment under the seat or on the floor.

_____ 18. My report is going to be about one of these topics: South America's writers or modern plays.

_____ 19. We mow lawns clip hedges and water plants for a fair price.

_____ 20. I have a headache because I just took a long crowded noisy bus ride.

PUNCTUATING INDEPENDENT CLAUSES

20h   Use a comma before *and, but, or, nor, for, so*, and *yet* when they join independent clauses.

EXAMPLES   Claudia wanted to catch the bus**,** **but** it had already left.
I want to visit the museum**, and** Jaki wants to go with me.

NOTE   The comma may be left out before *and, but, or,* and *nor* if the independent clauses are very short or if the sentence cannot be misunderstood.

EXAMPLE   I studied and I did well.

Don't confuse a compound sentence with a simple sentence that has a compound verb.

SIMPLE SENTENCE   Ricardo **performs** with the marching band but **conducts** the orchestra. [one independent clause with a compound verb]
COMPOUND SENTENCE   Ricardo performs with the marching band**,** but he conducts the orchestra. [two independent clauses]

20i   Independent clauses in a series are usually separated by semicolons. However, commas may separate short independent clauses.

EXAMPLES   Before the afternoon tea we put flowers in the vases**;** we vacuumed the rugs**;** and we put linen napkins on each table.
All day long we dusted**,** we polished**,** and we vacuumed.

EXERCISE 4   Correcting Compound Sentences by Adding Commas and Semicolons

In the following sentences, add commas and semicolons where they belong. If a sentence is correct, write *C* on the line before it. [Note: There may be more than one correct way to punctuate a sentence.]

EX.   _____ 1. Lorraine loves animals, yet she doesn't own one.

_____ 1. Randy opened the box he removed its contents and he put the box in the recycling bin.

_____ 2. Will you answer the door and listen for the phone?

_____ 3. I love cool weather but Lexi prefers warmer weather.

_____ 4. Roxanne goes for a jog each morning for she wants to stay healthy and strong.

_____ 5. Akim worked hard and he saved his money.

_____ 6. I showed the kitten her new toy yet she didn't seem as interested as I had hoped.

_____ 7. Harriet Tubman ran into many obstacles but she succeeded in making the Underground Railroad a success.

_____ 8. I enjoy writing poetry and listening to different types of music.

_____ 9. We cleaned the room we set up tables and we hung a big sign.

_____ 10. Danya knows the way to the new variety store and she offered to draw a map for us.

_____ 11. I ordered spring rolls and mixed vegetables and I shared them with everyone.

_____ 12. My neighbor Monique has traveled a great deal yet she hasn't taken many photographs.

_____ 13. My friend Estrella moved here from Mexico last year and she often misses her friends back home.

_____ 14. Manatees are large, gentle sea mammals and they are frequently injured by passing motorboats.

_____ 15. Mr. Avery creates beautiful rugs but he rarely sells any of them.

_____ 16. Angie planted the flower seeds and she watered them.

_____ 17. As a child Wilma Rudolph didn't have the use of one of her legs but she later became the gold medalist in track at the 1960 Olympics.

_____ 18. Go to the other vegetable stand because they have the freshest produce they have the best variety and they have the best prices.

_____ 19. "I wanted to attend the reading but I couldn't find the address," Charese said.

_____ 20. Paco dances and he sings.

_____ 21. My cousins from Germany are visiting us for two weeks so we are planning several day trips to show them our historical sites.

_____ 22. Nine pole-vaulters tried to clear the bar but only one succeeded.

_____ 23. The hikers chose an inviting spot near a stream and set up their campsite for no one realized that a skunk family lived nearby.

_____ 24. Jared opened a small restaurant and invited his friends to enjoy a meal at half price.

_____ 25. The visitors were impressed by the empty land the local people took it for granted but all were awed by the Grand Canyon.

COMMAS WITH NONESSENTIAL ELEMENTS

20j **Use commas to set off nonessential clauses and nonessential participial phrases.**

A *nonessential* (or *nonrestrictive*) clause or participial phrase is one containing information that isn't needed to understand the main idea of the sentence.

NONESSENTIAL PHRASE   My cousin, **walking home one day,** found a large snapping turtle.

NONESSENTIAL CLAUSE   That scarf, **which is real silk,** was made in India.

An *essential* (or *restrictive*) phrase or clause is one that cannot be left out without changing the meaning of the sentence. Essential clauses and phrases are not set off by commas. Notice how leaving out the essential clause or phrase would change the meaning of the following sentences.

ESSENTIAL PHRASE   A book **written by Maxine Hong Kingston** is about growing up as a Chinese American woman.

ESSENTIAL CLAUSE   Vehicles **that do not pass inspection** must be taken off the roads.

NOTE   Adjective clauses beginning with *that,* like the one in the example above, are nearly always essential.

EXERCISE 5   Correcting Sentences by Adding Commas

Insert commas where necessary in the following sentences. Then identify each italicized phrase or clause by writing *e.* for *essential* or *n.e.* for *nonessential* on the line before each sentence.

EX.   __*e.*__ 1. The police officer *who was directing traffic* is my aunt.

_____ 1. Frederick Douglass *who taught himself to read and write* was one of the most effective speakers of his time.

_____ 2. The shirt *hanging on the doorknob* belongs to Maris.

_____ 3. Crowds *that are not kept under control* can be dangerous.

_____ 4. Genevieve *who plays the flute and oboe* is in a concert tonight at the town hall.

_____ 5. Have you learned the vocabulary words for the test *which is today?*

_____ 6. Jimmy Carter *who was the thirty-ninth president of the United States* was from Georgia.

_____ 7. I've read wonderful poetry *written by Elizabeth Bishop.*

_____ 8. This tasty recipe *which is made with spinach noodles* is Marta's favorite meal.

_____ 9. How long do you expect this storm *which sounds like a hurricane* to be passing over our town?

_____ 10. The blue-and-white plates *sitting on the table* were given as a gift.

_____ 11. My mother *leaning against the counter* announced that she didn't feel well.

_____ 12. The boy *who is working part time at the market* will be joining us later.

_____ 13. Meals from southern India *which are often vegetarian* are sometimes made with grated coconut.

_____ 14. The basket *woven by my grandfather* sits on the table by the front door.

_____ 15. Any letters *that you place in the mailbox* will definitely go out this afternoon.

_____ 16. The antiques *that are the most valuable* are in the back of the store.

_____ 17. Jasper *swimming in the pond one afternoon* found some beautiful lily pads.

_____ 18. That medication *which is for my allergies* is in the refrigerator drawer.

_____ 19. Erin often makes plans *that change at the last minute.*

_____ 20. Have any of you seen the new monument *which is in the center of the town square?*

_____ 21. The football game *that was on TV on Thanksgiving Day* was as muddy as any I'd ever seen.

_____ 22. The waves *that crashed against the rocky shore* were lovely to hear and to see.

_____ 23. Penelope learned embroidery *which is a difficult skill to learn.*

_____ 24. Washington, D.C. *which is the U.S. capital* is a busy city.

_____ 25. Martín *who walks to school with me* is moving to Kentucky.

COMMAS WITH INTRODUCTORY ELEMENTS

20k   Use a comma after certain introductory elements.

(1) At the beginning of a sentence, use a comma after *yes*, *no*, and mild exclamations such as *well* and *why*. Interjections such as *wow*, *yikes*, and *hey*, if not followed by an exclamation point, are also set off by commas.

EXAMPLES   No, the restaurant is not closing early this evening.
Well, I was hoping to be home by then.
Hey, didn't we meet at the carnival last year?

(2) Use a comma after an introductory participial phrase.

EXAMPLES   **Practicing her guitar one day,** Pasha taught herself to play that song.
Frightened by the loud noise, the baby cried for an hour before falling back to sleep.

(3) Use a comma after two or more introductory prepositional phrases.

EXAMPLE   **On the sidewalk behind the school,** squirrels gathered to look for food.

(4) Use a comma after an introductory adverb clause.

EXAMPLE   **After you come home from band practice,** please prepare dinner for the family.

EXERCISE 6   Using Commas in Sentences with Introductory Elements

On the line before each of the following sentences, write the word that comes before the missing comma, and place the comma after it. Write *C* if the sentence is correct.

EX.   _____Yes,_____1. Yes I do know that poem by heart.

_____ 1. Practicing every day I learned to speak Spanish well.

_____ 2. In the garbage cans behind our house we had ants.

_____ 3. Wow I didn't think so many people would arrive for the presentation.

_____ 4. In the back of the store's parking lot we saw an interesting purple convertible.

_____ 5. Well you look relaxed today.

_____ 6. After the meeting adjourned everyone helped prepare a snack at my apartment.

_____ 7. At midnight we heard a loud thunderstorm.

_____ 8. Singing an original song Raul impressed the spectators.

_____ 9. Staring at a beetle the cat crouched and prepared to pounce.

_____ 10. Next to my locker somebody spilled a container of juice.

_____ 11. When the prairies burned the fire seemed like red buffalo.

_____ 12. In Afghanistan Muslim brides often wear green, the symbol of hope.

_____ 13. Yes that scientist did win an important award.

_____ 14. As you answer each question keep track of your time.

_____ 15. Why that must be the famous movie actor.

_____ 16. In the back of the room the children hung their finger paintings.

_____ 17. Over the front door we hung a watercolor.

_____ 18. Yikes I didn't think anyone was in here!

_____ 19. In the park near the school the boys helped build a short footpath.

_____ 20. Long before the British settled Labrador the Innu people hunted caribou there.

_____ 21. Sailing through the jumps the horse and rider were quite impressive.

_____ 22. After the town meeting people were satisfied.

_____ 23. After we shared many interesting ideas we came up with a plan.

_____ 24. Calling an old friend I dialed the wrong number.

_____ 25. Sarah said, "No I don't need any more help."

_____ 26. Fishing for compliments Elena commented that her hair looked awful.

_____ 27. Running and lifting weights every day Lewis built up his endurance and strength.

_____ 28. Sure I'd be happy to take Sally to the carnival.

_____ 29. Digging through the ice the scientists uncovered the remains of a woolly mammoth.

_____ 30. In the ditch beside the road Danny found a gold coin.

COMMAS WITH OTHER SENTENCE INTERRUPTERS

20l   **Use commas to set off elements that interrupt a sentence.**

(1) Appositives and appositive phrases are usually set off by commas.

An *appositive* is a noun or pronoun that follows another noun or pronoun to identify or explain it. When you set off an appositive element, be sure to include all the words that are part of it.

EXAMPLES   Cheryl**, the class president,** is giving a speech today.
I spoke with him**, the teacher,** in the back row.

Sometimes an appositive is used to specify a particular person, place, thing, or idea. Such an appositive is called a *restrictive appositive*. Commas are not used to set off restrictive appositives.

EXAMPLES   My cousin **Liam** is going to a new high school. [The writer has more than one cousin. The appositive *Liam* specifies which cousin.]
Have you read the novel *A Separate Peace*? [The appositive *A Separate Peace* specifies the particular novel.]

(2) Use commas to set off words used in direct address.

EXAMPLES   **Ida,** do you have my sneakers?
Thank you, **Kalil,** for your dedication and hard work.

(3) Use commas to set off parenthetical expressions.

A *parenthetical expression* is a side remark that adds information or relates ideas. Some parenthetical expressions include *nevertheless, for instance, however, that is,* and *therefore.*

EXAMPLES   Jackson**, on the other hand,** would make a great assistant.
For instance, he is kind and charitable.

 NOTE   A contrasting expression introduced by *not* or *yet* is parenthetical and should be set off by commas.

EXAMPLE   His solo provided a simple**, yet elegant,** end to the recital.

EXERCISE 7   Correcting Sentences by Adding Commas

Add commas where they belong in the following sentences. If a sentence is correct, write *C* on the line before the sentence.

EX.   _____ 1. Melita of course will help you answer any questions.

_____   1. The 984-foot Eiffel Tower in Paris was built for the International Exposition of 1889.

_____ 2. Will you be visiting us again soon Ramón?

_____ 3. I talked with Fatima my new science partner.

_____ 4. I know in fact that parking places will be difficult to find on the day after Thanksgiving.

_____ 5. Have you seen the movie *My Girl* in the video stores?

_____ 6. Tiffany how long will the sale at Parelli's be going on?

_____ 7. We may on the other hand get better seats at the next show if we wait.

_____ 8. It was Petra not Gary who came up with that clever and very workable plan.

_____ 9. Stella the manager is going to have a word with those uncooperative employees.

_____ 10. Meanwhile everyone will be wondering what is going on.

_____ 11. How many blocks of cheese Meredith will we need for the picnic?

_____ 12. I enjoyed reading the novel *The Chocolate War*.

_____ 13. Generally speaking voter turnout in our town was excellent this year.

_____ 14. I now understand the equation the one on the blackboard better.

_____ 15. "How far north does this train travel Sir?" Mario asked the conductor.

_____ 16. At any rate we have to decide on a new school song for future years.

_____ 17. Mr. Carter that candle maker on Jackson Street is truly a fascinating man.

_____ 18. On the contrary I believe you would be perfect for that role Julian.

_____ 19. Have you seen our affectionate yet independent Scottish terrier?

_____ 20. Cameron please deliver these books to the library at the end of the street.

OTHER USES OF COMMAS

20m   Use commas to separate items in dates and addresses.

EXAMPLES   President Abraham Lincoln's Emancipation Proclamation
took effect on January 1, 1863.
Thomas Edison opened the world's first motion picture
studio on February 1, 1893, in West Orange, New Jersey.
On Friday, October 22, 1 will take a road trip.
Jacob lives at 4405 Paulsen Street, Savannah, GA 31405.
Send it to Mr. Lu, 12 West Sixth Street, New York, NY 10019.

No comma separates the month from the day, the house number from the
street name, or the ZIP Code from the two-letter state code. If the day is
given before the month or if only the month and the year are given, no
comma is used.

EXAMPLES   The date on the wedding invitation is 18 September 2008.
The last time my grandmother visited us was April 2006.

**20n   Use a comma after the salutation of a friendly letter and after the
closing of any letter.**

EXAMPLES   Dear Aunt Lucy,   Sincerely,

**20o   Use a comma after a name followed by an abbreviation such as
Jr., Sr., or *M.D.* and after the abbreviation when it is used in a
sentence.**

EXAMPLE   Angelina Valdez, M.D.
Martin Luther King, Jr., was a civil rights leader.

EXERCISE 8   **Proofreading Dates, Addresses, and Parts of a Letter for
Correct Use of Commas**

Add commas where they belong in the following items.

EX.   1.   200 Madison Avenue, New York, NY 10016

1.   P.O. Box 1813 Cambridge MA 02238

2.   August 29 1980 in New Haven Connecticut

3.   Sincerely yours

4.   From September 1 2008 through July 31 2009

5.   Circum-Pacific Map Project in Menlo Park CA 94025

6.   Dearest Tracey

7.   Until January 9 2009

8.   Downtown Philadelphia Pennsylvania

9.   Teresa Franklin M.D.

10.   Dear Marike

11.   Talk to Ed Baker Sr. about the window.

12.   524 San Anselmo Avenue Sail Anselmo California

13.   All the best

14.   Rural Route 12 Lindale Texas

15.   P.O. Box 47012 St. Petersburg FL 33743

16.   April 9 2008 at 4:00 P.M.

17.   Efrem Zimbalist Jr.

18.   My Dear Aunt Pepina

19.   Dinosaur National Monument in Jensen UT 84035

20.   Saturday July 18 through Wednesday August 6

21.   Best wishes

22.   1501 Montgomery Street Fort Worth TX 76107

23.   University of Wisconsin at 1215 West Dayton Street Madison WI 53706

24.   on January 1 2010

25.   Macon County North Carolina

EXERCISE 9   **Proofreading a Letter for Correct Use of Commas**
Insert commas where needed in the letter below.

1   June 20 2008

2   Dear Nora

3   This July I will be staying at 2420 Haftrey Avenue Evanston

4   IL 60202. This is the home of our family friend Juana.

5   Remember when I told you about Dr. Juana Delano the

6   veterinarian and her amazing cats? In August I will be visiting

7   my cousins at 1550 Oak Circle Wilmette IL 60091, and I'll be

8   home after that.

9   Fondly,

10   Tabia

CHAPTER REVIEW

A. Proofreading Sentences for Correct Punctuation

Insert commas and periods and other end marks where needed in the sentences below. If a sentence is correct, write C on the line before it.

EX. _____ 1. I bought a large, floppy canvas hat.

_____ 1. Tyrone have you been to Michigan which is a state near the Great Lakes

_____ 2. Yes I went to the Bailey-Matthews Shell Museum at 2440 Palm Ridge Road Sanibel Island Florida.

_____ 3. Traveling on a whale-watching ship we saw whales dolphins and many other types of marine life

_____ 4. Dr Jane Goodall a scientist from England went to Africa to study chimpanzees.

_____ 5. Well I invited Catalina Mendez MD to the conference but she already had plans

_____ 6. Wow This old bumpy dusty road needs to be repaved very soon.

_____ 7. After lunch we took the elevator to the top floor and viewed the city.

_____ 8. I want you Lee and Trenell to clean up your desks now

_____ 9. The tourists photographed historical sites ate in local restaurants and bought souvenir postcards.

_____ 10. On Friday January 15 a representative from Profits, Inc will speak to the PTA about fund-raising.

B. Proofreading a Paragraph for Correct Punctuation

In the following paragraph, insert commas where they are needed.

EX. [1] Sitting in a park on a windy day, we saw many kites.

[1] Chung Yang Chieh the Kiteflying Holiday is a special day in China. [2] At dawn boys and their fathers uncles grandfathers and other male relatives climb hills and mountains near their towns. [3] Standing on the mountains they spend the day flying beautiful kites. [4] The kites are

brightly colored and people often spend weeks creating them.

[5] Most kites are made of paper some are made of silk and many have intricate designs. [6] One popular design for example is a bat which symbolizes happiness and long life. [7] Instead of counting by months and days the Chinese calendar counts time by the moon so holidays occur on the sixth day of the Sixth Moon or the fourth day of the Fourth Moon. [8] The Kiteflying Holiday occurs on the ninth day of the Ninth Moon which is also called the Chrysanthemum Moon. [9] Yes this holiday is over two thousand years old and it celebrates the legend of a brave family whose village was destroyed. [10] Escaping to the top of the mountain the family survived and lived a prosperous life.

C. Cooperating to Write a Business Plan

You are planning to open a new business. Work with a partner to invent a business name and logo. Then, together, write a brief report to the City Business Council about your plans. Your report might include job descriptions for employees, an analysis of prospective customers, a slogan, and a list of possible products or services. Write ten complete sentences demonstrating at least five of the rules from this chapter.

EX.   Name of business: Homesweet Homes

1. Employees, we believe, are the heart of the company and should be treated well.

B.C. by Johnny Hart. By permission of Johnny Hart and Creators Syndicate.

SEMICOLONS

21a Use a semicolon between independent clauses in a sentence if they are not joined by *and, but, or, nor, for, so,* or *yet*.

EXAMPLE   Everyone else in my family loves swimming**;** I prefer hiking.

When the thoughts in two short sentences are closely related, a semicolon can take the place of the period between them.

EXAMPLES   The river is rising rapidly. It's expected to crest by noon. [two simple sentences]
The river is rising rapidly**;** it's expected to crest by noon.

21b Use a semicolon between independent clauses joined by conjunctive adverbs or transitional expressions.

EXAMPLE   Ariel is planning to go to medical school**; however,** she is also interested in ballet.

Commonly Used Conjunctive Adverbs			
accordingly	furthermore	instead	nevertheless
besides	however	meanwhile	otherwise
consequently	indeed	morever	therefore

Commonly Used Transitional Expressions			
as a result	for instance	in fact	in conclusion
for example	in addition	that is	in other words

21c A semicolon (rather than a comma) may be needed to separate independent clauses joined by a coordinating conjunction if commas appear within the clauses.

CONFUSING   Karen, Scott, and Jerome went to the concert, but Felicity, Marcus, and Joan went to the play.

CLEAR   Karen, Scott, and Jerome went to the concert**;** but Felicity, Marcus, and Joan went to the play.

21d Use a semicolon between items in a series if the items contain commas.

EXAMPLE   The International Club will meet on Tuesday, September 16**;** Tuesday, September 23**;** Tuesday, September 30**;** and Tuesday, October 7.

EXERCISE 1   Correcting Sentences by Adding Semicolons

In each sentence below, replace each incorrect comma with a semicolon.

EX.   1.   Usually we go to the mountains in the summer however, this year we went to the ocean.

1.   Sharks have a fearsome reputation, however, many kinds of sharks are harmless to people.

2.   Mickey Mouse participated in World War II his name was the Allies' password on D-day in 1944.

3.   Nakai does his homework as soon as he gets home, otherwise, he would have to fit it in between his chores and his job at the market.

4.   The first ascent by humans in a balloon was in 1783 it lasted about twenty-five minutes.

5.   Alana has visited Mexico, Guatemala, and Costa Rica, and next year her family is going to Belize and Honduras.

6.   I have received letters from my pen pals in London, England; Moscow, Russia; Nairobi, Kenya, and Suva, Fiji.

7.   Boudicca was a queen in ancient Britain, she led a revolt against the Romans.

8.   Jonas likes the rain, consequently, you can always find him outside during a storm.

9.   The native people who live in the Arctic have been called Eskimos by other Native Americans, however, the different Arctic people call themselves by specific tribal names, such as Inuit and Inupiat.

10.   When Lady Murasaki Shikibu wrote *The Tale of Genji* around 1000 A.D., Chinese was the official language of Japan, only working people and women were allowed to speak Japanese.

11.   Some important wildlife preservation parks are Salonga Reserve, Zaire; Fjordland National Park, New Zealand, Snowdonia National Park, Wales; and the Royal Chiawan Sanctuary, Nepal.

12.   First we had dinner, then we went to a movie.

13.   The blue whale is the largest mammal, the pigmy shrew and the bumblebee bat are the smallest mammals.

14.   More than forty thousand times each year, some part of the earth shakes, moreover, a major earthquake occurs about once a month.

15.   Copper, zinc, silver, and mercury are found in Mexico, in addition, in 1974, reserves of oil were discovered.

COLONS

21e   Use a colon to mean "note what follows."

(1) Use a colon before a list of items, especially after expressions like *the following* **and** *as follows.*

EXAMPLE   You will need the following items**:** a jacket, sturdy boots, a bag lunch, and insect repellent.

NOTE   Do not use a colon before a list immediately following a verb or a preposition.

INCORRECT   Additional supplies are**:** a pocketknife, a first-aid kit, a change of clothes, and a snack.

CORRECT   Additional supplies are a pocketknife, a first-aid kit, a change of clothes, and a snack.

(2) Use a colon before a long, formal statement or a long quotation.

EXAMPLE   In Lorna's opinion, the twenty-first century will bring many new developments**:** there will be new cures in medicine, new methods of communication, and improved methods of transportation.

21f   Use a colon in certain conventional situations.

(1) Use a colon between the hour and minute.

EXAMPLES   9**:**30 A.M.   8**:**00 P.M.

(2) Use a colon between chapter and verse in referring to passages from the Bible.

EXAMPLES   Esther 3**:**5   John 3**:**16–21

(3) Use a colon after the salutation of a business letter.

EXAMPLES   Dear Ms. De Rosa**:**   Dear Madam or Sir**:**

EXERCISE 2   Correcting Sentences by Adding Colons

In each of the following sentences, add the missing colon. Some sentences may be correct.

EX.   1.   These are my favorite writers Jane Austen, Jack London, and Mark Twain.

1.   The sermon last Sunday was based on Exodus 7 16.

2. At the market you need to buy these foods eggs, tortillas, tomatoes, and mangoes.

3. The meeting lasted from 1 30 P.M. until 3 45 P.M.

4. When we went whale watching, we saw two types of whales humpback and minke.

5. In her talk, Dr. Jackson quoted these poets Shakespeare, Shelley, Dickinson, and Frost.

6. It is Leviticus 19 18 that talks about loving our neighbors.

7. The bus will leave at 9 30 A.M.

8. I enjoy the following sports skiing, hiking, and rock climbing.

9. When it is 7 00 A.M. in New York City, it is 3 00 P.M. in Moscow.

10. These religions are practiced in China Buddhism, Confucianism, Taoism, and Islam.

11. Some specialities in medicine are psychiatry, dermatology, and pediatrics.

12. For the camping trip you will need to provide these items a sleeping bag, a backpack, and eating utensils.

13. Juanita pointed out these constellations Pegasus, Draco, and Ursa Minor.

14. Food crops in Mexico include beans, corn, and avocados.

15. Write "Dear Mayor Tobey" for the salutation of your business letter.

16. The bus will leave promptly at 6 00 A.M.

17. These are famous American painters Jackson Pollock, Georgia O'Keeffe, and Mary Cassatt.

18. The ancient Inca Empire consisted of much of these present-day countries Ecuador, Peru, Bolivia, and Chile.

19. On our trip we drove through the following states Arizona, Texas, and New Mexico.

20. The senator believes that his district needs funding "What we propose are improvements for the only clinic in the area, a new heating system for the high school, and a central sewage system for the entire district."

UNDERLINING (ITALICS)

21g Use underlining (italics) for titles of books, plays, periodicals, films, television series, works of art, long musical compositions, ships, aircraft, and spacecraft.

Type of Name	Examples
Books	*Invisible Man, The Rest of Life*
Plays	*The Tempest, Later Life*
Periodicals	*Utah Today, The Boston Globe*
Films	*A Christmas Story, Godzilla*
Television series	*Lost, Mystery!*
Work of art	*The Thinker, The Ballet Class*
long musical Composition	*The Magic Flute, Tommy*
Ships	*Mayflower,* USS *Iowa*
Aircraft	*Spirit of St Louis, Dreamliner*
Spacecraft	*Discovery, Phoenix*

 NOTE Underline (italicize) the title of a poem long enough to be published in a separate volume.

EXAMPLE My older brother is reading John Milton's *Paradise Lost*.

21h Use underlining (italics) for words, letters, and figures referred to as such, and for foreign words.

EXAMPLES The word *Halloween* has two *l*'s and two *e*'s.
The *6* on that address looks like an *8*.
Luminarias are part of the Mexican Christmas tradition.

EXERCISE 3 **Correcting Sentences by Adding Underlining (Italics)**

Underline all the words and word groups that should be italicized in the following sentences.

EX. 1. For my birthday I got a subscription to <u>National Geographic</u>.

1. Did you see 60 Minutes last night?

2.   The Titanic sank after it hit an iceberg.

3.   The astronauts landed on the moon in the lunar module Eagle.

4.   Her older sister likes to read Popular Science.

5.   At the festival they served moo shi, a well known Chinese dish.

6.   It was a great thrill to see Salvador Dali's painting The Persistence of Memory.

7.   We were lucky to get tickets to see the play Miss Saigon.

8.   José wrote a book report about Born Free, the story of Elsa, the lion cub.

9.   At the fair this summer, the first prize was a cruise on the Island Queen.

10. My mother subscribes to The New York Times.

11. Some people mistake the 7 on this sign for a 1.

12. "I will prepare my favorite dessert, Surprise à l'Orange," Nicole said.

13. Lonesome Dove is a western that takes place in the 1800s.

14. One of Pablo Picasso's most famous works is the painting Guernica.

15. You can probably look up that word in The Oxford English Dictionary.

16. Shalom means "hello," "good-bye," and "peace" in Hebrew.

17. Although it has been many years since the book was written, people still enjoy reading the novel Great Expectations.

18. The president travels on Air Force One.

19. At the end of the birthday party, they showed the movie Tron.

20. I can never remember if commitment has one t or two.

21. We enjoy watching the cooking lessons that Rachael Ray presents on 30-Minute Meals

22. Edith Wharton's book The Age of Innocence was made into a movie starring Daniel Day-Lewis and Michelle Pfeiffer.

23. When she was nine, Christina's favorite book was Stuart Little.

24. Do you know anyone who has sailed on the Queen Elizabeth 2?

25. During the weekend, Tomás read three chapters from I Know Why the Caged Bird Sings.

QUOTATION MARKS

21i **Use quotation marks both before and after a direct quotation. Begin the quotation with a capital letter.**

EXAMPLE **"M**aybe this is the place," Kerry said.

Do not use quotation marks for *indirect quotations.*

DIRECT QUOTATION "May I go now?" Tranh asked. [his exact words]
INDIRECT QUOTATION Tranh asked if he could leave.

21j **When a quoted sentence is divided into two parts by an interrupting expression, the second part begins with a small letter.**

EXAMPLE "I asked the same question twice," she said, "**a**nd I got two different answers."

 NOTE An interrupting expression is not part of a quotation and should never be inside quotation marks. If, however, the second part of a divided quotation is a sentence, it begins with a capital letter.

EXAMPLE "Look at that," Amy said. "**A** light is flashing at sea."

21k **A direct quotation is set off from the rest of the sentence by a comma, a question mark, or an exclamation point, but not by a period.**

EXAMPLE Jerome said**,** "The books are packed and ready to be moved."

21l **When used with quotation marks, the other marks of punctuation are placed according to the following rules.**

(1) A period or comma should always be placed inside the closing quotation marks.

EXAMPLES Josie said, "That's a beautiful weaving**.**"
"I made it myself**,**" Emma replied.

(2) Colons and semicolons are always placed outside closing quotation marks.

EXAMPLE These people have been nominated for "Student of the Year"**:** Tyrone, Marilyn, Barry, Annika, and Vernon.

(3) Question marks and exclamation points are placed inside the closing quotation marks if the quotation is a question or an exclamation; otherwise, they are placed outside.

EXAMPLES "It's cold in here**!**" Joe exclaimed.
Why did you choose to read "Mending Wall"**?**

21m When you write dialogue (conversation), begin a new paragraph every time the speaker changes.

EXAMPLE   "Did you see that light?" Cecilia asked.
               "Yes," Frank admitted reluctantly. They stopped on the trail and looked at each other doubtfully.
               "What do you think it was?" she whispered.

21n When a quoted passage consists of more than one paragraph, put quotation marks at the beginning of each paragraph and at the end of the entire passage.

EXAMPLE   The news story reported, **"**Late last night police discovered a broken window at the Cupboard Restaurant.
               "The case is still being investigated. Further reports will be published as they become available.**"**

EXERCISE 4   Proofreading Sentences for Quotation Marks

Add quotation marks where they are needed in the sentences below. Some sentences may be correct.

EX.   1. Grandfather said, "I will tell you about the festival of Gai Jatra."

1. Stop! he shouted.

2. Maya said that she is going to make a bird feeder.

3. If you wish, Mrs. Osaka said, I can tell you how the Japanese celebrate Tanabata.

4. Those videos have all been sold, the salesperson said. We may get more later.

5. Don't ever say, I quit!

6. Why did you say, The Martians have landed?

7. Naomi said It's time to light the candles; then she set the candlesticks on the table.

8. Do you like reggae? she asked.
    I don't know he answered. I'm not sure that I know what reggae is.

9. Earthquake! someone shouted, as the ground began to tremble.

10. The detective said, We have looked into these cases, and the first one was easy to solve.
     However, the second case was much more complicated, and I can't promise any answers soon.

21o   Use quotation marks to enclose titles of articles, short stories, essays, poems, songs, individual episodes of TV series, and chapters and other parts of books and periodicals.

EXAMPLES   We read O. Henry's short story "The Gift of the Magi."
Do you know the poem "Mother to Son" by Langston Hughes?

NOTE   The titles of long poems and long musical compositions are italicized, not enclosed in quotation marks.

21p   Use quotation marks to enclose slang words, technical terms, and other unusual uses of words.

EXAMPLE   The technician said he had to check the "wow" and "flutter" on the sound system.

21q   Use single quotation marks to enclose a quotation within a quotation.

EXAMPLE   She said, "In reply, I will quote our mayor: 'Recycling is a community effort.'"

EXERCISE 5   Correcting Sentences by Adding Quotation Marks

Add quotation marks where they are needed in the following sentences.

EX.   1.   She quoted from Robert Frost's poem "The Gift Outright."

1. Rob told me, She said No when I asked if we were disturbing her.

2. Abi memorized Gwendolyn Brooks's poem The Bean Eaters.

3. Sometimes I think awesome is the only adjective my brother knows.

4. Carlos read aloud Chapter 2, When the Lights Went Out.

5. Do you like using the mouse on this computer?

6. Everyone liked Pete's version of You've Got a Friend.

7. Next week we will study Unit 6, The Geography of Latin America.

8. Your job is to yell Boo! when the lights go out, Alyssa said.

9. Have you read Cassandra, a poem by Louise Bogan?

10. The Storyteller is one of my favorite tales by Saki.

REVIEW EXERCISE

A. Correcting Sentences by Adding Underlining (Italics)

In each of the sentences below, underline all the words and word groups that should be italicized.

EX. 1. My father reads <u>Sports Illustrated</u> every week.

1. We stood in line a long time to see the painting the Mona Lisa.

2. Daria always watches the reruns of the TV show This Old House.

3. Although it is nearly four centuries old, The Tragedy of Romeo and Juliet is still popular.

4. Carey made a mistake spelling Guadalajara.

5. Do you know if this number is an 8 or a 3?

6. I read an interesting article in Newsweek.

7. To prepare for his role, Daryl read The Miracle Worker twice.

8. This article tells about the 1957 launching of the satellite Sputnik.

9. The movie theater will present a special showing of Casablanca.

10. She described famous shipwrecks, including the sinking of the Titanic.

B. Correcting Sentences by Adding Quotation Marks

In each of the sentences below, add quotation marks where they are needed.

EX. 1. She sang "Sunny Skies."

1. Look out! a voice called as rocks began to fall.

2. Bianca asked, Where is the shop that sells pottery?

3. Rob suggested, Let's try holding a carwash. That usually earns money.

4. I asked Mrs. Savio, Belinda said, and she said, If it rains, the tour will be postponed.

5. Why, he asked, did you cut your hair?

6. Julian replied, Chogna Choeba is a Tibetan festival.

7. Why did he say Be here at nine?

8. In class we studied T. S. Eliot's poem The Love Song of J. Alfred Prufrock.

9. He said that the disk drive was in hyperdrive, or something like that.

10. These students will read Denise Levertov's poem The Quarry Pool: Jena, Pete, and Marcus.

APOSTROPHES

The *possessive case* of a noun or a pronoun shows ownership or relationship.

21r **To form the possessive case of a singular noun, add an apostrophe and an s. To form the possessive case of a plural noun ending in s, add only the apostrophe.**

SINGULAR	neighbor's house	Allan's job	bird's nest
PLURAL	dogs' owners	teams' fans	girls' hats

(1) The few plural nouns that do not end in s form the possessive case by adding an apostrophe and an s.

EXAMPLES   children's toys   mice's food

(2) A proper name ending in s may add only an apostrophe if the name has two or more syllables *and* if the addition of s after the apostrophe would make the name awkward to pronounce.

EXAMPLES   Achilles' armor   City of Taos' mayor

(3) Many proper names and common nouns ending in s add the apostrophe and s if the added s is pronounced as a separate syllable.

EXAMPLES   Chris's locker   bus's driver

21s **Possessive personal pronouns and the relative pronoun *whose* do not require an apostrophe.**

EXAMPLES   This is **my** plan.   **Whose** idea was this?

21t **Indefinite pronouns in the possessive case require an apostrophe and an s.**

EXAMPLES   anyone's choice   everyone's idea

21u **In compound words, names of organizations and business firms, and words showing joint possession, only the last word is possessive in form.**

EXAMPLES   Paul and Raoul's science project
            the board of directors' report

21v **When two or more persons possess something individually, each of their names is possessive in form.**

EXAMPLES   Michael's and Lily's books
            the dog's and the cat's collars

EXERCISE 6   Correcting Phrases by Adding Apostrophes

For each of the following phrases, add apostrophes where they are needed. Some phrases may be correct.

EX.   1.   a week's pay

1. my uncles book
2. Dan and Marlas class
3. everyones rights
4. Shakespeares sonnets
5. Maviss bicycle
6. Mexicos coastline
7. Kittys and Maxs schedules
8. the hours of practicing
9. the presidents speech
10. Ulysses voyage

11. womens group
12. American Legions pamphlet
13. someones backpack
14. Charless project
15. the Sierra Clubs membership
16. whose pencil
17. the Jenkins house
18. oxens work
19. brother-in-laws new car
20. the two mountaineers courage

EXERCISE 7   Proofreading for Correct Use of Apostrophes

In the following sentences, add apostrophes where they are needed. Some sentences are correct and will need no apostrophe.

EX.   1.   Once more, that cat has taken the dog's bone.

1. The editor in chiefs decision is final.
2. Who the winner will be is anyones guess.
3. Do you know if Arkansas capital is Eureka Springs?
4. This mornings paper has a full report about the fire.
5. Joan said, "Those books are ours."
6. Janice and Gwens trip included stops in Moscow and Gorky.
7. Does anyone in your family know the Cherokee language?
8. According to the weather reports, the winds speed was greater than eighty miles per hour.
9. I wrote my report about Xerxes reign in Persia.
10. The mens tennis team will practice at three o'clock.

DASHES AND PARENTHESES

Most parenthetical elements are set off by commas or by parentheses. Sometimes, though, such elements call for a sharper separation from the rest of the sentence. In such cases, a dash is used.

21w Use a dash to indicate an abrupt break in thought or speech or an unfinished statement or question.

EXAMPLES   "Who——" Rhoda began as the door slowly opened.
The results—I am happy to say—are favorable.

21x Use a dash to mean *namely, that is, in other words,* and similar expressions that come before an explanation.

EXAMPLES   I speak two other languages—French and Spanish. [*namely*]
The weather was cool—in the seventies—for the first time in weeks. [*that is*]

NOTE   Either a dash or a colon is acceptable in the first example above.

21y Use parentheses to enclose material of minor importance in a sentence.

EXAMPLES   The child's question ("Why is the sky blue?") stumped his parents.
Our neighbors' three-year-old daughter (she loves the water) swims in the pool with her parents.

EXERCISE 8 Correcting Sentences by Using Dashes and Parentheses

On the line after each of the following sentences, show where dashes and parentheses are needed by writing the word before, the enclosed material, and the word after each set of marks.

EX. 1. Jerome agreed to listen to an opera what a shock if his parents would listen to his rap records.

    opera—what a shock—if

1. Shirley is worried that her grade-point average it's 3.6 is not high enough for her to win a scholarship to the Naval Academy.

2. To assemble this machine the instructions are included takes only an hour.

3. C. S. Lewis Gloria has read all of his books is her favorite author.

_____

4. They decided they had time to visit two places Belize and Costa Rica.

_____

5. We went to Oakland it's just across the bay from San Francisco to see the exhibition.

_____

6. The date I'm sorry I forgot to tell you has been changed to next week.

_____

7. "Why why didn't you tell me?" she asked.

_____

8. The cost of the dinner including the tip was much more than Derek had expected.

_____

9. They celebrate April First April Fool's Day with great enthusiasm.

_____

10. When the plane landed in Israel the flight took thirteen hours, everyone was eager to walk around and breathe the fresh air.

_____

11. We went to Quebec the majority of French-speaking Canadians live there to practice our French.

_____

12. Her suggestion it was to serve chile con carne and enchiladas was a popular one.

_____

13. Han's poem he has just started writing poetry was accepted by the school's literary publication.

_____

14. Because the weather was so cold it was below freezing at night we were glad we had warm clothing.

_____

15. Do you ever wonder I often do why winter seems to last so long?

_____

CHAPTER REVIEW

A. Correcting Sentences by Adding Underlining (Italics), Quotation Marks, Colons, or Semicolons

For each of the sentences below, add underlining (italics), quotation marks, colons, or semicolons where they are needed.

EX.   1.   We decided to watch the movie Happy Feet again.

1.   In its opening performance of the season, the ballet presented Sleeping Beauty.

2.   Denise advised, Bring a coat; however, I forgot.

3.   Lian said, Grandmother told me; it was fortunate that I asked.

4.   He didn't know any Spanish phrases except por favor.

5.   As the parade came closer, the people applauded and shouted Hoorah!

6.   For the test, you need the following items a pencil, an eraser, scratch paper, and a calculator.

7.   That beach is popular in the summer in other words, if you go there, plan to arrive early to get a good spot.

8.   The assignment for tomorrow is to read Chapter 13, Earthquakes and Volcanoes.

9.   The plane arrived at 4 15 P.M. exactly.

10.   Let's go on, Haki said. The summit can't be far from here.

B. Proofreading for Errors in Punctuation

For each of the following sentences, correct errors in punctuation by adding apostrophes (include s if necessary), dashes, quotation marks, or parentheses where they are needed. Write the sentences on your own paper. If the sentence is correct, write C.

EX.   [l] The doors were already closed I was only ten minutes late when I arrived.

1.   The doors were already closed (I was only ten minutes late) when I arrived.

[l] Let me tell you about yesterday school was closed for in-service teacher workshops when Iris wanted me to go cycling with her and her friend, Zuri.

[2] She said, We don't have to go far, Chris; however, I should have known better.

[3] I knew that Zuri and Iris idea of a short ride would be different from mine, but I went along anyway. [4] We rode to the lake a quick hours ride. [5] Then their plans changed.

[6] We could go on to Markleville for lunch, Iris suggested. It's only another ten miles.

[7] What do you think, Zuri? she continued. She wouldn't ask me because I had stretched out in the sun to rest.

[8] I think we should go around the lake first, Zuri answered, then we could ride the back roads they're prettier than the main road to Markleville.

[9] I pointed out that Iris and Zuris bicycles were newer than mine, but I knew nothing would change their minds nothing does when they get an idea. [10] By my tally, we rode fifty miles on their short bike trip.

C. Writing Slogans

You are the owner of a bumper-sticker shop, and you are creating new slogans for your stickers. You need slogans for the following topics:

favorite sports teams	vacation spots
water conservation	clean air
recycling	favorite pets
school	

For five of the topics above, write a slogan at least two lines long. Use at least one of the following marks of punctuation in each slogan: semicolons, colons, italics, quotation marks, apostrophes, dashes, and parentheses. Use a variety of punctuation marks in your slogans.

EX. 1. Clean air—
     Dear Sir or Madam (as the case may be):
     Do you want clean air? Then plant a tree.

A dictionary entry is divided into several parts. Study the parts of the sample dictionary entry below

im•prove (im proov'), *vt.* –proved', –prov'ing [earlier *improw* < Anglo-Fr *emprower* < *en-*, in + *prou*, gain, advantage] **1.** to raise to a better quality or condition; make better [to *improve* a method] **2.** to make (land or structures) more valuable by cultivation, construction, etc. **3.** [Now Rare] to use profitably or to good advantage —*vi.* to become better in quality or condition —**improve on** (or **upon**) to do or make better than, as by additions or changes —**im•prov'a•bil'i•ty** *n.* —**im•prov'a•ble** *adj.* —**im•prov'•er** *n.*

SYN. better, ameliorate ANT. worsen, impair

1. **Entry word.** The entry word shows how the word is spelled and how it is divided into syllables. The entry word may also show capitalization and alternate spellings.
2. **Pronunciation.** The pronunciation is shown by the use of accent marks, phonetic symbols, or diacritical marks. A pronounciation key explains the meaning of diacritical marks and other phonetic symbols.
3. **Part-of-speech labels.** These labels are usually abbreviated and show how the entry word should be used in a sentence. Some words may be used as more than one part of speech. In this case, a part-of-speech label is placed in front of each numbered or lettered series.
4. **Other forms.** An entry may also show spellings of plural forms of nouns, tenses of verbs, or the comparative forms of adjectives and adverbs.

5. **Etymology.** The *etymology* is the origin and history of a word. It tells how the word (or its parts) came into the English language and how the word has changed over time.
6. **Definitions.** If there is more than one meaning, definitions are numbered or lettered.
7. **Sample usage.** Phrases or sentences may demonstrate how the defined word is used.
8. **Special usage labels.** These labels identify words that have special meanings or are used in special ways in certain situations.
9. **Related word forms.** These are various forms of the entry word, usually created by adding suffixes or prefixes.
10. **Synonyms and antonyms.** Words similar in meaning are *synonyms*. Words opposite in meaning are *antonyms*. Synonyms and antonyms may appear at the ends of some word entries.

EXERCISE 1   Using a Dictionary

Use a dictionary to answer the following questions.

EX.   1. How many syllables are in the word *spectacular*? ___four___

1. What is the spelling for the plural form of *tomato*? _____

2. How is the word *humorous* divided into syllables? _____

    _____

3. What is the past tense of *awake?* _____

4. Give three different meanings for the word *box*. _____

    _____

5. What is the etymology of the word *kindergarten*? _____

    _____

EXERCISE 2   Writing Words with Alternate Spellings

For each word below, write the alternate spellings on the line before the word.

EX. ___encyclopaedia___ 1. encyclopedia

_____ 1. monolog   _____ 4. enthrall

_____ 2. eerie   _____ 5. theater

_____ 3. Hanukkah

SPELLING RULES

---

ie and *ei*

22a Write *ie* when the sound is long *e*, except after *c*.

LONG E	believe	chief	field	niece
AFTER C	conceit	deceive	perceive	receipt
EXCEPTIONS	either	leisure	neither	seize

22b Write *ei* when the sound is not long *e* and especially when the sound is long *a*.

EXAMPLES	forfeit	freight	height	neighbor
EXCEPTIONS	friend	lie	mischief	pie

–cede, –ceed, and *–sede*

22c The only English word that ends in *–sede* is *supersede*. The only words that end in *–ceed* are *exceed, proceed,* and *succeed*. All other words with this sound end in *–cede*.

EXAMPLES	concede	intercede	precede	recede

EXERCISE 3 Writing Words with *ie* and *ei*

On the line in each word, write the letters *ie* or *ei* to spell each word correctly. Use a dictionary as needed.

EX. 1. for __ei__ gn

1. p _____ ce
2. w _____ rd
3. cash _____ r
4. _____ ght
5. sh _____ ld
6. gr _____ f
7. br _____ f

8. h _____ r
9. th _____ f
10. dec _____ t
11. y _____ ld
12. rec _____ ve
13. b _____ ge
14. conc _____ t

15. c _____ ling
16. th _____ r
17. v _____ l
18. counterf _____ t
19. p _____ rce
20. sl _____ gh

EXERCISE 4   Proofreading a Paragraph to Correct Spelling Errors

In the paragraph below, draw a line through the ten incorrectly spelled words. Write the correct spelling above each incorrect word.

EX.   [1] My *friend* ~~freind~~ Ashanti and I want to visit the South Pole.

[1] It may seem wierd that we want to spend time in a place that averages -72° Fahrenheit in the winter. [2] However, we both want to sucede in the field of astronomy someday. [3] The South Pole has been recieving attention from astronomers all over the world. [4] Astronomers beleive that Antarctica, the land area surrounding the South Pole, is one of the best places in the world for astronomical observations. [5] The area's altitude, or hieght above sea level, is one reason it provides such accurate observations. [6] Ashanti read a breif article about how the area's low temperatures also improve observations. [7] Scientists do conceed that some of their instruments may not work as well in this extreme cold. [8] Niether Ashanti nor I can imagine what it would be like to visit a place that is always covered with ice. [9] A freindly professor at a nearby college showed us pictures of the Amundsen-Scott South Pole Base, which will eventually have one of the first research facilities in Antarctica. [10] Once Ashanti and I get to the South Pole, maybe we will procede to work there.

PREFIXES AND SUFFIXES

22d When a prefix is added to a word, the spelling of the original word remains the same.

EXAMPLES   mis + spell = **mis**spell   il + legible = **il**legible
             un + sure = **un**sure   dis + advantage = **dis**advantage

22e When the suffix _–ly_ or _–ness_ is added to a word, the spelling of the original word usually remains the same.

EXAMPLES   fit + ness = fit**ness**   kind + ness = kind**ness**
             swift + ly = swift**ly**   usual + ly = usual**ly**
             dry + ly = dry**ly**   shy + ness = shy**ness**

EXCEPTION   For most words that end in _y_ and have more than one syllable, change the _y_ to _i_ before adding _–ly_ or _–ness._

             EXAMPLES   steady + ness = stead**iness**   busy + ly = bus**ily**

22f Drop the final silent _e_ before adding a suffix that begins with a vowel.

EXAMPLES   tame + est = tam**est**   bake + ing = bak**ing**
             remove + able = remov**able**   safe + er = saf**er**

EXCEPTION   Keep the silent _e_ in words ending in _ce_ and _ge_ before a suffix beginning with _a_ or _o._

             EXAMPLES   service + able = servic**eable**
                          advantage + ous = advantag**eous**

EXCEPTION   To avoid confusion with other words, keep the final silent _e_ in some words.

             EXAMPLES   dy**e**ing, dying
                          sing**e**ing, singing

22g Keep the final silent _e_ before adding a suffix that begins with a consonant.

EXAMPLES   use + less = us**eless**   advertise + ment = advertis**ement**
             late + ly = lat**ely**

EXCEPTIONS   judge + ment = judg**ment**   true + ly = tru**ly**

EXERCISE 5   Spelling Words with Prefixes and Suffixes

On the lines below, add the given prefix or suffix to each of the words.

EX.   1. il + legal   _illegal_

1. sincere + ly   _____   11. im + mature   _____

2. un + sure   _____   12. careful + ly   _____

3. sudden + ly   _____   13. un + nerve   _____

4. ir + responsible   _____   14. ready + ness   _____

5. thoughtful + ly   _____   15. re + arrange   _____

6. writ + ing   _____   16. over + run   _____

7. mis + understand   _____   17. paste + ing   _____

8. insure + er   _____   18. happy + ly   _____

9. rake + ing   _____   19. dis + satisfied   _____

10. de + compress   _____   20. waste + ed   _____

EXERCISE 6   Spelling Words with Suffixes

On the lines below, add the given suffix to each of the words.

EX.   1. nice + er   _nicer_

1. excite + ment   _____   11. approve + al   _____

2. dye + ing   _____   12. mine + ed   _____

3. slow + ly   _____   13. vote + ing   _____

4. advance + ing   _____   14. safe + est   _____

5. type + ist   _____   15. usual + ly   _____

6. cold + ness   _____   16. nine + ty   _____

7. make + ing   _____   17. page + ing   _____

8. true + ly   _____   18. gentle + ness   _____

9. take + en   _____   19. love + able   _____

10. courage + ous   _____   20. hope + ful   _____

22h When a word ends in *y* preceded by a consonant, change the *y* to *i* before any suffix except one beginning with *i*.

EXAMPLES   study + ing = study**ing**   bury + al = bur**ial**
                 lively + er = livel**ier**   tasty + est = tast**iest**

22i When a word ends in *y* preceded by a vowel, simply add the suffix.

EXAMPLES   pay + ment = pay**ment**   stay + ed = stay**ed**
EXCEPTIONS say + ed = sa**id**   day + ly = da**ily**

22j Double the final consonant before a suffix that begins with a vowel if the word (1) has only one syllable or is accented on the last syllable *and* (2) ends in a *single* consonant preceded by a *single* vowel.

EXAMPLES   mad + est = ma**ddest**   begin + ing = begin**ning**
                 ship + ed = shi**pped**   stop + er = stop**per**

Otherwise, simply add the suffix.

EXAMPLES   differ + ence = difference   cold + er = colder
                 near + est = nearest   sail + ing = sailing

EXERCISE 7   Spelling Words with Suffixes

On the lines below, add the given suffix to each of the words.

EX.   1. glad + est   *gladdest*

1. trap + ed   _____

2. misty + er   _____

3. think + ing   _____

4. gay + ly   _____

5. worry + ing   _____

6. mop + ing   _____

7. sip + ing   _____

8. clean + er   _____

9. fluffy + er   _____

10. stoop + ed   _____

EXERCISE 8   Proofreading to Correct Spelling in a Paragraph

In the paragraph below, draw a line through each incorrectly spelled word. Write the correct spelling above the incorrect word. [Note: Not every sentence contains a spelling error.]

EX.   [1] One afternoon Kavon and I found a ~~beautyful~~ *beautiful* kitten alone in an alley.

[1] The animal was busyly cleaning its paws with its rough tongue.

[2] The idea that someone would abandon this helpless creature was inconceivable to us, so we tryed to find the owner. [3] We brought the black-and-white kitten some food and a rubber ball, and it seemed happyer. [4] Kavon made some flyers, and he was hopeful that the owner would see one of them. [5] Days went by, however, and we were begining to think we'd need another plan. [6] The kitten would wait for us anxioussly each day and would hungryly nibble the cat food. [7] We pitied the animal, but neither one of us was able to provide a home, since my brother had allergies and Kavon owned two dogs. [8] Eventually, we received a call from someone who wanted to adopt the kitten.

[9] The caller, who owned a small bookstore, sayed the cat might be happy climbing on the shelves, lookking out the front window, and lounging in front of the store's wood-burning stove. [10] Now, when we walk by the store dayly on our way home from school, the kitten stares fiercely out the store window, as if to guard its interesting new home.

PLURALS OF NOUNS

22k   Form the plurals of most English nouns by adding –s.

SINGULAR	pen	arcade	book	rabbit	clock	plate
PLURAL	pens	arcades	books	rabbits	clocks	plates

22l   To form the plurals of other nouns, follow these rules.

(1) If the noun ends in *s, x, z, ch,* or *sh,* add –es.

SINGULAR	glass	box	waltz	bench	wish
PLURAL	glass**es**	box**es**	waltz**es**	bench**es**	wish**es**

 NOTE   Proper nouns usually follow these rules, too.

EXAMPLES   the Jordens**es**   the Manx**es**
the Sánchez**es**   the Frankovich**es**

(2) If the noun ends in *y* preceded by a consonant, change the *y* to *i* and add –es. If the noun ends in *y* preceded by a vowel, add *s.*

SINGULAR	city	jury	penny	spy	essay	Sunday
PLURAL	cit**ies**	jur**ies**	penn**ies**	sp**ies**	essays	Sundays

EXCEPTION   The plurals of proper nouns: the Kennedys, the Lipskys

(3) For some nouns ending in *f* or *fe,* change the *f* to *v* and add –s or –es.

SINGULAR	belief	fife	knife	leaf	wife
PLURAL	beliefs	fif**es**	kni**ves**	lea**ves**	wi**ves**

NOTE   Noticing how the plural is pronounced will help you remember whether to change the *f* to *v.*

(4) If the noun ends in *o* preceded by a consonant, add –es. If the noun ends in *o* preceded by a vowel, add *s.*

SINGULAR	tomato	hero	patio	rodeo
PLURAL	tomato**es**	hero**es**	patios	rode**os**

Nouns for musical terms that end in *o* preceded by a consonant form their plurals by adding –s.

SINGULAR	solo	cello	contralto
PLURAL	solos	cellos	contraltos

Some nouns that end in *o* preceded by a consonant have two plural forms.

EXAMPLES   mosquito**es** *or* mosquitos   cargo**es** *or* cargos

(5) The plurals of some nouns are formed in irregular ways.

SINGULAR   child   foot   ox   tooth   woman
 PLURAL   child**ren**   f**ee**t   ox**en**   t**ee**th   w**o**men

(6) Some nouns have the same form in both the singular and the plural.

EXAMPLES   deer   falafel   Japanese   trout

(7) If a compound noun is written as one word, form the plural by adding –s or –es.

SINGULAR   fistful   oilskin   toolbox
 PLURAL   fistful**s**   oilskin**s**   toolbox**es**

(8) If a compound noun is hyphenated, or is written as two or three words, make the modified noun plural.

SINGULAR   editor in chief   runner-up   sea gull
 PLURAL   editor**s** in chief   runner**s**-up   sea gull**s**

(9) Some nouns borrowed from other languages form their plurals as they do in the original language.

SINGULAR   alumnus   datum   vertebra
 PLURAL   alumn**i**   dat**a**   vertebr**ae**

(10) To form the plurals of numerals, most capital letters, symbols, and words used as words, add either –s or an apostrophe and –s.

EXAMPLES   Are all of your *t*s (*or* *t*'s) crossed?
    Pinga studied the politics of the late 1960**s** (*or* 1960**'s**).

To prevent confusion, always use both an apostrophe and an *s* to form the plurals of lowercase letters, certain capital letters, and some words used as words.

EXAMPLES   The word *Mississippi* has four *s*'s and four *i*'s. [Without an apostrophe, the plural of the the letter *i* would look like the word *is*.]
    All the *her*'s in his letter have clear antecedents. [Without the apostrophe, the plural of the word *her* could be confused with the possessive pronoun *hers*.]

EXERCISE 9   Spelling the Plurals of Nouns

On your own paper, write the correct plural form of each of the following nouns.

EX. 1. ax
    1. axes

1. trench	6. valley	11. blue jay	16. echo
2. area	7. Daly	12. father-in-law	17. stereo
3. Pérez	8. woman	13. crisis	18. *e*
4. soprano	9. sheep	14. 1800	19. *&*
5. life	10. spoonful	15. rash	20. checkbook

EXERCISE 10   Identifying Incorrect Spelling

Each sentence below contains at least two spelling errors. Draw a line through each incorrectly spelled word, and write the correct spelling above the misspelled word.

EX. 1. When the ~~Katz~~ *Katzes* went on vacation, they had to find someone to take care of their ~~gooses~~ *geese* and goats.

1. The twinses worked for two days on their taxs.

2. All over town, people tuned their radioes to the local station to hear Ella sing her soloes.

3. Mr. Reilly went with the other Reillies to pick berrys.

4. Under the pile of branchs, Irma found a family of mouses.

5. It seemed as though all the childs in those two classes were missing front tooths.

6. Ruth's sister-in-laws spent the morning raking and burning leafs.

7. The Japaneses staying in town for the summer are very fond of Mrs. Myers' apple pie's.

8. The mens arrived promptly at seven, carrying their toolsbox.

9. Keep adding fistsful of soil until the gladiolus are snug in the ground.

10. At the reunion, the alumnuses will enjoy remembering the 1970es.

11. Inside the main building on campus, there is one room where the awardes and trophys of the college teams are displayed.

12. All the six-years-old enjoyed playing with the puppys.

13. With lunch, Mavis had two bunchs of grapes and two handsful of raisins.

14. To set a place for everyone at the table, you will need six knifes and six forkes.

15. In her vegetable garden, Tanya grew tomatos, peppers, and radishs.

SPELLING NUMBERS

22m Always spell out a number that begins a sentence.

EXAMPLE   **Four hundred fifty** students filed into the auditorium.

22n Within a sentence, spell out numbers that can be written in one or two words; use numerals for other numbers.

EXAMPLES   Wyatt baked **twenty-five** loaves of bread last weekend.
I guessed that the cheese wheel weighed **125** pounds.

EXCEPTION   If you have some numbers of one or two words and some of more than two words, use numerals for all of them.

EXAMPLE   The count shows **143** votes for and **80** votes against.

22o Spell out numbers used to indicate order.

EXAMPLE   The field hockey team is **fourth** in the division.

EXCEPTION   Use numerals for dates when you include the name of the month.

EXAMPLE   Grandmother was born on July **4, 1929**.

EXERCISE 11 Spelling Numbers

On your own paper, write five original sentences, following the directions provided below.

EX.   1. Include information about your pet winning the top prize in the pet show.
    1. My dog Sherman won first prize in the pet show this fall.

1. Begin the sentence with a number.
2. Include two numbers that can be written in one or two words.
3. Include three numbers, one of which can be written in one or two words and two of which can be written in more than two words.
4. Use a number to indicate the place, or rank in class, of a person graduating from high school.
5. Give the month and date of your birthday.

CHAPTER REVIEW

A. Correcting Spelling Errors in Sentences

Draw a line through the misspelled word in each sentence below, and write the misspelled word correctly on the line before the sentence.

EX. _____foreign_____ 1. Molly wants to collect ~~foriegn~~ coins.

_____ 1. Many citys will have a parade on Thanksgiving Day.

_____ 2. The Martínezs fed the family cat while we were away last month.

_____ 3. Vanessa will be haveing a recital in December.

_____ 4. The audience proceded to the lobby for refreshments.

_____ 5. We collected a large amount of datums for our history presentation.

_____ 6. I bought two wooden jewelry boxs at the craft fair.

_____ 7. My baby brother will be steadyer on his feet in another few months.

_____ 8. "The weather is usualy warmer this time of year," the announcer stated.

_____ 9. Kylie and Miguel are both editor in chiefs of the school literary magazine.

_____ 10. My freind Gloria moved here last year from El Salvador.

B. Proofreading a Paragraph to Correct Spelling Errors

In the following paragraph, draw a line through each misspelled word. Write the correct spelling above the misspelled word.

EX.   [1] One of my sister's birthday wishes
                                    ~~wishs~~ was to take a trip to New York City.

[1] My sister was the happyest person in the world as we took a

liesurely drive to the city. [2] When we arrived, she was still decideing

whether to visit the Statue of Liberty first or to go souvenir shoping.

[3] Then we came across an advertisment for the Liberty Science Center

close by in Jersey City, New Jersey. [4] My sister decided that visitting this center, which opened on January twenty-fourth, 1993, would be a great way to spend part of her special day. [5] My parents agreed, and we ended up stayying there the entire day. [6] It was an exciting place because most of the displayes provided hands-on experience. [7] The top floor focussed on the environment, and looker-ons could handle small animals and learn how to predict weather. [8] Other floors had unnusual exhibits about health and inventtions. [9] The center also had a theater with a screen that was eight storys tall. [10] My sister's favorite part of the visit was talking with the "bug lady," an insect speciallist who had a fascinating collection of spiders and giant cockroachs.

C. Using Correct Spelling

You are an exchange student in a foreign country, and you have been assigned to run a spelling workshop for students your age who are learning English. Select two spelling rules from this chapter to teach to the students. On your own paper, write each rule, and provide examples and an exercise to check students' understanding of the rule. Each exercise should contain five questions or items for students to complete. Write answers for each exercise on a separate piece of paper.

EX.   1.   RULE: To form the plural of a noun that ends in y preceded by a
              consonant, change the y to i and add –es.

      EXAMPLES: city   spy   penny
                 cities   spies   pennies

      EXCEPTIONS: The plurals of proper nouns: the Bailys

      EXERCISE: Form plurals of the following words.
      1. fly   3. cry   5. Murphy
      2. sty   4. jelly

      ANSWERS:
      1. flies   3. cries   5. Murphys
      2. sties   4. jellies

A

abbreviations, 275
abstract noun, 101
accept, except, 249
action (*or* nonlinking) verb
    defined, 113
    linking verb used as, 115
active voice, 231
adjective
    comma used to separate
      two or more, 277
    defined, 107
    modified by adverbs, 121
    noun used as, 109
    participle used as, 153
    predicate, 141
    pronoun used as, 109
    proper, 109, 263
adjective clause
    defined, 171
    placement of, 245
    used to combine sentences,
      83
adjective phrase, 151
adverb
    conjunctive, 74, 82, 291
    defined, 119
    relative, 171
    there or *here* used as, 135
    used to modify adjectives
      and other adverbs, 121
adverb clause
    comma used after, 283
    defined, 173
    placement of, 245
    used to combine sentences,
      83
adverb phrase, 151
advice letter
    model of, 59–60
    writing, 59–66
affect, effect, 249
agreement
    of collective nouns, 191
    with compound subject,
      189
    with indefinite pronouns,
      187
    with intervening phrases,
      185
    number, 181
    pronoun, 197
    subject-verb, 183, 189, 193
all the farther, all the faster, 249
allusion, illusion, 249

ambiguous reference, 215
among, between, 249
and etc., 249
anecdote, 29
antecedent
    agreement with pronoun,
      197
    defined, 105, 197
antonyms, in a dictionary
    entry, 308
anywheres, everywheres,
    nowheres, somewheres, 250
apostrophe, 301
appositive
    commas used to set off,
      285
    defined, 165, 213, 285
    pronoun used as, 213
    restrictive, 285
appositive phrase
    commas used to set off, 285
    defined, 69, 165
    used to combine sentences,
      79
arranging ideas, 6
article, 107
as, as if, like, 253
asking questions, 3
at, 250
auxiliary (*or* helping) verb,
    117, 183
awards, capitalization of, 267

B

base form of a verb, 219
be, forms of, 115
being as, being that, 251
between, among, 249
brainstorming, 2
brand names of business
    products, capitalization
      of, 267
buildings, capitalization
    of, 265
businesses, capitalization
    of, 265
bust, busted, 251

C

capitalization, 261-69
    of brand names of
      business products, 267
    of the first word in every
      sentence, 263

of geographical names, 261
of the interjection *O*, 263
of names of historical
    events and periods,
    special events and
    holidays, and other
    calendar items, 267
of names of
    nationalities, races, and
    peoples, 265
of names of persons, 261
of names of religions
    and their followers, holy
    days and celebrations,
    sacred writings, and
    specific deities, 266
of names of school
    subjects, 263
of names of ships,
    monuments, awards,
    planets, and any other
    particular places, things,
    or events, 267
of the pronoun *I*, 263
of proper nouns and
    proper adjectives, 263
of teams, organizations,
    businesses, institutions,
    buildings, and
    government bodies, 265
of titles, 269
case
    defined, 201
    nominative, 201, 203, 211
    of object of a preposition,
      207
    objective, 201, 205, 207, 211
    possessive, 201, 301
    of predicate nominative,
      203
    of pronouns, 201–207
    of *who* and *whom*, 211
cause and effect, using
    narration to explain, 24
–cede, –ceed, and *–sede,*
    spelling rules, 309
chronological order
    defined, 6
    used in an early plan, 27
    used in an I-Search paper,
      52
    used in narration, 23
    used to create coherence,
      18